SUITCASES
from
Heaven

SUITCASES

from

Heaven

A Mother's Journey of Hope
Through Her Daughter-in-Law's Cancer

CINDY SEATON HENSON

REDEMPTION
PRESS

Published by Redemption Press, PO Box 427, Enumclaw, WA 98022. Toll-Free (844) 2REDEEM (273-3336)

Redemption Press is honored to present this title in partnership with the author. The views expressed or implied in this work are those of the author. Redemption Press provides our imprint seal representing design excellence, creative content, and high-quality production.

The author has tried to recreate events, locales, and conversations from memories of them. In order to maintain their anonymity, in some instances the names of individuals, some identifying characteristics, and some details may have been changed, such as physical properties, occupations, and places of residence.

ISBN 13: 978-1-64645-835-6 (Paperback)
978-1-64645-833-2 (ePub)
978-1-951350-28-4 (Audiobook)
Library of Congress Catalog Card Number: 2023907554

DEDICATION

To Sherie and Charlene,
mothers who lovingly carried their daughters
through their battle with cancer.
And to all mothers who have loved and lost children
and are looking for healing
amid their sorrow.

Why I Wrote This Book

*I*F YOU OPENED THIS book hoping to be entertained, I would tell you to find a novel. Between these pages is a love story— not one of fairy tales, silly infatuations, or shallow romance but of deep, abiding love.

After going through twenty-five years of bitterness toward God, I had finally given up on the idea of my son Kyle getting a miracle and being healed of severe autism. Ten years ago, I was added to the prayer group of a family who had a sixteen-year-old son, Victor, who had become a paraplegic after having a brain tumor removed. Victor was taught to sign with his fingers, which he could move slightly. He made it clear to his parents, Jay and Laura Hottel, that he still loved God and trusted Him with his life.

At the time, Kyle was an adult, living under a blanket in his room each day, constantly smearing poop from floor to ceiling. The doctors didn't know what was wrong with him. We spoon-fed him meals because he had too much anxiety to eat. Kyle pounded his walls with his fists all night long. Vance and I hardly slept for two years straight. I was at an extreme low in my bitterness with God.

At four in the morning, I sat in front of my computer alone, reading Victor's story again. He had a horrible life of suffering, yet his love for God had not wavered in the slightest. Which struck a chord in my heart. God showed me how my love for Him was only based on one outcome. If God healed Kyle, I would love Him, and if He didn't, I would hate Him. It didn't matter what else God had done for me, not even that His Son had died on the cross for my sins.

None of that mattered to me—it was all about the miracle.

But now my eyes were open to my sin and self-centeredness, and I sat weeping as I realized what I had done to my Savior. The Holy Spirit came over me, and my heart was filled with an unexplainable joy, one I had not felt in twenty-two years. It changed me so much that friends and family commented on the incredible transformation in me.

I thought I had hidden the bitterness, but apparently I hadn't. After my change of heart, friends and family encouraged me to write a book. My first book, *Beauty from Ashes*, was born out of my pain and brought me a beautiful ministry to women around the world.

I had made my peace with God.

Then my son Eythan fell in love with Jazmin, who was diagnosed at age seventeen with stage 4 adrenocortical carcinoma. She had a tumor the size of a grapefruit removed from her tummy when she was sixteen. Jazmin was sent to Sick Kids Hospital in Toronto, Ontario, to have the mass removed, and the tumor was sent to a lab to be assessed.

Three months later, Sherie, Jazmin's mom, called their doctor to see if the results had come back. The doctors had known for a while that the tumor had tested positive for cancer. They just didn't know how or what to tell Jazmin's family since there wasn't a solid treatment plan for the aggressive cancer.

The doctor told Sherie that Jazmin was terminally ill. Her type of cancer was untreatable. They could try chemo, but the chance of it killing the cancer was so small that Jazmin would most likely be sick from chemo but not get the results she wanted.

Jazmin came fluttering into our home, speaking of healing and miracles. I didn't know how to tell her I didn't believe in that nonsense.

I had jumped on a miracle train twenty-five years before and landed with a suitcase full of bitterness. I thought the kindest thing I could do was help Jazmin accept that she was dying. Instead, God used Jazmin to teach me that the best way to live a fragile life is with hope and belief that miracles still happen every day.

> Jazmin came fluttering into our home, speaking of healing and miracles. I didn't know how to tell her I didn't believe in that nonsense.

While Jazmin kept her unwavering candle of hope burning brightly, I secretly began to write her love story with God as it unfolded.

These chapters are filled with her love, and they will change your life if you have the courage to read this story to the end. Jazmin was willing to suffer in hopes that her trials and tribulations during her battle with cancer would draw one person to Jesus Christ and into the abiding love He generously gave her. I hope you are that person.

CHAPTER ONE

Love Is Blind

I don't need to have it all together, because God is strong when I am weak. I can rely on Him to get me through it.

—JAZMIN HENSON

Canada
September 2016

I HOPPED INTO OUR WHITE SUV and watched my youngest child, Eythan, walk in front of the car. He opened the door and hopped into the passenger seat, and I backed the car into the turnaround, then scooted out of our long gravel driveway, the last one on our dead-end street. We chatted as we drove through the curtain of gorgeous fall colors lining our country road.

As we drove to church, I asked Eythan, "Are you sure you did the right thing?"

He had gone through a breakup recently and assured me that the one-and-a-half-year relationship was over. He and his ex-girlfriend would not be dating again.

I saw his jaw flex.

Eythan was only nineteen and had already experienced a broken heart. I wanted to find a Band-Aid in my mom-purse and place it over his wounded heart. This wasn't something I could fix with a quick solution. I hoped he would return to his fun-loving, prankster self before he thought of dating again. I felt words stringing together in my heart and I almost kept them to myself, but they flowed freely from my lips.

"Eythan, I believe God has a girl picked out for you, and she'll bring you great joy, but you're going to have to wait for her."

I looked at Eythan and could tell he wasn't in the mood for this conversation. I let it go.

Two weeks later, Eythan returned home from a college-and-career weekend at Aush-Bik-Koong Bible camp. We were standing at our kitchen island. Our heads hovered together as he showed me pictures on his phone. He quickly scrolled through about twenty photos from the weekend. The last one was of him in a larger group, and Eythan was standing on the end with his arm around a girl.

Really?

My teeth gritted together, and a mix of anger and anxiety brewed in my chest. Speechless, I walked away and wiped down the mess on the counter left from supper.

Had my son forgotten so quickly what he had put Vance and me through in the last year and a half? We had continuously worried about him as we watched him spiral into sadness.

Was my son so thickheaded and clueless?

Later that night I hopped into bed, still burning with anger. Are all boys this foolish, or just my son? I lay beside my husband, and we talked in hushed tones about Eythan's lack of discernment. We agreed that he had completely lost his marbles.

Lord, help us!

12

Then we shifted our thinking. What if Eythan was serious about this girl? We could support him or hinder him, and we never wanted to hinder what God might be doing, even if our feelings didn't align with our children's decisions.

The next morning my son Devyn, who was three years older, was up first. He had also been at the camp for the weekend. I pulled him aside in the hallway before he went into the bathroom. I kept my voice low. "Devyn, who is the girl I saw Eythan with his arm around in a photo?"

"That's Jazmin."

"Is she a nice girl?" My eyes darted back and forth as I studied Devyn's expressions. He couldn't lie; his face always betrayed his feelings.

"Mom, have you ever met someone who has an angel inside them?" His face showed beautiful emotions. "That's Jazmin." Devyn's big brown eyes looked sincere.

Tension eased in my shoulders.

"But, Mom, she has cancer," he added in a hushed tone.

That didn't faze me in the least. I just wanted Eythan to marry someone who adored our family and loved him.

When Eythan woke, I asked him about Jazmin, and he got a big grin on his face as he described the lovely girl. Then he told me she had cancer.

"I'm not concerned about that. We can handle it. But what if you fall in love with Jazmin and she dies? I don't want you to become bitter with God." Eythan had just met the girl he thought was the woman of his dreams. How could I say anything to a boy who thought this was love at first sight?

"I won't be bitter if she dies, Mom."

"Well, then, you have my and Dad's blessing to date Jazmin."

Technically it wasn't love at first sight, since he had seen Jazmin at ABK when they were younger. He thought she was a sweet girl then, and Jazmin thought Eythan was a cute boy, but it hadn't gone any further than that.

Three years later, in April 2014, Jazmin had a six-inch tumor removed from her left adrenal gland. Shortly after surgery a lung biopsy discovered more than forty tiny metastatic tumors in her lungs. She was diagnosed with stage 4 ACC cancer at age sixteen.

Later that summer, Eythan and Jazmin worked at Aush-Bik-Koong Bible camp. During a chapel service, Eythan heard Jazmin share with the young girls about her diagnosis and her desire to trust God with her cancer.

Eythan sat in the chapel, which overlooked Sugar Lake, and was struck by Jazmin's spiritual maturity and also her beauty. They were awkward teenagers and managed to only say a sentence or two to each other that week. Then they went their separate ways.

Jazmin returned home to deal with cancer, and Eythan came home to live in our house of chaos where severe autism ruled every moment of our family's life. Little did they know that one day they would fall in love. Love is blind, thankfully. But how would they survive the years ahead? Could they face the beast of cancer together?

I suppose we were all blind. Only God knew.

The Lord gives sight to the blind,
the Lord lifts up those who are bowed down,
the Lord loves the righteous.

(Psalm 146:8)

CHAPTER TWO

Miracles and Nonsense

*I'm not thankful for having cancer. I want it gone,
and I pray God will completely heal my body. I am,
however, very thankful for everything that I have learned
by going through this experience.*

—JAZMIN HENSON

October 2016

ETHAN INVITED JAZMIN TO our city to meet his family. Vance and I had been out looking at a house. We pulled into our driveway and saw Jazmin's car parked in the turnaround. Vance and I stepped onto our beautiful wraparound porch and walked in the front door of our big dark-blue two-story home.

Jazmin was sitting on one of the barstools at the kitchen island. Her auburn-haired head turned, and I saw the face of an angel.

We walked toward each other. Jazmin was petite but tall, and I took her into my arms, welcoming her to our home. The moment I hugged Jazmin, I just knew—I knew she was the one my mother-heart wanted for my son.

Our family fell in love with her instantly. Somehow we knew Eythan was going to marry this girl, or at least that we wanted him to marry her. Our kids—Devyn, Aryanna, Kyle, Charity, and her husband, Dan—all told Eythan they wanted him to make this relationship work. Our family agreed 110 percent that we wanted Jazmin to join our large clan.

"Eythan, if you mess up your relationship with Jazmin, I'm ditching you," I said jokingly.

He might have thought I was serious. Jazmin was a keeper. I wanted this relationship to work. How could it not? She was such a doll. Eythan grinned at me, and I think he was thankful that his family loved Jazmin so much and approved of his choice.

That first weekend, the kids were around often for meals, hoping to get to know Jazmin better. I was warmed by her desire to be wherever the noise was taking place. Rarely did she ask Eythan to be alone with her, and she embraced our family wholeheartedly.

We had a lot of time to get to know her, and the way she told stories brought rounds of laughter from everyone. Eythan just smiled, and I often caught him staring at Jazmin. Whenever she talked, her long slim fingers flew, her spine straightened, and her brown eyes, framed with thick long dark eyelashes, lit up her strikingly beautiful face.

Before I met Jazmin that weekend, Eythan had mentioned her testimony and how she believed she was going to get a miracle. I was glad he filled me in so I had time to prepare myself to respond in a neutral fashion. Of course, I had lots to say, but I zipped my lips. How could I burst Jazmin's bubble of hope? I had always determined that anyone who married into our family would feel fully embraced.

Jazmin shared with us that cancer had changed her in many ways. She sat at our table with a mug of hot coffee. "I used to be a snooty girl, and selfish. After I was diagnosed, it really made me think about the type of person I want to be, and God convicted me to be kind and caring and accepting of other people and their faults."

My heart warmed at how much God had done to bring Jazmin to a place of wanting to honor Him with her life. We couldn't imagine Jazmin not being the lovely young woman in front of us, and I was thankful God had transformed her, because she was going to make a wonderful wife and mother one day.

As I sat there listening to Jazmin talk about her hopeful miracle, my mind wandered to the years when Vance and I were engaged in a spiritual battle, praying for a miracle for our son Kyle, who was about five years old. Someone had told us God could heal Kyle of autism if only we had enough faith. Every ounce of energy we had went into this faith. And after years of trying to convince God to give Kyle a miracle, I gave up.

My faith plummeted, and I fell into a black abyss that I couldn't seem to come out of for a long time. Bitterness enveloped my heart as I realized God had the power to heal Kyle—He just needed to snap His fingers and it would be done—but chose not to. God decided not to make my son well. I was very angry with Him. How could a good and loving God let a helpless, innocent child suffer so much?

For twenty-two years, my bitterness gained momentum. It was a deep, dark secret I shared only with my husband. I spoke of God in the most hateful way. Yet to my kids, friends, and extended family, I proclaimed to be a Christian. I knew my bitterness was wrong, but I didn't care. If God wasn't going to give my son a miracle, He was going to listen to my hateful spewing every day until He did what I wanted.

When I was alone in my car, which was rare since I homeschooled our children for fourteen years, I screamed at the top of my lungs at

God. I can't repeat here what I said, because I wouldn't talk that way even to my worst enemy. But God had become the enemy.

My husband told me he was afraid to sit next to me when I was spewing at God, because he thought I might get struck by lightning. He didn't want to be killed too.

Then we met Jazmin.

From day one, she told us she was holding out for a miracle from God.

I found this extremely hard to watch. I didn't want to go back to that place only to have my hopes smashed into a thousand pieces. I didn't want Jazmin to fall into the deep pit of bitterness and anger I had fallen into if she didn't get her miracle. How could I stand by and watch her fall into the pit of depression I had sunk into?

Jazmin's fingers flew excitedly in front of her as she launched into another delightful story. As I watched her eyes brighten, resolve settled into my bones.

I would protect her from making the same mistake I had—trusting God for nonsense like miracles.

Dear Lord,

When darkness smothers us and threatens
to envelop our minds, protect us with your holy shield.
Lift us out of the miry pit and put our feet
on solid ground.

Amen.

CHAPTER THREE

After All, We Are Family

The blessings that Jesus has put in my life give me joy, and with Him I know that I'm not alone.

—JAZMIN HENSON

November–December 2016

WINTERS ARE LONG AND cold in northern Ontario. It's not uncommon for us to have six months of snow, which is five months longer than I want. On one of these snow-laden days, I was doing dishes at my kitchen sink. I looked out the window.

Jazmin and Eythan were sitting in the snow, chatting away, smiling and laughing. Jazmin's back was toward me, and I could see her long auburn hair peeking out of her toque.

Eythan tossed snow in Jazmin's face and laughed with a grin that reminded me of the sweet little boy who adored me when he was five.

Jazmin grabbed a handful of snow and gave him what he deserved.

I secretly cheered her on from my side of the window. "You go, girl!" I have a stubborn streak. I didn't want my boys to marry girls they could easily manipulate or control, since I knew this would make my sons more selfish.

Jazmin had a backbone and could hold her own, and I liked that! I knew my son had found his best friend. A girl who would hold him accountable and encourage him to be unselfish.

Sometimes Eythan just sat on the couch staring at Jazmin and smiling. He was completely enamored with her beauty and her sweet spirit. They were often found flirting or holding hands or snuggling on the couch with silly grins.

On one visit, Eythan was sick and was lying on the couch with a cushion behind his head. Jazmin found our guitar, which no one in our family knew how to play, and put one foot up on the couch with the guitar propped on her knee as she stood strumming a tune. She started singing a silly song to Eythan, stuck out her lip in a pout, and fluttered her big brown eyes at him. Eythan smiled at her.

Young love was so beautiful, sweet, and consuming.

She fell head over heels in love not only with Eythan but with our family too. Jazmin genuinely enjoyed being with us. Our five kids were born within seven and a half years, and we homeschooled for fourteen years. Our family was close knit. If one child was doing something they shouldn't, the other three made sure to tell them.

As a family we stood together to lend strength when someone fell into a situation that required them to be pulled back out. I knew our children would stand with Jazmin and Eythan in the journey ahead.

But could we do this together and survive whatever cancer brought our way? Would Jazmin and Eythan be able to survive what was ahead?

> He gives strength to the weary
> and increases the power of the weak.
>
> (Isaiah 40:29)

CHAPTER FOUR

Ice Cream and Sunshine Fill the Soul

Life is crazy and overwhelming and sometimes scary and depressing, but if you have no joy, then that's all your life will ever be—crazy, overwhelming, scary, depressing, and lonely. Jesus gives me a reason to be joyful. He loves me. Just that overwhelms me with joy!

—JAZMIN HENSON

Mother's Day, May 2017

THE DAY WAS RAINY and dark. The winds blew through our balcony door, ruffling the sheer white curtains. Vance and I were at a Jamaican resort, and I was watching the ocean from our balcony.

Little did we know a storm was about to break out in our lives.

Although I had spent the day with Vance laughing and dining, an anxious feeling settled in my chest. I couldn't put my finger on it. Somehow I seem to know when a tornado is brewing in the spiritual realm.

The ocean stirred and churned as I slipped into bed and fell asleep. During the night, my phone beeped. I anxiously sat up and grabbed my glasses to see who was texting me. It was my daughter Charity. She never messaged me in the night. I read the message.

Jazmin was in the hospital, and she was coughing up blood.

My heart pounded, and I felt confused.

We thought her cancer was stable. She'd had it for three and a half years, and doctors had thought it would kill her when she was originally diagnosed. Jazmin chose the natural route, seeing doctors in other countries and getting the cancer to settle down for a few years.

A heaviness pressed my chest as I drifted into a restless sleep, praying for Jazmin. I woke in the night again and discovered Charity had left me another message. X-rays had come back saying Jazmin had large tumors in her lungs. The CAT scan showed they were bleeding.

Charity and her husband, Dan, were staying at our house to care for Kyle. We were okay with Jazmin visiting while we were gone.

I had heard Jazmin had a tumor on her kidney and her adrenal gland, but I didn't know she also had tumors in her lungs. The extent of her cancer had never been discussed with us. (I later learned that Jazmin didn't talk about her cancer because she thought if she dwelled on it too much, it would affect her faith and the possibility of getting a miracle.)

The news of her lungs being full of cancerous tumors flabbergasted me, and I was in shock. My heart was completely broken knowing our sweet girl didn't stand a chance. I sat in the hotel bathroom, crying. The cold hard tiles would betray me if I cried too loudly, so I wept softly while my husband slept. Waking him wouldn't change the situation. When he woke, I told him what had transpired in the night.

Vance was quiet and serious. Jazmin had worked her way into every corner of our hearts. Vance felt protective of her. Usually we talked back and forth, but this somber morning, we sat quietly on the balcony.

After a while, we walked to the breakfast buffet. We passed the flowers, trees, lush bushes, and gorgeous blue-green ocean that seemed to blur. We were on auto pilot as we contemplated the future of Jazmin's life.

We ate in silence.

Neither of us knew what to say.

I needed to tell my mom before anyone else did. I went to the bathroom nearest the buffet and dialed.

"Hi, Mom."

"Wow, you're calling me from Jamaica. I feel special," Mom said in a cheerful tone.

"I wish I was calling with good news. Jazmin is at the hospital. Her lungs are full of tumors, and they're bleeding."

"What?"

"Apparently they have been full of tumors for a while now, but no one told Vance or me that." I sniffled as I wiped my tears.

"Oh, Cindy, are you okay?" Mom's voice was soft, laced with concern.

"Vance and I are in shock. I have no clue why Eythan or Jazmin never told us. We were under the impression her cancer was stable." I thought I heard a noise in the bathroom, but I was pretty sure I was the only one in the room.

"How's Eythan doing?"

"I don't know. I've only been messaging with Charity. Eythan's so quiet he hardly talks about stuff like this."

Mom and I cried.

My youngest is silent as the grave most times. He's not a talkative child; he's the quietest one of them all. I rarely know what he's thinking. Our other kids tell us everything. I worry about Eythan. I want him to spill what's on his heart out to me so I know how to help him through his worries.

I heard the toilet in the next stall flush. Gosh, I didn't want the whole world to hear me! I leaned forward and pressed my eye to the crack in the stall door and saw one of the Jamaican staff.

"Cindy?" Mom prompted.

"Sorry. I just realized there was someone in the bathroom this whole time."

"You're in a public washroom?"

"Yeah. I needed to call you before anyone else told you."

Mom and I giggled. The funny bone in our family is hereditary.

"I will be praying for all of you, especially Eythan and Jazmin."

"Thanks, Mom." I took comfort in her words. Sometimes I think my mom has a phone in her apartment that's linked directly to Jesus.

I sneaked out of the bathroom and leaned against the door, trying to stay inconspicuous as I scanned the room for the lady from the bathroom. When all was clear, I snuck back to Vance and sat down.

Charity called us later that night. Vance and I were propped up in our bed with the phone between us on speaker mode.

"When we took Jazmin to the hospital last night, she looked very sick. But by morning she looked great."

Vance and I looked at each other, confused. "How is she now?" I asked.

"Good!" Charity said cheerfully. "I think God may have done a miracle. If you could have seen how terrible she looked, you'd believe me."

She had been at the hospital with Jazmin and Eythan when the doctor came into the room after doing X-rays. "Um . . . you have some masses in your lungs." The doctor sounded very concerned.

"Yes, I know," Jazmin said calmly.

"Are you getting treatment?" He was taken aback by her relaxed demeanor.

"I decided to forgo chemo since my physician said the chance of it helping was low." Jazmin showed no emotion and just answered the question matter-of-factly.

The doctor strongly suggested she get the chemo.

Jazmin was used to this drill. She was a solid rock, not wavering in her countenance as she thanked the doctor for his advice.

"Sherie and Aaron are coming for a visit," Charity said. "They want to check on Jazmin." We hadn't met her parents yet. I imagined that drive would seem like three years instead of three hours. They had poured their time, love, and savings into preserving Jazmin's life.

Before we hung up, I said, "Clean the house!"

I was mortified thinking about the mess that was probably strewn throughout our home. I didn't want Sherie and Aaron Ayotte to see the *real* way we lived, or they might take their daughter and run. Living with severe autism is messy business, and most parents wouldn't want their sick daughter staying in a place with as many germs as our home had accumulated.

(We learned months later that Sherie and Aaron's goal was to do everything in their power to save Jazmin's life. If it meant trips around the world to see the best doctors or regimens of strict healthy diets, they would do it.)

I walked through the white sheer curtains and onto the balcony, where the waters below and the clouds above were dark and looming. Stepping into the spiritual realm awaiting me, I felt a heaviness in my soul. A thick fog of fear enveloped me. Would my son lose the love of his life before he married her? Charity thought a miracle had happened, but I had my doubts.

I sent messages to our friends Sue and Dean and Wendell and Lila, asking them to pray for Jazmin. Wendell and Lila pastored our church. Wendell had been Vance's closest friend for over twenty-six years. Sue and I had been close friends for ten years.

Charity messaged us that Jazmin and Eythan were going to speed up their wedding date, which was supposed to be August 19. They wanted to get married now.

Our daughters, Charity and Aryanna, used to watch the movie *A Walk to Remember.* Mandy Moore plays a high school girl with cancer who falls in love with a rebellious teenage boy in her school, and they decide to get married even though she has a short time to live.

Never in a million years did we think we'd be living a similar story.

We called Charity and put her on speaker mode.

"Hi, Mom and Dad!"

"How is everyone doing?" I asked as we sat on the bed.

"Well, Eythan and Jazmin have decided to elope!" She giggled with excitement.

Vance and I smiled at each other.

"Can you ask them to at least wait until we get home?"

She laughed. "I think they plan on having all the parents and siblings there to see them get married. And they still plan on having a big celebration in August."

"Oh, I'm so happy for them!" My heart warmed as I thought about them being able to have some time together as husband and wife before Jazmin passed away.

We would have a new bonus daughter quicker than we thought. We hung up and breathed a sigh of relief.

Then it dawned on me that Jazmin's parents hadn't heard these plans yet. I hoped they felt at peace about the kids eloping. They had allowed Jazmin to make her own decisions, but her parents' blessing would be crucial to them moving their wedding date up. Jazmin didn't want to disappoint her mom and dad, so whatever Sherie and Aaron said would have a big influence on what the kids did.

Vance and I headed to the pool and tried to relax in the beautiful Jamaican sunshine. I plunked our beach bag down on the cobblestones, kicked off my flip-flops, and sat down on my beach chair.

Another text from Charity: "Jazmin's CAT scan came back. No new cancer. No new growth since a year ago."

My heart fluttered. This was good news! I took a deep breath, exhaled my worries, let out all the tension, leaned back in my chair, and lifted my face to the glorious sunshine.

When I opened my eyes, a mother and her young son were sitting across from us with strawberry ice cream cones. Their moment together was peaceful and normal. Simplicity sat in front of me. The beauty of family, love, and life.

I felt like I had attended a funeral and won the lottery within five hours' time. The prize? Being able to keep Jazmin on this earth a little longer. Their treat appeared brighter and more wonderful than I ever remembered ice cream cones looking. I wanted this wonderful, simple, beautiful life for Jazmin and Eythan.

I embraced the moment, and a glimmer of hope sparked in my soul. Maybe Jazmin would get better. Maybe Sherie and Aaron would be okay with Jazmin and Eythan marrying early.

Back on our ocean resort balcony, I wondered how Aaron and Sherie did it. They were our age and had lived in complete chaos the past two years as they were constantly traveling with Jazmin to see doctors. How did they ride this roller coaster called cancer year after year with their daughter?

Jazmin had already survived past the time most people with this type of cancer had lived. She was at the two-year mark, and she was thin but had clear skin and thick hair. She didn't look sick. A glimmer of hope warmed me.

As I pondered such deep and weighty thoughts, I heard a familiar whisper in my soul.

Cindy, come walk on water with Me.

I knew what God was asking of me: to have faith in Him, to believe in Him, to know He could carry Jazmin and Eythan through all the uncertain days ahead . . . to let go.

Could I trust Him? Would I be disappointed with the outcome?

Closing my eyes, I saw Jesus holding out His hand to me.

I put my hand in His.

Mother's Day weekend ended with a mother's prayer.

Dear God,

I give Jazmin to You, and I'm going to choose to put my blind trust in You. Help me to walk on water with You. I'm terrified. Panicked. Uncertain. Please give Jazmin more time so she and Eythan can get married. If it is Your will for them to get married now, let Sherie and Aaron give them their blessing.

CHAPTER FIVE

Through the Desert

When I was a young girl, my dad told me,
"First you go to school, then you get married, and then you
have babies . . . in that order!" And I said, "Okay, Daddy."
When I got a little older and he told me the order for my life,
I said with a grin, "Okay. First I'll have babies, then I'll go to
school, and then I'll get married!" I laughed my head off as he
frantically said, "No, no, no, no, no! You've got it all wrong!"
But I knew he was right. School, then marriage,
then babies. Got it!

—JAZMIN HENSON

June 2017

CHARITY CALLED AND TOLD us how the visit went after Sherie and Aaron arrived.

Jazmin was home from the hospital. She looked good, but her parents inquired about her appearance because when they had first received the call, Jazmin was doing terrible.

Imagine their shock to see her sitting at our kitchen table looking perfectly normal after coughing up lots of blood the day before and feeling like she was going to die.

Both being schoolteachers and watching out for Jazmin as much as possible, Aaron and Sherie went through the usual drill with their daughter:

"Are you taking care of yourself?"

"Are you eating healthy?"

"Are you drinking enough?"

"Are you getting enough rest?"

They needed to know she could keep living at our house for the next month and still take care of her health.

Jazmin had been going to our maple forest each day. I was concerned about the physical activity of snowshoeing up hills and through thick bushes to tap trees. But she could not be deterred. Wherever Eythan was, she wanted to be there.

Eythan and Jazmin had been enjoying watching movies in the evenings and eating chocolate bars and candy. Jazmin loved candy! The typical things young adults took for granted were not activities she was supposed to be doing.

Sitting at our kitchen table, Jazmin's parents encouraged her to either move the wedding up to a closer date or wait until August and get married on their original date instead of going to the courthouse.

Jazmin and Eythan talked about the options. They decided to stick to their original plan to marry in August. I was worried she might not make it another seven months. But Jazmin kept living like she didn't have cancer. And I kept watching the clock, knowing she was running out of time.

Jazmin believed God was going to give her a complete healing from cancer, and I believed I was supposed to help her get to the point where she would accept she wasn't going to get a miracle. It would become my best-kept secret that Jazmin would never know.

At the time, I honestly believed it was the kindest thing I could do for Jazmin. But God knew the best thing for me was to give me a daughter-in-law who would teach me a whole new way to live, to believe, to hope, and to never give up on God's ability to heal.

Jazmin's faith bolstered mine during some of my hardest days. I had been sick for years due to toxic mold in our home, and I was especially sick during the year after we met Jazmin.

One Sunday in church, our pastor, Wendell, had just finished preaching and said, "Let's pray."

I was sitting in the front row, and as I bowed my head to pray, something started pooling out of my nose. I cupped my hand under it to catch it. I looked down—blood. It scared me! I'd never in all my life had a bloody nose. I wasn't scared because it was blood but because it was the straw that broke the camel's back.

Vance and I went to the emergency room at our local hospital. I was fortunate to have the sweetest doctor, but he was stumped as to what could be going on in my body. He ran a massive number of tests. Everything was perfect, even my hemoglobin.

I thought for sure I had cancer, a brain tumor, diabetes, thyroid disease—I had googled it all in the past year. A different disease was diagnosed every week by Doctor Me.

The real doctor said he couldn't find anything, yet somehow I knew he believed me that something was wrong. This is the same story many people who have been through toxic mold have shared. I left the hospital frustrated and feeling a bit hopeless.

My naturopathic doctor encouraged me to get our home tested for mold.

The mold experts came into our house and took samples. Weeks later, we got the lab results back. Two deadly toxic molds. This happened during a five-year span as a result of Kyle flooding his toilet by stuffing household items in it and flushing until water flowed throughout our home.

I've wondered many times why God allowed me to go through all that. Now I know He wanted me to be still. To hear His voice. In His care, God was nursing me, teaching me, speaking to me by my bedside each day.

I love people, and I like to move. Being still used to drive me crazy! If I had my choice of a dream job, it would be to work in a café every day, talking to the people who come in and sip warm mugs of delicious lattes and cappuccinos while they chat with their friends. Or I'd be a hippie, traveling the world in my van, wearing bohemian dresses, with my family seeing all the wonders this world has to offer. Kyle would be free of autism, and our family could experience the simplicities of normal life.

I was stuck in a moldy house for a year, with no friends, no outings, no fun . . . just sickness. I still mustered energy once in a blue moon to go see my friends Kyna and Sue. Sometimes I came home right after and rolled into bed. But I faithfully got up every morning at 4:30, grabbed a coffee, and started writing. (I had written *Beauty from Ashes* the year I was sick, when we met Jazmin. She helped me format my book to upload it to Amazon. She was a godsend! That was right before we went to Jamaica.) The days I didn't write, I still took care of my family.

When Jazmin came into our lives, she shared how God told her to get out of bed every day in faith and not look at how she was feeling but to put one foot in front of the other, trusting God instead of believing her symptoms. That struck me profoundly since I was obsessing over my symptoms and she was living in faith. I took Jazmin's advice and tried to get out more and not let my illness rule my life.

But I had to ask, *Where is God in all this?*

He was carrying me and calling me. He was asking me to come to Him and believe He had a beautiful plan for my suffering.

God allowed me to be sick as I sat writing my life story, *Beauty from Ashes*. I'd already had a horrendous life before I got sick. I didn't need more drama piled on. Every day I prayed for God to restore me, but He brought me into the desert, and I spent a year with Him.

Writing.

Crying.

Praying.

Confessing.

Forgiving.

Healing.

God still had so much for me to learn, and He would teach me through Jazmin's suffering and battle with cancer. How could I lean into Him when I didn't have answers and trust His plan for my life— and for Jazmin's life?

Those who know your name trust in you, for you, LORD,
have never forsaken those who seek you.

(Psalm 9:10)

33

CHAPTER SIX

Poker-Faced Lies

I'm going to say something very important.
DON'T EVER TAKE DISHWASHERS FOR GRANTED!
I have never been happier to load up a dishwasher in my life.
The things I took for granted when I lived at home with my
parents became so evident when I began apartment living.

—JAZMIN HENSON

May 2017

E HAD RETURNED FROM Jamaica. I was painting my cupboards a beautiful off-white linen color called Vanilla Frosting.

Vance came into the kitchen and stood beside me. "Do you want me to fix that broken drawer?" The front face of the drawer had a crack through it. But my husband is the size of New York City when he's standing in a room. If I'm working in the kitchen, I don't usually want him in my space because it takes five minutes to walk around his big strong shoulders.

I lifted my brush and looked up at him. "No. I want to leave it like that. It's the one Eythan broke."

"When?"

"He was eight and too short to reach the plastic drinking cups. He would open this drawer and use it as a stepladder." My heart warmed as I pictured my little blond-haired boy.

As I painted the cupboards, my thoughts were on Eythan moving to Sudbury to begin his new life with Jazmin. He was starting a new job and was going to live on his own until Jazmin moved in with him after they were married. I was excited for him. But I had been a bit teary-eyed the weeks before at the thought of him leaving home.

I looked in the drawer, and memories flooded back of the little boy with blond hair and crystal-blue eyes who used to sit on my knee and think his world revolved around me.

I remembered the day we moved into this house. The kids went running in to see their rooms. I walked into the kitchen and found Eythan standing in front of the dishwasher, his arms around the front of it.

He had his eyes closed and a huge smile across his face. "I love you, dishwasher."

I smiled. We had rented a house and lived in it for a year while we were building our new home. There was no dishwasher, and all the kids took turns doing dishes. Eythan loathed doing dishes.

Eythan was a cuddle bug when he was small. Every chance he had, he cuddled on my lap. He loved it when Vance worked out of town because that meant he could sleep in Mom and Dad's bed. He snuggled up next to me and fell asleep.

Eythan struggled with telling the truth until he was twelve years old. I had a hard time believing anything he said held an ounce of truth. One day, his cousin Scott came over to play. Scott is my nephew. His mom, Kyna, Vance's cousin and my best friend, set me up with Vance when we were teenagers.

Kyna and I had an errand to run, and before we went out the door, the boys asked if they could go out Eythan's bedroom window and run around on the roof of our two-story house.

"Absolutely not!" was my proper response.

When we returned home, I saw a flash of red move across the roof.

I marched into the house with Kyna on my heels, prepared to go toe to toe with the lying boys.

I yelled upstairs, "Why were you two on the roof?"

"We weren't on the roof," Eythan said with a straight face.

I could strike it rich if this kid became a professional poker player. "Yes, you were. I saw Scott's red shirt."

Scott wasn't quite as talented at lying. His eyes shifted to Eythan, then to me.

"No, we weren't!" Eythan stuck to his statement.

We went back and forth for a few minutes, then I said, "Eythan, if you lie to me about this, why would I believe you any other time?"

Eythan grew quiet.

Eventually Vance told me to let him deal with Eythan's lies and gave me a break. I was able to share a lot of good moments with Eythan rather than always trying to go toe to toe with him in a battle of poker faces.

When Eythan was much older, he told me that day was pivotal because he realized he didn't want to grow up to be a man who couldn't be trusted. After Eythan met Jazmin, I knew she would be good for him and would hold him accountable to be the honest man he was and continued to strive to be. She treated my son with respect, and he adored her.

But I knew I would miss my "Eeffer." I was hoping Eythan would live a peaceful, quiet life. Isn't that what every mother dreams?

I didn't know what his future held, but Vance and I always hoped our children would find peace no matter what life brought them.

What Eythan would face in the coming years was far from a quiet, peaceful life.

Lord,
when chaos is all we know, help us to find a place to retreat to, so we can hear your voice and feel your peace.

Amen.

CHAPTER SEVEN

Rope Swings, Mud Slides, and a $100,000 Miracle

My full name is Jazmin Faith Henson. My mom said that when I was born, I went unnamed for three days. My parents finally agreed on the name Jazmin as long as it was spelled with a z. My middle name, Faith, was given to me because my parents felt that God's plan for my life would heavily involve faith in Him. Boy, were they right.

—JAZMIN HENSON

June–July 2017

I GOT A TEXT FROM Sherie, Jazmin's mom. "Had to call an ambulance for Jazmin please pray!"

Immediately I sent a text to Eythan, telling him I was praying for him and Jazmin, knowing he'd text me when he could since everyone was running to the hospital.

I didn't know if she had passed out, was in severe pain, or was even alive. I hated not knowing when something happened to Jazmin.

I felt completely undone. To think of her in any kind of pain broke my heart.

Soon Sherie sent an update and said Jazmin was in a lot of pain.

I sat in my bedroom, crying—again.

While Jazmin was at the hospital, the doctors tried different medications to manage the pain. Finally, around suppertime, we heard Jazmin had fallen asleep.

Relief washed over me.

Many evenings when she was visiting, Jazmin had carried her heated beanbag to the couch, scrunched up into a small ball, and dozed off.

Sometimes sadness and a feeling of helplessness washed over me because there was nothing I could do for her. I wanted to grab on to her faith and cling to it for dear life. But I felt bogged down with worry.

A video I saw on *America's Funniest Videos* featured a heavyset woman at the top of a mud bank overlooking a lake. She grabbed a rope and attempted to swing, but her body was too heavy. Almost as soon as she lifted her feet, she lost her grip and spiraled down the mud slide, face-first. The video showed others who barely made it into the lake. They face-planted in the mud on the shore.

The weight of cancer was heavy. Would I make it to the cool, refreshing lake or sink into a thick, murky abyss?

I knew God had placed Jazmin in Eythan's life, and him in hers. My son was going to mature in his faith more than most young men his age. He would need to lean into God to get him and his future wife through the dark valleys of cancer. I prayed he had the strength to hold on dearly to Jesus so he could help carry Jazmin through the days ahead.

One afternoon, I got a text from Sherie that caused my heart to race.

The painkiller the hospital had sent Jazmin home with the previous day had caused her to throw up everything for twenty-four hours. Now they had her on an IV for dehydration.

My hope fizzled. Was this the end?

Their wedding was still three months away. It might as well be thirty years away.

The next day Vance and I drove to Sudbury to see Jazmin and Eythan.

Vance always teases me that I don't drive, I sleep in the driver's seat. I prop my pillow against the SUV window, close my eyes, and wake up in a different city. It's like being transported in time.

We wound our way through the twisty, unkempt roads of Sudbury to the hospital and walked hand in hand across the parking lot. Vance and I took the elevator up to Jazmin's floor and looked for her room.

There she was, small and frail, dark circles around her eyes.

I kept my composure as I hugged my sweet future daughter, and it felt so good to have her in my arms. How I loved this precious girl! I turned and hugged Eythan, and he looked the best I had seen him in years.

Jazmin was exhausted, since her hemoglobin had dropped twenty points in one night. She slept while we visited.

This was our first time meeting Aaron. When we walked into the room, he was sitting on the windowsill with Sherie. Both rose to hug us.

If there was any mother on this earth who would do everything in her power to save her child, Sherie was it. I saw worry in her blue eyes. Sherie was pretty, with a dazzling white smile. I could see where Jazmin's beauty came from. Anything Jazmin needed Sherie would get for her.

Aaron was a husky man, about six feet tall, with the same color hair as Jazmin. He had a big grin that came easily.

Sherie and Aaron were both teachers. Aaron taught physical education, and Sherie taught home economics to kids with special needs. I could tell her heart was tender, and she was a compassionate woman. It seemed as though Sherie and Jazmin had run nonstop for a month. Whenever we saw Sherie, she had a big smile and hug for us, and she seemed to see the positive side in negative situations. Aaron could make a person laugh no matter how serious a situation might be. Jazmin's sister, Vangie, was the same. Her contagious laughter and beautiful smile were evident during Jazmin's stay in the hospital. They had learned to laugh on their hardest days and to embrace life in the moment, because today might be Jazmin's last day.

Hope was a solid rock in the Ayotte family. Today was a new day, and they were going to let the difficulties in life roll off their backs.

But Sherie and Aaron appeared tired and worried.

We learned that the doctor suggested radiation. It wouldn't save Jazmin's life; it would just halt the progression of one of the tumors. The Ayotte family didn't feel good about this. They were praying that God would provide another solution. But nothing was appearing.

What we didn't realize was that God was on the move.

I sat on the window seat, leaned close to Sherie, and whispered, "Has Jazmin told you about her friend Gayle, who's getting treatment in Arizona, and the success she's having?"

"No." Sherie's eyes widened.

I had her undivided attention. "I know her dad and stepmom. They grew up in my hometown. I follow them on Facebook. They're feeling hopeful that this new treatment may shrink Gayle's cancer."

Sherie rubbed her tired eyes. "Well, we are looking for options, and I know nothing is impossible with God!" She grabbed her knees and took in a deep breath.

When I showed her Gayle's Facebook page, Sherie was flabbergasted and asked for more information.

I messaged my friend Charlene Katzenback, Gayle's stepmother, who contacted Sherie and put her in touch with Gayle's doctor. Sherie found out that the initial testing would cost 36,000, US dollars. The entire treatment would cost $100,000.

"We don't have that kind of money," Sherie said. "So if God wants Jazzy to go to Arizona, He is going to have to send us the money."

Charity started a GoFundMe page for Jazmin. Within twenty-four hours, $2,000 had been donated.

God was moving everything into place for Jazmin to go to Arizona. I could see Sherie and Aaron were touched by how much people were giving.

Within forty-eight hours, $26,000 was in Sherie's hands.

Sherie and Aaron were speechless. Their hope was bolstered as they watched God do His thing.

> Sherie and Aaron were speechless. Their hope was bolstered as they watched God do His thing.

Aaron sat quietly in the hospital room most of the time, staring at Jazmin. It wrenched our hearts. His daughter was dying, and there was nothing he could do about it. We could see the helpless feeling in his worried eyes.

After days of nausea, Jazmin finally got hungry and ate half a waffle. Aaron was so excited you would have thought she had won the Nobel Peace Prize. Aaron speaks one volume: really loud.

Jazmin tried to hush him. "Dad, the whole hospital can hear you!"

"Well, sweetheart, you ate a waffle. I haven't seen you eat that much in a long time!" Aaron grinned from ear to ear.

One evening, Jazmin's older sister, Vangie, came to the hospital for a visit. We sat around telling funny stories and riddles where you had to figure out the missing piece.

Vangie has long curly hair like her mom and a mischievous grin like her dad. She loves to laugh, and sometimes she giggled so hard she cried, especially at her father when he was trying to tell a riddle but had it backward.

I couldn't figure out if we were laughing at Aaron or at Vangie because she was laughing so hard.

We spent an hour having a wonderful time as the seven of us bonded. Jazmin sat in her bed watching us, in between dozing off to sleep. She lay quietly, her hands across her abdomen. At one point Eythan bugged her by reaching his big toe out and hitting the button that made Jazmin's bed go up. He sent her up five feet in the air, and she grinned at him with a you're-such-a-bug look. Eythan smiled back. The two of them sent silent messages back and forth. Eythan kept things fun for Jazmin. He was the calm when the world around her was a storm.

I thought of the timing of their relationship and was amazed that God had brought them together when He did. Eythan had been able to support her through the hardest part of her life and could make her smile on her toughest days. He teased Jazmin relentlessly and was always poking her or tickling her, and Jazmin just smiled or giggled.

Sherie told me that Eythan seemed to be what Jazmin wanted and needed and he brought her peace and comfort. My mother-heart swelled with pride when I heard her express gratefulness for my son.

But Jazmin had done the same for Eythan, and his heart was completely smitten with her. I told Sherie that Eythan and our family were in this for the long haul, no matter what happened to Jazmin. We wanted Sherie and Aaron to know they weren't alone and that we wanted to be a support to their family as they prayed, cared for, and worried about their daughter.

We met Eythan for breakfast the next morning at a restaurant a block from the hospital. The waitress poured Vance and me mugs of hot coffee. The three of us chatted while we waited for our food.

At one point, Eythan flipped open his phone and said, "Fifty-five more days until we get married."

I was so proud of him. His fiancé was dying, but he had not lost hope. I didn't care what my son did or didn't accomplish in this life; I couldn't imagine being prouder of him than I did that day as he looked forward to Jazmin being his bride—cancer and all.

The next day we went back to the hospital to say goodbye. The blood transfusion had given Jazmin energy, but she felt yucky, warm, and restless. Her parents were concerned. We wanted to stay until Jazmin was more stable, but we had to get home. Charity and Devyn were watching Kyle, and we were already late and needed to get back so they could leave.

We prayed for Jazmin before we left, and I started to cry. I hoped she could get to Arizona for treatments. I also knew she could die before we saw her again—would we see her again?

We left heavy hearted and quiet, silently praying that God would spare Jazmin and carry her though until she received the new treatment.

After we left, Eythan filmed himself and Jazmin sitting on her hospital bed and posted the video on Facebook. He tagged a couple of friends and challenged them to tag their friends, asking them to do burpees for Jazmin and then donate to her fundraiser. They started a hashtag #burpeezforjaz.

The fundraiser spread like wildfire. Friends tagged athletes in the CrossFit community, the sport our family loved. CrossFit gyms started tagging one another.

Within another three days, GoFundMe had brought in another $9,500. They now had enough funds to head to Arizona for special treatments.

Jazmin was released from the hospital. She was still throwing up, but she wanted to go home.

The next day, she felt better. She and Eythan went furniture shopping for their apartment. Jazmin had fun at the mall. She loved fashion and home décor. They were counting down the days until they could sit on their new couch in their own apartment they called home.

Surely God is my salvation; I will trust and not be afraid.
The Lord, the Lord himself, is my strength and my defense;
he has become my salvation.

(Isaiah 12:2)

Provide for those who grieve in Zion—to bestow on them
a crown of beauty instead of ashes, the oil of joy instead
of mourning, and a garment of praise instead of a spirit
of despair. They will be called oaks of righteousness, a
planting of the Lord for the display of his splendor.

(Isaiah 61:3)

Lord,

When medicine has no answers, show us the solution. Give
our doctors guidance to make us well. Help us to trust You
when it looks like the end is near. You determine our days
and the length of them.

Amen.

CHAPTER EIGHT

Prayer and Pie

*The most important thing about me is my faith in Jesus.
He is my Lord and Savior and comforter. He is strong in my
weakness. Knowing that God loves me unconditionally
gets me through every single day.*

—JAZMIN HENSON

*Man oh man, I am so thankful that I have all the supports
that I do. In all forms, from family to friends,
to medical care, to support from machines,
and of course the comfort and peace of God.*

—JAZMIN HENSON

*Neither do people light a lamp and put it under a bowl.
Instead they put it on its stand, and it gives light to everyone
in the house. In the same way, let your light shine before
others, that they may see your good deeds and
glorify your Father in heaven.*

(MATTHEW 5:15–16)

July 2017

CHARITY AND I STARTED a Facebook prayer group called Jazmin Faith Ayotte's God Is on the Move. This way Sherie could text us updates from Arizona. And we could post them on her prayer page so people could pray for Jazmin and also see God's amazing power to provide her with everything she needed for treatment.

Sherie shared Jazmin's history so we could start the group:

After being given no prognosis from the medical community, she has tried numerous natural therapies out of country. She has since had further metastasis in her kidney and diaphragm and considerable growth in her lung tumors. Jazmin was recently in the hospital to manage extreme pain caused by tumors in her kidney.

Her family has recently learned of a doctor in Arizona who does state-of-the-art testing and treatments that preserve the immune system and target specific rare and aggressive cancers like Jazmin's. One of her peers who was given months to live is being treated there and is getting great results. We would like the opportunity to take Jazmin there.

Her Facebook prayer group had hundreds of people added to it. I don't think Sherie knew what she got herself into when she met the Hensons. We were a capable social media family, and we had Jazmin's story flying everywhere—fast. Sherie's head was spinning and so was her heart. She couldn't believe how quickly God moved in Jazmin's situation and how public it went. I think Sherie might have felt a bit like Mary Poppins, with her umbrella of faith sweeping her off to places she never thought possible.

The Ayotte family had been very quiet and protective of Jazmin's cancer journey. Sherie didn't want people to say the wrong thing to Jazmin and affect her faith and belief in getting a miracle.

But there is power in stories. If our current struggle could help someone else with their relationship with God, isn't our story worth telling?

I wrote blog posts about Eythan and Jazmin on my website, www.cindyseaton.com, and the women who wrote me were always touched by Jazmin's strength and hope.

> But there is power in stories. If our current struggle could help someone else with their relationship with God, isn't our story worth telling?

More people began to pray for her as her story spread around the world in churches, families, and the community. Sherie had thought God was going to heal Jazmin in a quiet setting through alternative treatments, not publicly for all to see.

We continued to pray, asking God what else we could do to raise money for Jazmin's continued treatments in Arizona.

"Let's throw a stag and doe fundraiser for Jazmin and Eythan!" Charity said to me one day when we were eating a snack at the kitchen counter.

My hand stopped halfway to my mouth. Could God pull off a fundraiser in three weeks? As my mind reeled, I heard His quiet voice whisper, "Just watch Me move!"

I called my friend Sue. "I'm planning a fundraiser for Jazmin and Eythan."

"What can I do to help?" Sue, my friend with a heart of gold, and her husband, Dean, would do whatever they could.

Two weeks before the stag and doe, Jazmin and Sherie headed to Arizona for Jazmin to have her pretesting done.

When Sherie and Jazmin came home from Arizona, we had the stag and doe. Our kids and some of their friends helped decorate and set up booths that required the guests to use either their brains or their brawn. Sue sold raffle tickets at the front door, and I'm convinced she could sell lipstick to a gorilla. With her big smile and bright blue eyes, people have a hard time saying no to her.

Charity had spent a significant amount of time working on the event. She was great with social media, and the stag and doe reached many people. She spent many hours designing the booths and decorating on the day of the event. Our son Devyn, our daughter Aryanna, and Charity's husband, Dan, helped with decorating too.

The theme of the stag and doe was Brains or Brawn. Jazmin was feeling good that night, and she was dressed in a lab coat with a pair of big glasses taped around the bridge and her hair in pigtails. She was the perfect-looking brainiac. Eythan wore a muscle shirt and a headband and had all the brawn he could muster going on.

Sherie and Aaron had driven up for the event. They had a lot of fun meeting many of our friends and family. I watched Sheri from the booth I was hosting play Ping-Pong in her knee-length dress, her ponytail bouncing. Her giggle and smile told me she was enjoying the evening.

Jazmin and Eythan mingled with friends and family and played games with the guests. For one game, we had labeled two jars Bride and Groom, which circled throughout the crowd. Guests could put money into the jar of the person they wanted to see get a pie in the face.

Of course, by the end of the evening, Eythan's jar had a significant amount of money.

He sat perched on a chair while Jazmin took a whipped-cream pie and, with great gusto and delight, smashed Eythan's face with it. The two of them laughed.

The crowd gave a big cheer, and the room filled with laughter.

That night we gained many happy memories with Jazmin. Would we have more happy memories like these? I hoped so.

The kids had helped me and Vance, along with Sue and Dean, to host a successful fundraiser in a short amount of time. God did not disappoint us. In three weeks, He pulled off an event that usually takes three months to plan. A small miracle.

But could God pull off a bigger miracle and heal Jazmin of cancer too? She thought so, as did Sherie. I had my doubts. Wasn't I the logical one? Time would tell.

For now, we had more money for the treatment, and maybe by some miracle, it would work.

But could God pull off a bigger miracle and heal Jazmin of cancer too? She thought so, as did Sherie. I had my doubts. Wasn't I the logical one? Time would tell.

Dear Lord,

When we have no faith that You can do big miracles, show us little miracles to build our faith so we can believe You can do something even greater!

Amen.

CHAPTER NINE

Wedding Bells

*I am married to my best friend, who is the most caring man
in the world. Eythan Henson became my husband
on August 19, 2017. He is a man devoted to God.
I couldn't imagine my life without him.*

—JAZMIN HENSON

August 2017

A FEW WEEKS LATER, WE were traveling to Sudbury for the wedding. On this trip, I stayed awake, gabbing excitedly with Vance about the upcoming wedding weekend. We had arranged three nights of care for Kyle, and it was a real treat for us to get away on a mini vacation. We would have a weekend in a hotel, a rehearsal dinner, and a day to celebrate Jazmin and Eythan's wedding and marriage.

Vance and I spent Friday morning with Sherie and Aaron, helping a volunteer decorator prepare the hall for the reception in our hotel. Weeks before, the original decorator had to cancel, but God provided another woman who stepped up to the plate and offered her services. God showed us over and over how He could take care of anything that fell through.

For hours we unwound white tulle and carefully laid white linen napkins on the table and hung white lanterns from the ceiling. An abundance of twinkling miniature lights were spread throughout the large room. When we stood back and admired the magic, it looked beautiful! We had helped the decorator transform a rather dull-looking ballroom into a fairy-tale mirage.

Sherie and I ran errands Friday afternoon. I had barely spent any time with her before the wedding, so I was looking forward to getting to know her better as we scooted around the city in my truck.

Sherie turned in the passenger seat and looked at me with teary eyes. Jazmin had been in pain all day. "Oh, Cindy, why does it have to be this way? Jazmin has been through so much. Can't she be pain free on her wedding day?"

I tried not to cry myself. "Sherie, tomorrow is a new day. Let's put our hope in that and believe she is going to be well for the wedding." As the words came out of my mouth, peace settled in my heart.

"You're right, Cindy. We need to have faith in God." Sherie took a deep breath, let out a long slow breath, and dried her eyes.

Sherie didn't hide her emotions and was very real with her feelings. I liked that about her.

We pulled ourselves together. Two moms on a mission to see our kids have a joy-filled wedding day. I had a lot of fun with Sherie. Our friendship was going forward in tiny steps. It was important to Vance and me that we connect with the families our children married into. We wanted to spend time together on special occasions and not always feel like strangers or be awkward with one another if we only visited a couple of times a year.

That afternoon we had the rehearsal at the little church. Jazmin wore a knee-length floral dress, and Eythan wore a dress shirt and pants. Jazmin had quite a bit of pain as the wedding party rehearsed. She had taken medication but wanted to rush through so she could sit down and give the pills time to alleviate the pain. Jazmin held her hand around her side, pressing into her kidney. Her face was serious and drawn, and she was curt as she directed everyone quickly through the practice run.

I felt the tension in the room as everyone walked on eggshells around the bride-to-be. Would she be okay tomorrow, or would this pain carry over?

After the rehearsal, we drove to a local restaurant for dinner. Our evening was relaxed and fun as we saw Jazmin return to her normal, happy self. We sat in high-back chairs at one long table, and we laughed, visited, and ate for a couple of hours.

Before we went to bed, I posted in Jazmin's prayer group, asking people to pray for her to have a pain-free wedding day. In the morning, I texted Sherie, asking how Jazmin was doing.

"Good!" she texted back.

A big smile spread across my face. My heart rejoiced. Today was going to be a great day! I could feel it in my soul.

Sherie messaged me again, asking if I had booked a hairdresser for myself for the wedding.

I told her I hadn't.

Sheri had heard of a shop that had a renowned hairdresser and made us both an appointment.

I agreed to meet her at the shop. Vance dropped me off after breakfast, and he went off to do something with Aaron. I had no clue what Aaron had planned for him and Vance, but Aaron always had something up his sleeve that involved Vance later telling me funny stories about weird adventures.

I hopped out of the car. "Sherie will drive me back to her house after." I leaned in through his window and gave him a quick kiss.

He raised his eyebrows at me. "Bye, beautiful." He always calls me that. Not a day since we got married has he forgotten to tell me I'm beautiful.

I hurried away to get my fabulous makeover. I walked toward the three-store plaza and stepped into a dark space. The shop was predominately one color: black.

Sherie stood at the front desk, and we gave each other a hug.

The friendly lady behind the desk greeted us and told us to have a seat.

We plunked down into two chairs in front of the big picture window and talked about Jazmin and last-minute details. Then Sherie confided in me, "I'm really excited to have been fortunate enough to book this hairdresser. I never get my hair done. Jazmin usually trims it for me, and rarely do I even do that."

"This is so exciting, Sherie. I can't wait to see what he does with your long curly hair!" What style would she choose? Long straight hair flat-ironed out? An updo of curls?

After a few minutes, an elderly gentleman came out and called Sherie's name. He was about five and a half feet tall and pleasantly plump. Was this the famous hairdresser? He definitely didn't look like a young and hip stylist you might see in a movie set in Paris. I had pictured a man in his thirties with a black tam on his head, positioned slightly to one side, a scarf around his neck, and a thin mustache.

Sherie grabbed her purse and followed the adorable little man as he shuffled to his chair.

A few minutes later, a tall slim woman in her twenties called my name. I sat in her chair. She wrapped a black poncho around me, took out my ponytail, and began to comb out my curly hair. "What style would you like?"

"A bun with soft curls around my face." I reached up and ran my fingers through my silky blond hair.

As my hairdresser grabbed her curling iron, I looked into the mirror and saw Sherie behind me, her chair perpendicular to mine.

The little gentleman was brushing through her tight curls. He had created a massive amount of frizz. It reminded me of the static metal balls at a science fair you can put your hand on and all your hair goes out from your head in a wide circle. He managed to take the frizz, give it a few twists, and clip the giant mass to the back of her head. I gasped when I saw one long piece of frizz down Sherie's back.

My hairdresser's gaze darted nervously from my reflection to Sherie's.

Nervous thoughts swirled in my head. Was that the hairdo Sherie asked for? If so, what would I say if she asked if I liked it? What if she liked it, then changed her mind if I told her I didn't?

I mulled over ways I could be kind but honest. I was horrible at this! My relationship with Sherie was new, and I didn't want to ruin it by insulting her.

Maybe the hairdresser was going to unclip it and do something else. I prayed he would because I didn't want to have an awkward conversation with Sherie, especially in front of my hairdresser.

I looked up again, and the gentlemen had whipped off her poncho and was shaking it out.

Sherie stood and brushed off her clothing.

My eyes grew big. Was that really the finished product? *Dear God, please don't let her ask me what I think.*

Sherie rushed over to my chair, leaned close to me, and whispered, "Cindy, I've got to go!" Her face said it all—she was not the least bit happy with her frizz bomb. She looked like Ms. Frizzle from the *Magic School Bus*, and I knew that wasn't the style she had dreamed of when she'd lain in bed the night before, envisioning herself walking down the aisle looking like she'd been featured on the cover of *Vogue* magazine. Sherie rushed out the door. I heard her car start up, and she drove away.

Oh, great. She was my ride. How was I going to get to her house?

My phone chimed.

"Sorry for ditching you, but I'm heading to find another hairdresser. Can you ask Vance to pick you up?"

I messaged her back telling her yes, then texted Vance.

An hour later I was walking out of the shop toward my husband. Vance always raises his eyebrows when he likes the way I look. Today the look in his eyes did not say, *Hey, gorgeous!*

I hopped into the car. "What? You don't like my hairdo?"

"Do you?" he asked.

I love the way he deflects the inevitable. I flipped down the visor and looked in the mirror. "Well, it looks better than when I walked into the shop." I turned to him and said, "Okay, why don't you like my hair?"

He looked sheepish. He's a smart man. Answering this question is like answering the question, *Do I look fat in this dress?* A husband can't win no matter how he answers. Vance looked at me blankly. "You still look beautiful, but you look much older than forty-eight."

I looked in the mirror again. My bun was pulled tight like a librarian's, with some perfect curls from the 1800s around my face. "You're right." I sighed. "What am I going to do?"

"Can you find another hairdresser?"

"It's too late." I was stuck with this stern-looking concoction.

We headed back to Sherie and Aaron's.

I walked up the four stairs and into the kitchen of their side-split house. I heard giggling and loud voices as the six bridesmaids, Jazmin, and Sherie all talked excitedly.

"Cindy!" Sherie called out to me.

I followed the voice to the bathroom and found Sherie sitting on a stool in front of the long vanity. Jazmin was doing her hair.

"My hair looked horrible!" Sherie said, looking at my reflection in the mirror.

Boy, was I glad she said it first. "I was wondering if you'd asked for that style, but I didn't want to say anything in case you liked it."

"Are you kidding me? It was the worst hairdo ever!"

I laughed.

"Jazmin told me to come home and she would do my hair."

Holding bobby pins between her lips and a curling iron in one hand, Jazmin mumbled about the mess the hairdresser had created.

By then, Charity had come into the bathroom. "Mom, do you want me to do your hair?"

"Are you sure you have time?" I patted my librarian bun.

"Yes. I'm ready; I just have to put on my dress." She had her hair and makeup done, and she looked beautiful. It seemed the bridal party had scored with the right hairdressers.

Half an hour later, my hair looked elegant. Charity had sideswept my hair into a bun and had given me soft, large curls around my face.

A makeup artist applied our makeup. The bridal party and the mothers were the loveliest entourage you could imagine, as if our fairy godmother had turned up and sprinkled us with fairy dust.

Two days before, Jazmin had called to make sure the flowers would be delivered on time, but no one had confirmed the order. Panic ensued when they didn't show up.

Sherie brought calm to the situation. "These details are out of my hands. God is going to have to take care of this."

Charity told Jazmin she would take care of the flower disaster. She called the first flower shop on the list. The owner agreed to make bouquets for the bridal party and twenty centerpieces for the reception. We wondered if the flowers would still be beautiful since they were ordered at the last minute.

The flowers arrived, and we all stood around the table, oohing and ahhing as we unwrapped each box. The bouquets of sage-green eucalyptus and white, pink, and red roses were even lovelier than the original bouquets Jazmin had ordered.

The bridal party changed into their soft pink gowns, and Jazmin came out in her mermaid-style white strapless gown. She was beautiful!

I asked the photographer to take a picture of me and my girls, Jazmin, Charity, and Aryanna, all looking elegant and feminine. Happiness bubbled in my tummy as we squeezed each other tightly and shared delightful, giggly smiles.

We all hopped into cars and drove the thirty minutes into town to the church and gathered in the vestibule at the back. Sherie and I walked down the aisle, each of us on one of Eythan's arms. We were the two happiest moms on earth at that moment, Sherie in her floor-length lavender dress and I in my gown with a white lace bodice and pink chiffon skirt.

Eythan left us on either side of the aisle with our husbands.

Vance squeezed my hand and whispered to me, "You look beautiful!" We stood by our chairs and turned to watch the bridal party walk down the aisle.

My lovely girls walked past me, followed by Jazmin's sister Vangie, Courtney, and her two best friends, Emily and Serena, all dressed in soft pink. The groomsmen matched in their gray suits.

Then Aaron came down the aisle with Jazmin, radiant and smiling at a grinning Eythan, who looked handsome in his navy-blue suit.

What a beautiful gift we were being given that day: a new daughter and a very happy son.

Jazmin came down the aisle looking like a porcelain doll. She was stunningly beautiful. I turned to look at my son. Emotions passed over his face, and I could tell he was trying not to cry. Jazmin smiled as she walked toward her groom. She hugged her dad, and he released her arm as she joined hands with Eythan. Contagious joy filled the room.

Our friend Dean stood under a wooden archway Aaron had built with Eythan. The guests sat in wooden pews, and the interior of the church was mostly stained wood. Everything around this ceremony had a solid surface, and we hoped this would be the same for the foundation of their marriage.

Eythan and Jazmin took the two steps up to the platform, and Dean married them in a beautiful ceremony.

Tears streamed down my face as my son, whom we had poured a thousand prayers into, married this wonderful young woman.

When Eythan was in high school, there were times when we wondered if he would make it to a day like this. He went through a period of testing in his Christian walk, and Vance and I had prayed fervently for him.

A week before the wedding, I sensed God asking me to concentrate on celebrating their union at the wedding and not think about how long they might have together before Jazmin died. God didn't want the day filled with sadness; he wanted it to be about His joy, which meant we had to trust His plan for our children's lives.

Outside the church, Sherie and I hugged and posed for a quick picture with our husbands. Both she and I felt the other had given us a gift. Vance and I were honored to have Jazmin as a daughter now, and they were delighted to finally have a son and a man who loved their daughter.

People had commented about what an amazing young man Eythan was to stick with a girl with cancer—and he was amazing, but not for that reason.

Eythan wasn't sticking with Jazmin to be a hero. She had brought him so much joy since the day he saw her across the dining hall at Aush-Bik-Koong Bible camp. She became his best friend and biggest cheerleader. She had also shown him what was truly important in life and not to sweat the small stuff.

Eythan's name means "strength and patience." When he was young, we waited for the patience to arrive because Eythan didn't have any, and I wondered if his name meant his parents would need mounds of patience and strength to raise him. Now I could see the strength and patience in him, and I felt very proud of my son.

Jazmin shared with us that she was not the same girl before she had cancer. She believed she was kinder and more patient, that she worried less and thought of others' needs instead of just her own. Our two kids had matured in the year before they married, and their love had grown immensely for each other as they faced one trial after another. It seemed as though they had experienced a thousand years of life in one short year.

When Eythan was small, Vance and I traveled to Italy for our fifteenth wedding anniversary. My little boy hopped onto my lap when I got home, cuddled up to me, and with tears in his blue eyes, said, "Mommy, when you die, I want to die!"

I was now happy that my son no longer felt this way, for he had transferred that love and devotion to Jazmin. As a mother, I wanted Eythan to love Jazmin a thousand times more than he had loved me.

I never wanted my daughters-in-law to feel like they had to compete with me for my sons' love or attention. I wanted to see my boys love their wives with all their heart, soul, and mind. If you love your children, give up the competition and encourage them to have a stronger relationship with their spouses than they have had with you.

A devoted marriage is a reflection of Christ's love for us. Someone once said the greatest thing a father can do for his children is to love their mother. Vance has been a tremendous example of a loving husband, and he gave Eythan a wonderful role model to follow.

Jazmin floated through the day on a prayer. Or maybe it was a thousand prayers? I'd lost count. Jazmin felt wonderful the day of her wedding. She danced until ten o'clock that night, and she and Eythan sneaked away with hardly anyone noticing.

Vance and I rolled into bed that night, exhausted from our long day but overjoyed by the wonderful way God had pulled through for us, for Sherie and Aaron, and especially for Jazmin and Eythan.

The imperfect hairdos, lovely decorations, and missing flowers paled in light of the love we had embraced that day. With love, you can conquer anything together and transform it into something beautiful. Trials and tribulations will test our love for each other and our faith in God. True love will withstand the storms that come. If you love someone more than you love yourself, your love will never fail.

Love is patient, love is kind. It does not envy,
it does not boast, it is not proud. It does not dishonor
others, it is not self-seeking, it is not easily angered,
it keeps no record of wrongs. Love does not delight in evil
but rejoices with the truth. It always protects, always trusts,
always hopes, always perseveres.

(1 Corinthians 13:4-7)

CHAPTER TEN

Newlyweds

I am an optimist in every aspect of life.
The glass is always half full in my eyes.

—JAZMIN HENSON

August 2017

"**W**E WANT TO GO on a cruise for our honeymoon." Eythan had blurted out a few months before their wedding as he scrolled his phone looking for vacation packages. How could I tell my adult son that was a horrible idea?

The day the kids said they wanted to leave the country for their honeymoon, Sherie and I were concerned. How could we persuade them to stay in Canada? They had no health insurance. If Jazmin fell ill and needed to be hospitalized, how would she get treatment on a cruise?

They left the safety of Canada, and we were worried sick. How would they manage Jazmin's pain if it got out of control in the middle of the ocean?

Sherie and I decided not to text the kids on their honeymoon. They would contact us if something went wrong. We did a lot of praying that week. I breathed a huge sigh of relief when Eythan and Jazmin landed back on Canadian soil.

I drove across the border into the US, twenty minutes to the airport, and waited excitedly outside the exit door. I saw the kids coming down the ramp. Jazmin wore a pair of ripped jeans and a black T-shirt. Eythan had on a muscle shirt and shorts, and he had a great tan. They looked very happy as they smiled through the window at me. When they came through the door, I hugged them and asked how their trip had gone.

On the drive home, Eythan and Jazmin excitedly filled me in on their week. As I looked at my new daughter-in-law, she seemed to be just as healthy as when they left. Why did I worry so much when God was perfectly capable of taking good care of her? Anxiety that I'd been carrying all week lifted from my mind.

Jazmin said she had some pain on and off, and Eythan had picked up a strange cough. But they had a lovely time, despite the bumps along the way. They went on and on about the food, the buffets, the dining room, and the ice cream. They'd enjoyed their honeymoon, and that made me one happy mama.

Within a week of getting home, they headed to Arizona again for cancer treatment. Which meant more traveling, moving, and uncertainty added to their life as newlyweds. This wasn't the ideal situation most couples want to face within a few weeks of saying, "I do."

They had been in Arizona for a few days when I texted Eythan to find out when Jazmin needed to return to Arizona after her month of treatment. We were trying to plan another fundraiser so she could go back when the doctor requested.

I sat on the porch heavyhearted. Forty-five thousand dollars had been raised so far. Thirty thousand dollars had been used already for the initial testing and for one week of treatment before the wedding. Jazmin had enough to get her through three more weeks, and they were going to throw in some of their own money from the wedding to be able to stay a whole month. How were we going to raise another $20,000 to get her through another month of treatment before Christmas? It seemed impossible!

Feeling discouraged, I went out on my porch one day to dump my feelings on God. We have an overly large front porch, and a couple of years ago, we screened in a portion of it so we could sit without the pesky mosquitoes chewing on us.

God and I have the best counseling sessions there as I listen to birds chirping to one another as the wind rustles our tall maple trees. "Father, I know You can drop a suitcase of money on my front porch. You can do the impossible—I know You can. Please do the impossible for Jazmin."

The next day, Jazmin texted us in our Henson Chat group. She told us her treatment costs had been reduced from $20,000 a month to $6,000! Our family cheered through Messenger and sent praises up to God. Instead of dropping a suitcase of money on our porch, God had drastically dropped the fees. Jazmin now had enough money for three months of treatment! Why had I doubted God's ability to do the impossible?

I was reminded of a story a friend told about a missionary couple who were on furlough when they were invited to their high school reunion. The couple really wanted to go, but the wife didn't own any fancy clothes, and the event was a formal one. They had no extra money to spend on a dress, so they asked God to provide appropriate clothes if He wanted them to attend.

A few days later, they were driving down the highway when they spotted a suitcase on the side of the road. They were in the middle of nowhere and couldn't see anyone nearby. The missionaries stopped, picked up the suitcase, and threw it into the car. When they got to where they were going, they opened the suitcase. Inside was a beautiful formal dress and shoes. The wife tried on the dress and shoes, and they fit perfectly. Since they couldn't find any ID in the luggage to return it to the owner, they knew God had answered their prayer in a mysterious way.

God also showed us He wasn't limited by our resources. He had friends in high places who could get these kids, who barely had two nickels to rub together, through expensive cancer treatments.

Beautiful clothes and money really can drop from the sky. Do you believe God can do these miracles? I do.

The newlyweds were heading into a very busy season of life, and traveling would be exhausting. But if God can drop miracles from heaven, He can help newlyweds who were forced to be gypsies get through the uncertain months ahead.

Sherie and I prayed these kids through their first year of marriage. God has a tender spot for moms who pray. He loves to draw them close to his heart.

Dear Lord,

I pray for the mom who is reading this book.
Show her how nothing is too hard for You.
Your provisions are unlimited. Help us to believe in Your
ability to provide what our kids need.

Amen.

CHAPTER ELEVEN

Suitcase Miracles

*Charlene, Jason, and Gayle did not stay strangers long.
I quickly felt close to them. Strangers became my family.*

—JAZMIN HENSON

September 2017–January 2018

HAVE YOU EVER WONDERED how many things in our lives are just random happenings or God arranging our circumstances in ways that seem bizarre and way out there? Can we trust Him when things look impossible?

Fifteen years ago, I was working in the kitchen at Aush-Bik-Koong Bible Camp (ABK). As I lifted the heavy trays of hot dishes out of the industrial dishwasher, a loud voice startled me. "Hey, are you Cindy Seaton?"

I whirled around to see a man close to my age smiling at me. I walked toward him. "Do I know you?"

He leaned one hip against the cafeteria window where the kids picked up food. He held a green melamine coffee mug. "I'm Jason Katzenback." He shifted and placed a palm on the countertop.

I studied him for a few seconds, trying to find the little boy I remembered from my childhood. I had played with his older sister Tomi when I was in fourth grade, and he was an annoying little bug with a freckled face and mischievous grin.

After a few seconds, I saw the resemblance. "Jason Katzenback, what are you doing at a Bible camp?" I felt embarrassed the moment those words flew out of my mouth. I honestly never thought the little troublemaker would make it to heaven's gates. But here he was, standing on holy ground.

He grinned and explained that he had become a Christian a few years before. He and his wife at the time, Audrey, were at ABK helping with youth camp. I was amazed at the transformation God had done in Jason's life, and I thought I would never see Jason again after Bible camp.

Over a year before we met Jazmin (fourteen years after I saw Jason at ABK), I awoke from a dream. Later that morning, when Vance and I were drinking our coffee, I shared my dream with him.

I had walked into a room full of people holding wine glasses and visiting with one another. I looked across the room and saw Jason Katzenback. I went to say hello, and he gave me a big hug.

Somehow I knew our lives were going to be intertwined with his, but I didn't know how or why. I had a million questions for God. But I let it go and trusted that one day I would understand.

Jason had remarried. His second wife, Charlene, had grown up in Wawa, Ontario, like Jason, Vance, and me. We all knew one another. Vance and I remembered Charlene as a sweet and shy child. We hadn't talked since moving away from Wawa over thirty years before.

When Sherie and Aaron decided to pursue treatment in Arizona for Jazmin after messaging Charlene about her stepdaughter's cancer treatment, I had an aha moment. I realized the dream I had the year before had been given to me to guide us on a path for Jazmin. But the dream happened before I met Jazmin. How does God plan so far ahead? He continually amazes me!

Charlene and Jason were pleased with Gayle's new treatment. Previously, Gayle was given six months to live when doctors discovered a cancerous tumor near her ear known as Ewing's sarcoma. After chemo and radiation, it seemed the cancer was gone. Sadly, it grew back and spread like wildfire throughout her body. The Katzenbacks turned to alternative treatment since there was nothing else that could be done for Gayle medically.

We had seen Charlene's posts on Facebook. She posted regularly in Gayle's prayer group. Charlene recommended Sherri and Aaron call the clinic and see if Jazmin could come to Arizona. Everything was arranged quickly and efficiently. Again we were surprised by how fast God pulled events together.

Gayle, Jazmin, and Eythan were close in age and knew one another through ABK. Charlene and Jason invited them to lodge in the house they had rented until Gayle was done with treatment. Another woman, Christie, who was a wife and mom of three and also getting treatment, would live in the rented house. Together the group became a patched-together family of seven.

The Katzenbacks had been working on a foundation so people like Jazmin could have their cancer treatment subsidized, making it affordable. We were humbled by their generosity and extra-large hearts filled with compassion for those who weren't in a financial position to pay for treatment.

For the first six months of their marriage, Jazmin and Eythan went back and forth between Arizona and home. First they packed up all their belongings and brought them to our house so they wouldn't have to pay rent on an apartment. The newlyweds were going to be living the life of gypsies with no real place to call their own and living with parents in between. Would it exhaust them? Would their marriage suffer from the lack of privacy? Everything seemed uncertain.

Treatments in Arizona were five days a week. Gayle, Jazmin, and Christie had theirs together. They had to sit in a variety of machines for unconventional therapies such as phototherapy, heat and magnetic therapies, and other experimental protocols. High-level vitamin C infusions were administered to each woman two to three times per week. They also took about fifty vitamins a day and had a very healthy diet.

Eventually Charlene and Jason's foundation, Moving Mountains, covered about 90 percent of the costs through fundraising or negotiating with the clinic. This was an incredible blessing and part of the "suitcase miracle."

Jazmin and Gayle did very well. Our hope gained momentum, as we believed the clinic might be able to help them fight cancer and live normal lives.

Gayle and Jazmin formed a strong friendship during Jazmin's stay in Arizona. Gayle was a sweet and unselfish young lady. The girls were only a year apart in age and were able to lean on each other for support as they battled cancer together.

Jazmin grew to love Charlene and Jason, as they devoted so much time and money to caring for the girls and handling all the politics and funding with the clinic. Charlene was a soft-spoken and sweet woman and protective stepmother, and Jason was a devoted husband and father.

Eythan and Jazmin spent some wonderful weeks enjoying the beautiful, sunny, warm weather in Arizona. Gayle, Jazmin, and Eythan spent a lot of time together and enjoyed the fellowship they shared as young adults. Eythan drove the three women to the clinic each day, and Charlene was able to concentrate on cooking healthy meals for them and also help Jason with the online business they owned.

Gayle had spent a lot of time away from friends and extended family as she went through her treatments. Having Jazmin and Eythan living with her family really helped with the loneliness.

Jazmin and Gayle were quite proud of themselves when they sneaked candy or ice cream past Charlene and Jason. They would tiptoe into the kitchen some nights when they couldn't sleep, giggling quietly as they munched on food the clinic had labeled "bad."

I laughed and rolled my eyes when Jazmin confessed their nighttime rebellion to me. They were like two five-year-olds sneaking cookies into bed and eating them under the covers. Jazmin said their midnight meetings in the kitchen gave her a chance to get to know Gayle better after long tiring days at the clinic.

We were relieved the girls seemed to be making progress in their health. But we wondered if the treatments would work long term. Were we just wasting time and money, chasing after suitcases in the wind, hoping to catch a medical miracle?

> We were relieved the girls seemed to be making progress in their health. But we wondered if the treatments would work long term. Were we just wasting time and money, chasing after suitcases in the wind, hoping to catch a medical miracle?

The dream about meeting Jason Katzenback and the story about the suitcase had confirmed to me that Jazmin was in God's will. He had provided the money, means, transportation, and lodging for a poor young married couple to live in another country for cancer treatment.

God had purposefully intertwined our lives with the Katzenbacks because he knew Jazmin would need them. He also knew Gayle needed a friend. He had gone above and beyond for both girls and their families.

Although I wanted to question God and have Him tell me whether the treatment would work, He showed me that nothing in life is random. He orchestrates the details, and we must learn to trust His plan for our lives.

Dear God,

I have no clue how You are going to work out this problem in my life, but I pray You will help me trust You to lead me where I am supposed to go.

Amen.

CHAPTER TWELVE

On the Road Again

*Dogs are God's best creation. The bigger the better. If I see a
dog in public, you bet I'm asking the owner if I can pet it.
Dogs bring me joy. Dogs are everything.*

—JAZMIN HENSON

Christmas 2018

EYTHAN AND JAZMIN WERE moving to Sudbury. He had been
hired by a gym to be a coach and personal trainer. They would
finally be living on their own and have the privacy they craved.

I shared in their joy of finally gaining their independence and
anticipated seeing their new apartment. But Vance and I worried
about whether they could financially stand on their own two feet
with only one income and Jazmin's medical needs. For most young
couples, both husband and wife work, and they don't have huge
medical bills. This was going to be a tremendous challenge.

Eythan and Jazmin packed everything they owned from our
house into Aaron's trailer and hauled it back to Sudbury. We made
the trip with Devyn, Dan, and Charity. We helped the traveling
gypsies, along with Sherie and Aaron, move into their home in a
large apartment building.

As we climbed the dark stairwell up to the second floor, I smelled marijuana. I felt a dark presence the closer we got to their apartment. The cold cement walls reminded me of a school or a prison.

Eythan opened the door, and the seven of us tried to squeeze into the empty apartment. I had never seen a space smaller than this one. Their kitchen and living room combined were the size of the closet and bathroom in my master suite. *This can't possibly be where they're going to live.*

I tried to be positive as I looked around the claustrophobic space. It wouldn't have seemed so small, but they also had a large dog, and everywhere I turned, Lacy was there.

I didn't say anything, since I didn't want to squash their happiness. Eythan's bedroom at home was the size of this whole apartment, and I was hoping he wouldn't find it too small now that he was sharing it with a wife and a dog.

Jazmin and Eythan were excited to finally be alone after living with other people for the first six months of their marriage. They had never complained. But now it seemed the real honeymoon could start.

Eythan isn't one to sit around. If his body isn't moving, his brain is moving. When he was small and I was schooling him at home, I thought of tying him to the chair to get him to sit still. Work was good for him.

The hours he worked were part time to start, and soon their money became tight. This stressed Eythan out greatly. He had grown up in a home where money was never a worry, and this was a new feeling and responsibility.

Jazmin was very supportive, and she told Eythan they had to trust God to provide. Their relationship became strained as money was sparse, Jazmin's needs were costly, and she couldn't contribute to the cost of living. The four walls of the micro-size apartment closed in on this young couple, and marital bliss was wearing thin.

Vance and I worried about them. Could their marriage survive the stress of being newlywed, poor, and sick? Our prayers went up to God as we asked him to give Eythan a full-time job.

Sure enough, God pulled through for Jazmin and Eythan, and he eventually worked full time. And Eythan learned a valuable lesson on how God can help when you are no longer relying on your parents for financial support and your wife needs a husband who can provide for her.

The couple became financially independent and were proud of themselves for having overcome being sick with cancer and financially broke. Jazmin encouraged Eythan to trust God to provide for them. God surprised them in many ways. Often money came their way that they weren't expecting.

It touched my heart to see the wonderful wife Jazmin was and how much she wanted to support Eythan in his career. God blessed her for her faithfulness to Eythan, and He always made sure their needs were met.

My God will meet all your needs
according to the riches of his glory in Christ Jesus.

(Philippians 4:19)

CHAPTER THIRTEEN

The Last Door Closed

*Sometimes you're so overwhelmed by the goodness
and light in your life that the darkness gets pushed down
deeper and deeper within you.*

—GAYLE KATZENBACK

January 2018

*L*IFE SHIFTED.

Christie, the mom of three who received treatment with Jazmin and Gayle, passed away. The sadness of losing her, especially since Christie had a family who loved her and needed her, fell upon everyone in the house in Arizona tremendously.

Fear gripped me as I realized there was no guarantee now that Jazmin or Gayle would get better. Would they both die too?

In March 2018, Gayle began to decline. She had severe pain in her neck. A scan revealed a tumor that had disintegrated the vertebrae in her neck. Doctors were shocked she was still mobile. A risky surgery was performed with the hope of making her more comfortable, but it was just too much for her weak body to recover from. She quickly declined.

With her family surrounding her and watching over her vigilantly, Gayle's fight was over, and she had finally won the battle over darkness. Gayle made her flight into the heavens at the age of twenty-one.

A little over a month before Gayle passed away, she posted this message on Facebook:

Last night, while I struggled to fall asleep, I vented through an Instagram caption, and I feel like sharing it here would be appropriate.

I like to call this a self-portrait. Not a selfie.

This month has been so eventful and eye-opening in so many ways. I am blessed beyond words by those who contributed to my gala, who contributed generously to my GoFundMe campaign and my T-shirt and hoodie campaign.

I've seen my community come together in support of me in my time of need, which is incredible. I've been blessed with opportunities that not many other people will ever be presented with. I am being watched, loved, and cared for immensely by so many people.

Sometimes, however, you're so overwhelmed by the goodness and light in your life that the darkness gets pushed down deeper and deeper within you. And although you may not see it, it brews inside you still—even when you place your best brave face on.

Most days we can forget to address the darkness and keep it bottled up within us, until we can't hold it together anymore. This is when it begins to pour freely out of the containers we once kept them bound in. The darkness and doubts begin to seep into your everyday life.

I guess what I'm saying is that it's not always easy to keep a brave face on. And though you try your best, sometimes it's okay to allow the sadness and doubt to surface.

I'm not always the brave face everyone sees. There are moments when I break down and cry. There are moments when I'm absolutely terrified about what lies ahead. However, these moments of sadness and fear can only make me stronger, as they are there to teach me.

I know, in the end, everything will work the way it is intended. And that gives me hope.

There is always hope.

#MovingMountains #GaylesFuture #GaylesGreaterThanCancer #GaylesFight4Life

Gayle's honesty and bravery were an inspiration to people around the world. Kids who never met Gayle but heard about her through other teens at school or through social media and followed her story were so upset after she died that schools set up special times to have the children receive counseling so they could process the grief.

Gayle's funeral was streamed for people around the world to watch online. She didn't seem to carry the bitterness many people have when they realize their life may end too soon. She continually pointed people to Jesus and His grace and was an inspiration to young and old alike.

Through it all Charlene, her stepmother and main caregiver, was the one I admired most. She was a quiet presence amid great turmoil. Her unwavering love and devotion to Gayle, even though she wasn't her child, sometimes caused me to choke up.

Gayle and her sister, Jillian, were both beautiful girls, and their sisterly bond seemed stronger than most. Gayle's mother, Audrey, also made trips to Arizona to care for her daughter. Both girls had beautiful feminine mannerisms and features from Audrey. She had a tall slim figure and a pretty smile.

But they had also been blessed by having a second mother, and Charlene's tender heart for her stepdaughters touched my soul deeply.

Charlene wrote the following excerpt about Jazmin and her role in their lives:

> This is where the unity of community came full circle. Cindy had been observing Gayle's journey online and reached out to me to inquire about alternative treatments. You see, Cindy's son, Eythan, had recently met and fallen in love with a girl named Jazmin, and they were soon to be married. However, Jazmin was beginning to show signs of fatigue and advancement of her cancer. Before the wedding, Jazmin and her mom flew to Arizona to see if what the clinic had to offer was something she would be interested in trying.
>
> When we heard that Jazmin was interested in trying these therapies, we were happy to be able to offer her and Eythan a place to stay, transportation to and from the clinic, and support however we could. Gayle was excited too. They had met a few times at ABK Bible camp, and she looked forward to having company her own age, but more importantly, someone who could relate to what she was living through. Gayle and Jazmin enjoyed shopping together and sharing stories during treatment. They surprised me one day with thoughtful gifts: flowers, a comfy cardigan, and fluffy socks. They said they wanted to show their appreciation. I smile every time I wear the sweater and socks, like getting a big hug from them both. We appreciated that Eythan and Jazmin were newlyweds, so we tried to give them their space, but we also shared some enjoyable moments together at the Christmas Festival of Lights, going out for dinner, and lounging around the pool.
>
> Another friend of ours came to the clinic. Christie shared a space with all of us in Arizona. She, too, had terminal cancer.

THE LAST DOOR CLOSED

Over the course of several months, we got to know and love Jazmin. She was very sweet, kind, soft spoken, and, most striking to me, strong in her faith. She was good for Gayle. I saw how her and Eythan's faith was helping Gayle to lean more into hers and me into mine. It was refreshing and enlightening to see such a young woman physically weakened yet so fearless in her relationship with God. She truly believed, and I hadn't witnessed this strength in faith from anyone her age before.

Jazmin was with us right up to the day Gayle was admitted to the Mayo Clinic. Although the treatments may have extended Gayle's life and likely helped her to feel healthier for longer, the cancer had metastasized even further. It had completely consumed one of her vertebrae. The doctors were shocked that she was able to walk into the clinic and was not already paralyzed. They operated, but it was futile, and unfortunately she never fully recovered. She passed away a month later.

Christie had passed away five months prior, and I believe the loss of both Gayle and Christie led to Jazmin and Eythan's decision to settle back in Canada. I am so glad they did! With the time Jazmin might have left, they could enjoy creating lifelong memories with each other, their friends, and family.

Jazmin and I were able to visit a number of times during that period, and I know I'm not alone in saying that I wanted Jazmin to get her miracle so desperately. Eighteen months after Gayle passed, I was diagnosed with breast cancer and began my own all-too-familiar journey with cancer. I asked Cindy to share the news when she felt Jazmin had the energy to hear it. I made it through my tough treatment days because of Gayle and Jazmin. The way they both handled their illness with such grace and invested faith was a true pillar of strength for me. I know our family will forever cherish our time with Jazmin and the extraordinary woman she was and continues to be through all those she touched.

83

Jazmin was beginning to feel pain every day, and sitting in one position or standing too long caused her more pain. She was on daily painkillers to try to combat the cancer's effects on her body.

Jazmin was also down to a hundred pounds on her five-foot-seven frame. I could tell she was in pain the day of the funeral, but she was determined to attend. She sat through the two-hour service and had also gone to the wake the night before. She and Eythan attended early so Jazmin wouldn't have to stand long.

The funeral was beautiful. At least four hundred people filled the room. The message was clear. Gayle loved Jesus, and she wanted others to love Him too. The funeral pointed people to Christ and to Gayle's desire to love Him through her battle with cancer.

Between the day Gayle died and the funeral, a deep sadness fell over Jazmin. She was distant for a few weeks after, and she seemed to be declining. Gayle's passing had affected her more deeply than she or we realized. Jazmin's faith had been shaken. The possibility of getting a miracle was dissipating with each woman's passing.

Finally Jazmin came out of her depression and told us God had asked her to keep trusting Him, that she needed to renew her hope in His ability to carry her through, no matter what happened.

Unlike Jazmin, though, my hope wasn't growing but was passing through a sieve as I began to understand that no one in the medical community had a cure for Jazmin.

Our last door had closed.

Since the treatment had not cured Gayle and Christie, Jazmin decided to stop her therapy treatments.

I was terrified that her time would soon end as well.

I didn't know what to do with this fear other than share it with my husband and with God. I pleaded with Jesus to give Jazmin more time. Over and over I banged on heaven's gates, asking my heavenly Father if He could spare our sweet Jazzy. Would He grant me my request? Would He heal Jazzy?

Between the tears and prayers of Charlene, Sherie, and me, I'm pretty sure we filled an ocean. I didn't know whether God would grant our requests, but I knew He cherished them and held them close to His heart. These thoughts brought me great comfort amid my continual fear of losing Jazmin.

> And when he had taken it, the four living creatures and the twenty-four elders fell down before the Lamb. Each one had a harp and they were holding golden bowls full of incense, which are the prayers of God's people.
>
> (Revelation 5:8)

CHAPTER FOURTEEN

Home Sweet Home

*You wouldn't believe how much a dishwasher has improved
our marriage, as we didn't have one in the apartment. Haha.
Joking aside, we really did take little things like that for
granted, and once we moved into the house,
we felt so thankful.*

—JAZMIN HENSON

April 2018

BEING SICK AND COOPED up in a micro apartment while Eythan was working took its toll on Jazmin, and she began to feel isolated and depressed. Her mental state was not good. Vance and I worried about her decline, and we knew something needed to change.

God provided her and Eythan with a newly renovated three-bedroom bungalow just five minutes from Jazmin's parents. They had been living forty minutes apart, and Sherie and Aaron wanted to be closer to the kids, and Jazmin and Eythan wanted the same. The two couples loved playing board games together and just hanging out when Jazmin needed company. Sherie and Aaron were fun and always up for a few rounds of Catan.

Friends of the family owned the bungalow and needed renters. The cost of renting the newly renovated house was only $100 a month more than the micro apartment, and it was just what Jazmin needed. We made the trip down to help the kids move, along with our son Devyn. Devyn is always so helpful, and whenever anyone needs a hand moving, he is one of the first to show up. This is one of Devyn's best character traits—to be a helping hand where he sees a need.

Sherie and Aaron were also there to help on moving day. Jazmin's health seemed to have been bolstered, and she had the energy to go all day. We pulled up to the neat and tidy bungalow, and I hopped out of our vehicle and climbed the three stairs up to the kitchen. One end of the room had an L shape of white cupboards on two walls and a matching island. At the other end, there was room for a small table and chairs next to the patio doors. A wall separated the side-by-side kitchen and living room with a large doorway between the two. The living room was generous in size and had a beautiful fireplace with a large wooden mantel at the end of the room and a large picture window with the front door beside it.

I walked past the kitchen and down a hall. Three bedrooms and a long narrow bathroom finished the upstairs. The house had wood-like laminate floors throughout and was cute and cozy. There was a rec room, a laundry room, and a sauna in the basement.

At the end of a long day of moving, our two families—tired but happy—sat crammed around the table in the kitchen, eating pizza and chatting. I looked over at Jazmin and Eythan. By their pleasant expressions, I could tell they truly felt God's hand upon them and His blessings in their life.

For two weeks Jazmin made a big turnaround, and she seemed to be getting better. The bright, cheery, and spacious three-bedroom bungalow lifted her spirits and caused her to feel like it was a real home for her, Eythan, and Lacey.

A few weeks later, I picked up Jazmin and drove her back to my house. Since Eythan had to work, he would come the day after. They were going to stay for the long weekend.

I loved having time alone with Jazmin. Conversation flowed easily between us. Up to this point, Jazmin had always talked of God giving her a miracle—she had claimed that from day one. But during our trip, I could tell her beliefs were shifting.

As I drove, I glanced at Jazmin from time to time. Her auburn hair glistened in the afternoon sunshine. Her thin arms moved with her hands as she talked. "Cindy, I have believed for a miracle for years now, and I always knew if I beat cancer, it was going to be miraculous so God could have all the glory. But in the past few months, my prayer has changed. I now pray, 'God, whether You heal me or take me to heaven, I want to glorify You either way.'"

> "I have believed for a miracle for years now, and I always knew if I beat cancer, it was going to be miraculous so God could have all the glory. But in the past few months, my prayer has changed. I now pray, 'God, whether You heal me or take me to heaven, I want to glorify You either way.'"

My heart warmed as I listened to Jazmin's confession. God was preparing her for her unknown future, and now I could relax and not worry about preparing her for dying.

After we chatted for a few hours, Jazmin was tired. She hopped into the back seat and lay down on her pillow for a nap. I glanced in my rearview mirror and saw her sleeping peacefully.

This precious child.

How was I gifted with such a beautiful soul for a daughter-in-law? I cannot even begin to explain how much I loved Jazmin. It was like she was always there. In my heart, Jazmin was one of my girls, sharing this special place with Charity and Aryanna—a space a mother holds for her daughters. My sons and my son-in-law, Dan, have the other side of my heart.

I smiled to myself as I drove in silence and took the time to ask God if He would give Jazmin a miracle. She had finally surrendered. Didn't that earn her a miracle? I thought it should. Relief filled me, and I took in a deep breath and let it out. God had answered my prayers. He was changing Jazmin's mind so I wouldn't have to be the one to burst her miracle-bubble. But I hoped he would answer Jazzy's prayers and give her the miracle she had asked for for many years.

Do not be anxious about anything, but in every situation,
by prayer and petition, with thanksgiving,
present your requests to God.

(Philippians 4:6)

CHAPTER FIFTEEN

Did You Say "Grandma"?

I'm so excited to be part of your family,
and I really do believe I have the best bonus mom ever!

—JAZMIN HENSON

May 2018

ITH ALL MY KIDS home, I was looking forward to Mother's Day weekend. My, Eythan's, and my mom's birthdays all fall within four days of one another every year at this time. Our kids piled into our home since Jazmin and Eythan were here. Charity and Dan happened to be staying with us while mold was removed from their apartment. Charity was two months pregnant.

A month before, I was overwhelmed when she and Dan surprised us with good news in a local restaurant. Vance and I were sitting at a tiny table across from Charity and Dan when they blurted out, "We're pregnant!" A thousand emotions ran through my heart. Happiness, anxiety, worry, joy, shock. Tears sprang to my eyes, and I hugged the kids as Vance and I congratulated them. We even had the waitress crying as our family's loud voices resonated off the walls of the small café.

I was in absolutely no rush to become a grandmother. Our home was the last place I would want small children or babies to visit. Kyle's unpredictable moods and outbursts could harm a child if he threw an object during an anxiety attack. How would we keep this baby safe? How could we babysit a baby with Kyle to care for too?

Charity had talked of nothing but adoption since she was eight years old. Our friends Ron and Christine, while they lived with us when Charity was young, had adopted a seven-year-old boy, Guillaume, from Haiti. This had inspired Charity to want to adopt children as well.

Children born to Charity and Dan were out of the question, and I was waiting for them to announce an adoption. They completely threw me for a loop with their announcement.

I didn't know how to process my thoughts on becoming a grandmother. Vance and I had planned to move to a new house, better suited to keep our grandbabies safe from the effects of autism. But as hard as we tried to look for another house, the doors kept closing. God was going to have to come through for us, because I didn't want my home to be somewhere my grandchildren didn't feel safe or were afraid to visit.

Charity called Jazmin on FaceTime to share her news. "You're going to be an aunt!"

Jazmin squealed and bounced in her chair. Since she couldn't be a mother unless she was healed of cancer, she kept encouraging Charity to have a baby instead so she could spoil a niece or nephew.

Over this weekend, the girls and I talked more about the baby to come. Jazmin was full of happiness as she chatted with Charity. Anything that helped boost Jazmin's spirits when she was experiencing lots of pain really helped her push through the hard days.

We spent Mother's Day weekend together and ate many meals as a family. One night we had a campfire. Jazmin and Eythan sat cuddled up in the hammock near the fire. Charity, Dan, Devyn, Aryanna, and her boyfriend, Daniel, sat in folding camp chairs.

As darkness fell, the miniature lights hanging in the forest surrounding our home twinkled. I captured this picture in my heart and held on to it dearly. All my children in one place laughing, roasting marshmallows, and living life to its fullest. The weekend was wonderful, and I sat in awe of all my blessings as a mother. Having children who love coming home and being together—there's no greater joy!

The day they were leaving to go home, Jazmin woke up and wasn't feeling well. She grabbed her beanbag and used extreme heat to distract her from the pain. The skin on her back was damaged and scarred, looking like the pattern of a giraffe from the beanbag burning her skin repeatedly. Jazmin felt in control of the pain when she needed it to take over the excruciating pain of cancer.

We helped Eythan load up the car, and they got ready to leave. We hugged them goodbye, and I wrapped Jazmin's tiny, hurting frame in a gentle hug. Each time they came, I wondered if l would see her again.

Vance and I stood together and waved until the kids were no longer in sight. We slowly made our way into the house with silent prayers for Jazmin. I would cherish this Mother's Day weekend as one of the dearest my heart would ever have.

The year before on Mother's Day, Jazmin had given me a card with a beautiful note inside: "I am so excited to soon have you as my bonus mom. You are such a great mother, and it is so evident that you strive to be a faithful servant of Christ. You continually demonstrate Christlike love to everyone around you. I have an immense amount of respect for both you and Vance as individuals and as a married couple. You and Vance have given Eythan an amazing example of how spouses should treat each other. I'm so excited to be part of your family, and I really do think I have the best bonus mom ever! Happy Mother's Day! Love, Jazmin."

Those words sat on my desk, and I read them over and over, and sometimes a tear would fall. Tears can hold sadness, but they can also hold joy and thankfulness.

Although our home was filled with the chaos of autism, and our years of parenting had many stressful moments, and we couldn't do the fun things most families did, God had blessed us with adult children who wanted to gather in our home and be close to their parents. He also blessed us with Dan and Jazmin, bonus kids who thought their in-laws were wonderful.

God made up to us what the locust had eaten, and we felt so blessed. I prayed He would make me a wonderful grandmother because I honestly didn't know how to handle the news. We had autism, cancer, and now a new baby coming. I was going to have to double up my prayers. Could God somehow work out all these different combinations and give us peace and rest? I had to believe he would, or I was going to be overwhelmed with the possibilities.

So do not fear, for I am with you; do not be dismayed, for I am your God. I will strengthen you and help you; I will uphold you with my righteous right hand.

(Isaiah 41:10)

CHAPTER SIXTEEN

Swirling Mind

Since I was diagnosed almost four years ago, I have absolutely loved this verse because of its relevance to my situation.

—JAZMIN HENSON

Trust in the Lord with all your heart and lean not on your own understanding; in all your ways submit to him, and he will make your paths straight.

(PROVERBS 3:5–6)

June 2018

ONE OF THE BIGGEST struggles of having a loved one who is gravely ill is the dreaded chime of a cell phone message. I'd go a few weeks without bad news, and I would begin to tuck away anxiety like Christmas ornaments stored until the next year.

One day while I was in my kitchen, my phone chimed with a text from Sherie. My heart raced. I held my breath as I opened the message.

"Jazmin woke up not being able to take in a full breath of air. Eythan took her to the hospital emergency room and tests revealed the tumors in Jazmin's lungs have moved into the lung lining. Jazmin is in pain and having breathing difficulties."

My hope collapsed. I felt completely devastated. Tears streamed down my face. Was this the end? Sherie was hoping for a miracle in the eleventh hour. If God awarded miracles according to people's faith, I didn't know a woman who was more deserving than her. She had stood her ground and not wavered in her faith that God was going to give Jazmin a miracle.

I texted, "I would be happy to come help and stay with Jazmin so you can return to work." Sherie's supervisor was generous with giving her time off, but she didn't want to take advantage of the situation.

"That would be helpful, but message Jazmin and ask her if she minds if you come and stay with her." Sherie was being respectful of Jazmin's feelings.

I flipped a text to Jazmin. "I heard about your trip to the hospital. Can I come hang out with you while your mom and Eythan are working?"

Jazmin wasn't one to be glued to her phone and sometimes took hours to message back. But within a few minutes, she responded, "Yes, I'd love that!"

I smiled. Her words warmed my heart. "I'm praying for you. I will see you tomorrow."

"Thanks, Mom!" She was bouncing between calling me Mom or Cindy. I loved it when she called me Mom.

When Vance came home from work, I filled him in on Jazmin's health. "I made arrangements to go stay with Jazmin for a week. I assumed you'd be okay with me going."

Vance looked serious, his face drawn and sad. "I think that's a good idea."

If you're a single woman and aren't married yet, look for a man who supports you when your loved ones need you. The gift Vance gave me of being able to care for Jazmin without putting his own needs first spoke volumes to me about his devotion to his family. I saw a Dear Abby letter on Facebook recently from a husband who was complaining about his wife always putting the kids ahead of his needs. Imagine making your wife feel guilty about meeting the needs of your own children. Vance considered Jazmin one of his daughters, and he wanted me to take care of her the best I could.

My heart felt light and heavy at the same time. I rolled into bed and cried that night. I was overwhelmed with the possibility that I could lose my daughter very soon, and my son would also lose his precious wife. They had only been married nine months.

While I was gone, Vance was going to care for Kyle on his own, morning and evening. He also needed to run a business. Having a child with autism makes it hard in situations that require us to drop everything and go. Vance and I couldn't both be there for our loved ones at the same time. When someone needed us, one of us had to stay with Kyle. We loved him and never wanted him to feel like he was a burden.

The next morning, I kissed Vance goodbye at the door. He gave me a big, warm hug. "I'm praying for you, Cindy, and for Jazmin. I love you."

"Thank you for letting me go. You are the best husband in the world!" I laid my head against his warm chest and tried not to cry. Vance's sacrifice for us girls made me love him more.

I stopped for a coffee at my favorite drive-through and hit the highway. The four-hour drive gave me time to pray. *Lord, please help me to be able to handle Jazmin dying. Help me not to panic or respond in a way that will scare Jazmin. Give me the strength I need to do this.*

I arrived at Jazmin and Eythan's by dinnertime.

I was expecting to hear Jazmin was in bed struggling for her life. But shockingly, she was up and moving about. She had made an incredible turnaround in twenty-four hours. She was so frail, I could tell she had lost weight and was most likely about ninety pounds. The day before she couldn't sit up, eat, or breathe well, and she was throwing up.

I had expected Eythan to look heavy hearted, but he seemed happy. I gave them each a big hug. My heart unloaded one hundred pounds of worry, and I dropped it to the floor like a heavy backpack.

Emily, one of Jazmin's best friends and her cousin, was visiting Jazmin when I arrived.

I plunked down on one of the couches, and Lacey hopped up on the couch beside me, wagging her tail. With her shiny black fur, dark-brown eyes, and wagging tail, she was adorable, well behaved, and quiet. Lacey would lie beside Jazmin in her bed on her worst days. Jazmin was known to try to take care of herself instead of calling family to stay with her when Eythan was working. Having Lacey lie with her in bed made her feel like she wasn't alone.

Emily, Jazmin, and I sat in the living room talking for a couple of hours while Eythan puttered around the house. It was fun to listen to the girls share stories about their childhood and their adventures with their other best friend, Serena. The girls talked quickly and finished each other's sentences. I smiled as I watched Jazmin forget she had been in the hospital the day before.

Around ten thirty I rolled into bed, two hours past my normal bedtime. I lay there thinking about how thin and tired Jazmin looked. She knew she was dying. But something had changed. Even though she had improved from the day before, I could feel something, and I couldn't put my finger on it. As I tossed and turned, my mind swirled in a dreamlike state. I didn't worry about my cell phone chiming since I was at Jazmin and Eythan's house. But death and cancer haunted me as I tried to catch a few hours of sleep.

How could I unload my worry to Jesus? It felt like it was pressing in on me even when I slept. I needed Him to overtake my thoughts and my sleep, because I was struggling to give my anxiety of Jazmin dying to Jesus.

Lord,

You promise to give us peace. When we don't know how to give our worries over to Your capable hands, help us to rest in Your presence. And please give us rest.

Amen.

CHAPTER SEVENTEEN

Funny Bones

A cheerful heart is good medicine,
but a crushed spirit dries up the bones.

(PROVERBS 17:22)

I WOKE UP AT 5:00 the next morning, tiptoed to the kitchen, put on a pot of coffee, and sat at the kitchen table, hoping to write for a few hours before the kids woke.

I thought about this crazy miracle Jazmin was hoping to have magically drop from the heavens. She was bouncing between trusting God with her life and believing she would get a miracle.

How can I help her accept the possibility of dying? I rubbed my face and tried to wake myself from the last bit of slumber. My mind swirled with the possibilities of the next few months and what could happen. I dropped my face into my hands and prayed. *Please, God, help Jazmin and her family come to grips with the truth that she is going to die.*

Wiping the tears from my eyes, I placed my fingers on the keyboard and got lost in my writing for a couple of hours, thoughts of death chased away.

I lifted my head when I heard the pounding footsteps of someone running. Jazmin came flying up the hallway and around the corner into the kitchen, with Lacey following. My brain was muddled as to why Jazmin would be frantically running into the kitchen. Was she sleepwalking? Was she afraid of something? I stared at her with my mouth wide open. She scrambled to open the patio doors to let Lacey out, but she fumbled with the lock.

"Open, stupid door!" she yelled.

Lacey gagged, and Jazmin pulled furiously at the patio door. Lacey threw up on the floor. Jazmin's face turned green. Her hands came to her mouth. She looked like she might toss her cookies.

"It's okay. You go back to bed, Jazmin. I've got this." I smiled at her as I held in the laughter that was ready to burst from my lips. I covered my mouth with my hand, trying to hide my grin. I could tell Jazmin wasn't in the mood for a good laugh.

"Thank you, Cindy!" Jazmin scooted to the bathroom.

I giggled as I recalled the size of Jazmin's eyes when she almost missed turning the corner into the kitchen. Her long skinny arms had frantically tried to balance her as her feet began to slide out from under her. I laughed for five minutes. My husband says I have a weird sense of humor. I believe I am perfectly normal in what tickles my funny bone.

Eythan told me later in the morning that by the time he rallied out of his sleep and realized the dog was gagging, Jazmin was already heading out of the bedroom. I laughed at his story, and he grinned at me. He's the one child who has my sense of humor, and he loves to pull pranks on people. He gets me.

Eythan was always tired due to Jazmin's restless nights, and he had a hard time waking most mornings. When I thought of the girl dying from cancer being the one who was able to fly out of the bedroom while he, the healthy, strong man, slumbered, I found it ironic and a tad funny.

Eythan and I ate breakfast together. He's my kid who can eat like you wouldn't believe. From the time he was small, Eythan was always hungry and slim. He struggled to gain weight but had managed to make it up to 165 pounds at five feet, ten inches, with a lot of effort. He had a very defined six-pack that most men have to work hard to get.

As I cooked him supper to take to work with him, we chatted for a bit. It was rare for me to have time alone with Eythan. Our house was always busy, with Kyle needing most of our attention. Usually the baby of the family steals the show, but Eythan had learned to find quiet places to hide when Kyle was having his hardest days. I enjoyed my morning with Eythan and cherished this time with him.

When Jazmin woke up, we relaxed for a bit. Then she said she wanted to go to the Dollar Store and a health food store and do some shopping. I had never gone with Jazmin anywhere by myself. With our large family, there's almost always more than one person with me. I was looking forward to us doing something together.

We parked the car and sauntered toward the Dollar Store. Jazmin was ahead of me, and her dress swayed as she slowly walked toward the door. Her shoulder bones poked through the top of the dress. She pushed on the door but wasn't strong enough to get it open, so I reached around her and opened it. Jazmin shuffled through the store, and I could tell the outing was draining her energy. Maybe we should go home. Could she make it back to the car? Was I strong enough to carry her? Finally Jazmin made her way to the car. I was relieved.

We stopped on the way home and picked up a pizza. Jazmin plunked onto the couch as soon as we came into the house.

Eythan had forgotten his supper and texted me, asking if I could drop it off for him.

"Jazmin, will you be okay on your own if I run Eythan his supper? He left it on the counter." I threw my purse over my shoulder.

"I'll be fine." She closed her eyes and put her head back on the couch.

"Do you promise not to move from that spot until I return? I don't want you falling while I'm gone."

She opened her eyes and smiled at me. "Riley is coming soon, so I won't be alone long."

"And you won't leave the couch until she comes?" I gave her my best mom look.

"I promise." She waved me off. Jazmin was a bit mischievous, so I had my doubts she would stay put. *Guaranteed she's going to leave that couch.*

I dropped off Eythan's supper half an hour away at the gym where he worked. He gave me a tour of the gym, and I met some of his coworkers. He was in his element working as a coach and personal trainer. Seeing his workplace brought me happiness. I wanted my kids to love their work and not dread their jobs each day.

I used my GPS to get back to their house. I have a horrible sense of direction and can't seem to remember the names of streets. I'm more of a landmark kind of girl—turn at the church, or drive past McDonald's and turn at the first street on the left.

Riley was there when I arrived, and we chatted for a few minutes. She's a lovely young woman with long thick brown hair and hazel eyes. After I chatted with them for a few minutes, she and Jazmin went out on the deck for a couple of hours and talked in the sunshine. Friends were starting to make visits. No one wanted to act as though it was a last goodbye, because that would be hard on Jazmin. They all knew she wanted them to believe in her miracle. Admitting she was dying was not part of the plan.

After Riley left, I asked Jazmin about her friend. "What's Riley like?"

"I love visiting with her. She doesn't beat around the bush and speaks her mind, but she is gracious."

I was thankful for the meaningful relationships Jazmin had with young women. I could tell with each visit her spirits seemed to lift.

Jazmin and I ate pizza and watched the home improvement channel. Watching someone take something ugly and turn it into something beautiful was a wonderful break from cancer. We commented back and forth on what we thought of each home, and Jaz and I clearly had different tastes in home decorating. She told me if she didn't like the same décor that I did, and her honesty was refreshing. Jazzy tried to be genuine and not compromise her beliefs for someone else's good opinion of her, and I admired that about her.

The heavy thoughts I had woken up with in the morning dissipated as I sat on the couch with Jazmin. At that moment we didn't have a care in the world—other than what color we would paint our living rooms.

I went to bed, and as I was dozing off to sleep, I saw Jazmin's green face and flailing arms as Lacey gagged up her dinner from the night before. I laughed and laughed and fell into a peaceful sleep. God gave me rest.

. . . a time to weep and a time to laugh, a time to mourn
and a time to dance.

(Ecclesiastes 3:4)

CHAPTER EIGHTEEN

Giving Up the Miracle

Everyone has struggles. My struggle right now is my illness,
but if it wasn't that, it would be something else.
Life is not easy for anyone. It's not supposed to be easy.
If it were, we wouldn't need God.

—JAZMIN HENSON

"ELLO!" I LOOKED UP from the show Jazmin and I were watching and saw Sherie walking into the living room. I jumped up and gave her a big hug. "Sherie, it's so nice to see you!" She always smelled like shampoo or perfume.

"Thank you for coming to take care of Jazmin." Her eyes shone with appreciation.

"Aww, I'm happy to be here." I warmed at her kindness.

Sherie let go of me and kissed Jazmin's cheek as she squeezed her. "Hi, honey!"

"Hi, Mom." Jazmin, sitting cross-legged on the plush yellow chair in front of the picture window, turned off the TV.

Sherie sat on the couch across from Jazmin. Lacey hopped up beside Sherie. She grabbed the dog's face, and her voice rose to the octave moms use on babies. "Oohh, Lacey, how are you doing? Good girl!"

Lacey wagged her tail and licked Sherie's face.

I wished I loved dogs as much as she did. Dogs loved me, and I didn't mind them; I just didn't want them under my feet or following me around the house.

I lowered myself to the love seat across from the gray stone fireplace that had not been fired up once since I arrived due to the warm summer days.

"My workplace has been wonderful, but I've taken way too much time off. You are a blessing, Cindy, being here this week." Sherie smoothed out her curly hair and put it back in a ponytail.

"I'm happy to help out wherever I can, and this way I get to spend some time with Jazmin." I smiled at my daughter-in-law and grabbed a cushion to hug.

Sherie and I were still getting to know each other, and our relationship hadn't reached an easy and relaxed place yet. I wanted to tread lightly and not enter spaces that were not mine to be in.

I felt uneasy invading all the conversations Jazmin was having with friends and family. The house was small, and it wasn't like I could disappear whenever people dropped in for a visit. Did they mind that I was here?

In the short time I had known Sherie, she had talked about the miracle Jazmin was going to get. I knew she worked hard to keep her faith at 100 percent every day. Sherie wasn't supposed to waver. She was the rock that held down the important paper on a windy day. She knew Jazmin could slip away from her if she wasn't diligent in her faith.

"Mom, my doctor is coming tomorrow, and she wants to discuss where I want to be when I die." Jazmin looked at her mom, keeping a steady gaze.

I sucked in a breath. *Wait, what? Did Jazmin just admit she might not get a miracle?* I was confused. Sometimes Jazmin just blurted things out. She didn't seem to have a filter for shocking news.

I nervously looked between the two of them. How was Sherie going to respond?

Sherie's lashes fluttered. She rubbed her face and took in a deep breath. "Umm, I wasn't expecting to hear that."

Jazmin's arms crossed over her abdomen. She often rubbed the tumor she could feel on her kidney. "Mom, we need to talk about the hard stuff. I want to be here at home in the end, not at the hospital."

Tears pooled in Jazmin's and Sherie's eyes. The clock seemed to stop ticking, and the air in the room became warm. I held my breath. It was an intimate moment, and I wanted to sink into a hole in the floor. *I shouldn't be listening to this conversation.*

Have you ever answered a call on your cell and realized someone had pocket-dialed you and you were listening in on a private conversation? I always hang up immediately. It feels wrong to keep listening. I hate overhearing conversations that are supposed to be private.

Maybe I could tiptoe from the room or say I need to use the bathroom. Honestly, Sherie and Jazmin might not have noticed if I had—mother and daughter were cocooned in a sacred moment. Five seconds of silence felt like hours.

Sherie looked down and slowly stroked Lacey's shiny black fur. She pulled her legs up on the couch and tucked them beside her, and Lacey moved. "Jazmin, Tom called me tonight and asked if I would come to his and Anita's house, because he had a word for me." Tom and Anita were close friends of Sherie and Aaron's.

Oh, no. More *if you have enough faith* nonsense. It made me angry. No one had the right to tell someone else that if they had enough faith, they would get a miracle. The person telling them that can muster up their own faith for a friend to get a miracle.

But Jazmin had opened up the conversation. Was Sherie going to shut the window?

Surprisingly, that wasn't what Tom had told Sherie.

"Tom said he had had a life-threatening disease when he was ten. His parents tried everything to get him a miracle and were exhausted from their efforts. Finally one day they gave up. God spoke to their hearts and asked them to have faith in Him and Him alone and believe, whether Tom lived or died, that He was good. Faith was believing in God and His plan—no matter what. Not necessarily believing for a miracle. Tom's parents gave God permission to take their son—if that was His good and perfect will."

Jazmin and I sat stunned. Neither of us knew what to say. I wondered if the miracle-spell had been broken. Was Sherie about to make a confession?

"Tom asked me to love God and trust Him even if He takes my daughter to heaven—to allow God to do what *He* thinks is right, not what I want." Sherie wiped tears from her cheek with her sleeve.

I grabbed a box of tissue off the coffee table and held it out to Sherie. She tugged a handful of tissues and blew her nose. I wiped my tears too.

Jazmin sat quietly, her lip trembling as she listened to her mother slowly coming to peace with the possibility that she might die young of cancer. Tears dropped from Jazmin's long black lashes down her pale cheeks, and she brushed them away. I held the box out to her, and she took what she needed.

Jazmin struggled to speak as she gulped air. "Mom, I'm so glad you've gotten to this point."

I'm pretty sure neither woman knew I was in the room anymore. I sat frozen, not moving, in case I interrupted this crossroad. Two lamps cast a soft glow, and the cozy room felt like the setting of a slow-motion dream.

God had used Tom's words and Anita's love to speak into Sherie's life.

"Why did it take so long for God to reach my heart?" Sherie asked me when Jazmin scooted to the washroom.

"Sherie, I went through everything you went through when Kyle wasn't healed of autism. I was so angry and bitter with God, I could have killed him with my bare hands—if that was possible! It took me over twenty years to get to a point of surrendering Kyle to God."

"Jazmin told me the other day," Sherie said, "'Mom, whether I die or get a miracle, it's going to be fast now. I can feel the urgency.'"

I was flabbergasted that Jazmin had had a complete change of heart and finally come to terms with the thought that she might die. I hoped her realization was permanent and she could be at peace knowing she would soon be walking in heaven's fields. My heart twinged at the bittersweet moment. If God was ready to take Jazmin, we had very little time left with her.

After Sherie left, Jazmin told me, "I'm so happy my mom is finally accepting the possibility that I might die. That is a huge relief to me."

The rock had been lifted from the paper.

God is gracious and gives us what we need even when our children are dying. He had met Sherie in her struggle and extended grace to His sweet daughter.

I wanted to make time stand still—just a little longer. How does one grab the clock of life and stop its hands from ticking? Holding on to Jazmin was like trying to hold water in my hands—she was slowly seeping through my fingers. But I knew I had to trust God's plan.

Lord,

When our loved ones are dying, help us to release them to You and not try to keep them here on earth any longer than You have planned. Help us to trust Your plan for their lives.

Amen.

CHAPTER NINETEEN

Hospice, Home Care, or Happiness

I had to decide to be joyful in difficult times when someone looking in might not see anything to be joyful about.

—JAZMIN HENSON

June 2018

I WENT TO BED WITH a heavy heart. Praying as my eyes closed, I drifted into a fitful sleep. The next morning I woke at four o'clock with the same cloud over my head. Darkness filled the room. As I sat on the edge of my bed, my hands came to my cheeks and caught my tears.

I'd never seen anyone I knew personally get a miracle and testify it was real.

Jazmin would be leaving us very soon. But there was a tiny spot in my heart that still held on. "God, please heal Jazmin. Don't let her die."

What else could I pray? Words didn't seem to come.

What could I do to make Jazmin's last days wonderful? *God, help me to do this—it's too hard for me.*

I'm a morning person. Like one of those really annoying morning people. I'm happy as soon as I wake up. It's probably because I'm heading to the coffeepot. But today happiness couldn't even be found in my favorite ceramic mug. I sat at my computer on the kitchen table, staring at the bright computer screen. I love writing. But on this morning, my brain was a complete muddle—emotional, messy, and upside down.

At seven o'clock, I grabbed my cell phone and called Vance. "I need to stay longer. Jazmin thinks she may die soon, and I don't want to leave Eythan here to cope with her dying by himself."

I was whispering so Jazmin couldn't hear me as I cried. "Jazmin is sad and feeling down." I was sitting on my bed and stared at my suitcase with all the clothes piled high. I never could keep a suitcase neat. Life felt like my suitcase: a big mess I couldn't sort through. No matter how hard I tried to look through the disaster, I couldn't find what I was looking for—hope, a miracle, a sign that Jazmin wouldn't die, anything. I was grasping at straws.

Silence hung between us, and I could hear Vance getting choked up. He loved Jazmin as much as our own girls, and I wished we were doing this together. I needed his strong arms and his barrel chest to lean into. There's no place on earth where I feel the stresses of this life fade away more than when I am in the arms of the man I love. Autism kept us apart many times when I had to go help a family member, and Vance wanted to be there too, but he needed to care for Kyle. I had to lean into God to find my strength.

"Cindy, stay as long as you need. I can take care of Kyle." This was the man I had left the hospital early for after having Kyle when I was twenty. I told the nurses I needed to be home to take care of my husband since he couldn't take care of himself. The nurses had rolled their eyes and sighed. Vance had come a long way in learning to serve others, and I was proud of him.

Eythan rose around nine o'clock.

I got out the eggs and bacon, and soon the kitchen filled with delicious smells. We ate breakfast together.

Today was the day Jazmin's doctor was going to come for a visit. She had planned to have "the talk" with her about how she wanted her last few weeks to look when she was dying. What would she decide? Did Eythan know what she chose? I didn't want to ask. Those were heavy questions requiring heavy answers.

"I'll do some shopping for a couple of hours while the doctor's here so you two can be alone with her."

Eythan nodded as he swallowed his eggs. He isn't someone who talks about his emotions. Our other children spilled their thoughts and feelings easily to Vance and me. But Jazmin was one of the few people Eythan shared his emotions with. I always believed it was partly due to his developmental years being filled with the chaos from autism. He had spent many afternoons after school hiding out in his bedroom to get away from the noise. He had learned to be quiet when autism overwhelmed our household.

Eythan planned to take the morning off so he could be with Jazmin when the doctor arrived. As the clock ticked, we waited for her to arrive. She messaged Jazmin saying she wouldn't arrive until the afternoon. Eythan had to head to work.

Jazmin and I sat together on the gray love seat and watched *Fixer Upper* for an hour. She slouched low on the couch with her arms crossed over her abdomen.

I got up to refill my coffee mug. Another dose of caffeine might help me get through the afternoon.

"Mom, would you like to stay when the doctor comes? She's bringing an intern with her. I don't want to be alone." I heard the vulnerability in her voice, and my heart tugged. How could I say no?

"Of course, Jazmin. I would be happy to be part of the conversation." No one wants to talk about dying. But I wanted to be there for Jazmin. I knew this would be one of the most difficult conversations to sit through. There was no way I could get out of this one. A loving mother would stay.

"How are you feeling today, Jazmin?" I asked her before I grabbed the coffee I desperately needed to boost my tired body.

Jazmin was still slouched down on the couch, her head leaning against the top of the cushion. She wore pajama pants and a favorite T-shirt. Jazmin owned what seemed like a hundred pairs of pajamas. Mostly due to the fact that she spent a lot of time in beds and on couches. "I'm feeling good!"

"Really?" My heart did a little two-skip dance.

"Something weird happened in the night. I woke up, and all of a sudden, I felt like I could breathe, and peacefulness fell over me. I went back to sleep, and when I got out of bed this morning, I felt like I'm going to be okay, like everything is going to be all right. The depression I felt the last few days has lifted." Jazmin's tone was relaxed, and there was no strain in her voice.

I stared at her, wondering if I had heard her right. Yesterday the plan was to die. Now she was feeling good? *I'm so confused. But let's grab this moment and run with it.*

My heart pulled a pretty floral blouse out of the hope-suitcase. I wore it the rest of the day.

I tried not to talk to Jazmin too much. She needed space and quiet to think and process what was happening. She would go through intense spiritual battles, and she'd have to fight the enveloping

116

darkness as the devil tried to persuade her to give up. But God had given our girl a strong resolution, and she would stand her ground. He would help her win each ferocious battle.

Jazmin was the extra-delicate thin paper, and she asked God to be the rock.

The devil would open the window on the windiest days and try to suck Jazmin out of her bed and into spiritual darkness. But God always seemed to hold her and shelter her beneath His wings.

I needed God to put a hold on me too, because I felt like I was floating wherever the wind blew me. My emotions easily changed with Jazmin's health.

"I'm going to hop in the shower and get ready for the doctor's visit." Jazmin jumped off the couch with more energy than she had the day before. Another tiny spark of hope ignited in my confused brain.

I grabbed my phone and texted my family and Sherie, letting them know Jazmin was having a really good day. The texts that came back were full of happy emojis and exclamation marks. It felt wonderful to spread good news!

A few hours later, Jazmin's doctor, a tall slim woman with blond hair to her shoulders, and the intern, a woman who looked to be in her late twenties, arrived around two o'clock. The doctor walked toward me in the bright, white kitchen with her hand extended. "Hi, I'm Lisa."

I was taken aback by her casual introduction and immediately felt formality leave the room. "I'm Cindy, Jazmin's mother-in-law. It's nice to meet you."

The intern also introduced herself with a friendly smile.

We invited the women into the living room and sat down. Jazmin and I sat in our usual places, her on the yellow chair and me on the love seat—a tiny bit of control in an out-of-control situation.

Lisa reached into her leather bag, pulled out a file, opened it, and placed it on her lap. "Jazmin, I have the results of the tests taken when you were in emergency."

Jazmin nodded, waiting for the verdict.

"The reason you're having trouble breathing is that a tumor has wrapped itself around a major artery in your lungs, squeezing the artery and making it harder to produce oxygen." She glanced from the file to Jazmin and held a compassionate gaze. Her tone was tender and graceful.

Jazmin sat cross-legged with her spine straight. Her face held no emotion. "Is there anything that can be done to improve my breathing?" She sounded matter-of-fact, and it threw me off.

I was stuck on the word *tumor.*

How did Jazmin act as though the doctor had just asked her if she wanted a blue or pink cast put on a broken arm? There was a tumor wrapped around an artery in her lungs that could suffocate her! I looked back and forth between the three of them. Was I the only one flabbergasted by the news?

"A stent could be put in to keep the artery open. The tumor is ten centimeters long. It was eight centimeters just a few months ago. There's also fluid around the tumor." Lisa's tone didn't change as she explained the details.

Jazmin kept nodding as Lisa went on. "There's a steroid I can prescribe to take down the swelling. I've also ordered oxygen for you to have at home to help when you're having difficulty breathing."

Jazmin and Lisa talked a bit more about these options, and Jazmin remained emotionless.

Lisa put her files back in her bag. She leaned her elbows on her knees and clasped her hands in front of her. "Jazmin, we need to discuss what you want the end to look like."

Did she want to be resuscitated?

Did she want to go to hospice?

Did she want homecare?

"I want to die at home." The words were flat and left no room for discussion.

I stared at Jazmin, and my heart sank. Panic climbed from my chest to my throat. She couldn't die at home. Everyone would be traumatized! There would be no nurse to help us if any of us felt panicked when she died. I wanted to shout, "No, you're not dying at home!"

Tears threatened to spill down my cheeks in a waterfall of emotions, and I clenched my jaw, trying to pull myself together. I didn't want Jazmin to know I believed she was going to die. I took deep but quiet breaths, pushing out my emotions, and they crawled back to the suitcase. I slammed it tight and calmed down.

Lisa looked at the intern, then back at Jazmin. "I'm amazed at your transformation. The emergency-room doctor said you were very ill when you came to the hospital. But you look good! Have you done anything different since then?" Both she and the intern stared at Jazmin for a logical answer.

Jazmin shook her head. "No, nothing."

Lisa looked surprised. "You obviously don't need homecare or hospice right now. Jazmin, continue to consider your options. If you change your mind and want to go to hospice in the end, let me know, and I can inform the center."

The word *die* was never used. Such a heavy word. Lisa knew how to talk about death without making it sound terrifying.

The visit went well, and I was impressed with how Lisa respected Jazmin's feelings and decisions. She spoke with tenderness and concern. Lisa was honest but made Jazmin feel comfortable.

We walked the women to the side entrance off the kitchen. Jazmin thanked the doctors for coming. As soon as they left, she whipped around and looked at me with a big grin. "Emily and Serena are coming over for a visit!"

When Jazmin was happy, she bounced and beamed. If happiness could be measured by human brilliance, her contagious joy could light up a whole room. How had we just talked about Jazmin dying and now she was bouncing on to happiness? I could barely keep up with the emotional roller coaster. It was like following a three-year-old around. A toddler is giggling one moment and crying her eyes out the next.

My heart joined hers as we did an emotional happy dance in celebration of her turnaround. I smiled at Jazmin, and she scooted down the hall to get ready for a visit with her favorite people.

Serena and Emily, Jazmin's best friends from the time they were all four, were coming with a truckload of silliness.

Jazmin flitted about the house getting ready. A few minutes later, I walked past the bathroom. She was perched like a tiny bird on the counter in front of the vanity mirror as she applied makeup to her pale skin. I didn't think I knew anyone who owned more makeup than Jaz—or could squat like her. She was a rare beauty and could go without a hint of cosmetics and still look gorgeous. Jazmin liked binge-watching tutorials on makeup. But she knew she didn't need makeup to be beautiful and wore her beauty lightly. Jaz knew she was pretty, but it didn't seem to be that important to her. She just thought it was fun to wear makeup and fashionable clothes.

She came out of the bathroom looking like she was ready for the runway.

My heart felt light and airy as I saw hope bloom before my eyes. On that day Jazmin wasn't a twenty-year-old sick woman—she was a silly teenage girl ready to have fun with her high school friends.

I drove into the city to do some shopping so I could give the girls some time alone, and I returned three hours later.

Jazmin, Serena, and Emily sat in the living room, laughing and talking, each one louder than the next.

Emily stood to leave around nine. She was the tallest of the three girls, with long blond hair. "I should be going. I have to go pick up Mattias at work."

Jazmin and Serena decided to go for the drive with Emily. Serena was the shortest of the three, with rich brown hair to her shoulders and blue eyes. All three girls were pretty but completely opposite of one another in appearance.

It was already an hour past my bedtime, and I felt sleepy. My pillow was calling my name.

Just before they left, Jazmin ran over to where I was sitting at the kitchen table, typing on my computer, and wrapped her arms around my neck. "I love you, Mom!" She kissed my cheek, and I reached up and squeezed her forearms.

Warmth spread through my arms and up to my neck. "I love you too, Jazmin."

My heart was harmonious with hers, and the world was wonderful. Life was beautiful. And our sweet girl was okay.

Jazmin bounced out of the kitchen and down the four steps, out the door, and into Emily's car.

I sat smiling.

How could someone go from almost dying at the beginning of a week to feeling on top of the world by the end of the week?

The power of prayer and the possibilities of hope.

Are you living each day on an emotional roller coaster with your feelings flying out of control with every loop-de-loop and health scare? It can crush a person emotionally and leave you drained of energy and joy. If your loved one's decisions about dying are not in your comfort zone, God can give you the grace and strength you need to be their support person. I was afraid of Jazmin dying at home. But God wasn't, because He had a plan.

> Cast all your anxiety on him because he cares for you.
>
> *(1 Peter 5:7)*

CHAPTER TWENTY

Sweet Christmas Addition

*There's always something in your life that God has graciously
blessed you with. Every good gift comes from Him.*

—JAZMIN HENSON

December 2018

T̶HE MONTH HAD FINALLY arrived when our grandchild
was supposed to be born. Jazmin made the trip a few weeks
before Charity's due date so she would be there to assist her
in the delivery room.

While we all waited for the baby to arrive, Aryanna, Charity,
Jazmin, and I spent time together cooking, talking about babies, and
enjoying one another's company as we gathered around the kitchen
island day after day.

Our eight-acre property was covered in a blanket of snow, and
tree branches were dusted in fluffy white powder. Christmas music
floated through our home, and a fire crackled in the fireplace.

Life was cozy. Jazmin had been stable since the summer. No
medical crisis had happened in months, other than the daily pain
that Jazmin managed. She strapped on her heated beanbag over

her kidney with a thick elastic belt. Dressed in her flannel pajama pants and hoodie, Jazzy perched her feet on a tall stool at the kitchen island and helped roll out dough and decorate cookies. We made an abundance of gluten-free Christmas goodies, and we ate it all within a few hours, which meant more baking the next day.

Devyn was there quite a bit in December. Having all the kids with us for meals when Jazmin and Eythan visited added to the fun of our family gatherings. They played board games, ate, and laughed. My heart filled with joy as my seven children gathered around our farmhouse table. Our children and their spouses got along well, and rarely did they fight or bicker.

On December 8, I woke early, checked my phone, and saw multiple texts from Charity. I immediately called her.

"Mom, your ringer must be off. Dan and I are at the hospital. My water broke. No hurry though. My contractions are mild right now."

Charity had spent so much time bouncing on a huge yoga ball, I was surprised the baby hadn't just fallen out on its own. (Apparently this is the new advice from midwives to help get the baby into place and possibly bring on contractions.)

I excitedly texted her back. "Jazmin and I will be there within the hour!"

Energy sparked my sleepy brain better than a giant mug of coffee. I was ready to go in ten minutes.

Jazmin reached the front door the same time I did, having received the same text. Grinning, we slipped out the door, trying not to wake Vance or Kyle. Since my huband's phone was off, I left him a text. I'd call him later and let him sleep. He couldn't come to the hospital until Kyle's staff arrived anyway.

Jazmin had taken a doula course and wanted to assist Charity when she had her baby. The two of them had sat at the kitchen table many times discussing birth plans. A beautiful bond formed as they worked together to come up with a plan for the new baby. Of course, having birthed five babies of my own, I knew plans pretty much went out the window once a woman went into labor. But I let them discuss the plan and believe it would go exactly as planned. To tell a mother otherwise can create a lot of anxiety, so I kept my opinions to myself.

Sure enough, the plan didn't happen. Charity needed a last-minute C-section, so Jazmin wasn't allowed in the delivery room.

Dan promised to text Jazmin as soon as the baby was born. She and I were ushered to the waiting room. Vance joined us a few hours later. The three of us sat in the small room, which was lined with colorful vinyl furniture.

Jazmin experienced pain throughout the day. She kept changing positions and shifting restlessly on the stiff furniture. She popped pain medication every few hours.

I took her beanbag to the tiny kitchen near the waiting room and microwaved it for her. It always smelled like something was on fire. When I overheard some nurses asking if there was a fire in the hospital, I popped my head out the doorway. "It's okay. I'm heating a beanbag in the microwave."

They laughed and asked why.

"My daughter-in-law has cancer and needs it for her pain."

The empathy on their faces told me they understood.

When I returned to the waiting room with the hot beanbag, she took it gratefully.

"I can drive you home and come back," Vance offered. "Charity will understand."

"No, I'm okay. I really want to see the baby as soon as possible after it's born."

Was she really okay? I didn't think so. Vance and I continued to monitor how often she changed positions. If her pain got too severe, it would be hard to get it back under control.

We waited anxiously for Dan's text. Jazmin checked her phone repeatedly.

When she went to the bathroom, Vance and I paced.

Through the large window in the waiting room, we saw Jazmin running toward us, skipping, jumping, and smiling.

And I knew. Her face and huge smile said it all.

"It's a girl!" Jazmin said as she burst into the waiting room, jumping up and down. The three of us laughed, cried, and embraced. Jazmin's pain was forgotten as happiness and joy swept over her.

Alice Jazmin Elliott.

Charity had told Jazmin that if it she had a girl, she would name her after Jazmin.

A half hour later, we rushed down the hall and into the birthing room. Dan looked up, holding a little bundle and wearing a huge smile. Pride radiated from his face. The most amazing father was born that day. His daughter would become the sun, moon, and stars to him.

I walked toward my new granddaughter. I looked down into a tiny face with rosebud lips that I knew I would love forever. Tears streamed down my cheeks.

I was a grandmother. How could I have ever doubted God's plan?

All the fears and worries I'd had dissipated into thin air, and my heart filled with indescribable love. The joy this child would bring me would counterbalance the painful days of cancer.

Vance and Jazmin took turns holding Alice, and both were smitten with her. Love radiated from their eyes as they cooed at the tiny baby girl.

Our children came to the hospital to see Alice. Devyn, Aryanna, and Eythan oohed and aahed over the new family member. Dan's parents, Don and Dixie, came and saw their first grandbaby, bursting with pride. Vance and I couldn't have asked for a sweeter couple to be Alice's other grandparents. This little girl was going to be loved by many.

Charity lay on the table, drugged and out of reality. (She says now she doesn't remember much about her stay in the hospital.)

Dan had been up since midnight the night before, and I offered to stay with Charity that night so he could go home and get some sleep. It took a lot of convincing, but I promised I would text him if anything happened.

Charity couldn't walk because of the effects of the epidural and drugs from the C-section. She also couldn't lift Alice from the hospital bassinette because her arms were numb, which was unusual.

Jazmin offered to stay too. But she was exhausted from trying to manage her pain. She rode home with Vance—the two of them ridiculously happy.

The weeks following Alice's birth were filled with trips to Charity and Dan's to bring food, to hold Alice while they slept, and to just sit and admire our grandbaby. Becoming grandparents was the best thing that had happened to us since we gained our bonus kids, Dan and Jazmin.

At family gatherings, we wanted so much to hold Alice we sometimes forgot to say hello to Charity and Dan when they walked into the house. Alice became our new favorite person. God had truly blessed us!

Jazmin and Eythan spent Christmas with us since her parents were in Minneapolis celebrating with Sherie's sister Lorie and her husband, CJ. We were overjoyed to have them spend the holiday with us two years in a row.

I had mixed emotions, though, as I wondered if this was going to be our last Christmas with Jazmin.

Our kids stayed overnight on Christmas Eve, and we went to bed with stomachs full of yummy treats. The next morning, I woke up around four o'clock, shuffled into the dark living room, turned on the lights, and gazed at the beautiful, glowing tree. I said the same prayer I pray every Christmas: "God, please heal Kyle from autism." Then I added, "And please heal Jazmin." I swallowed the lump in my throat and determined to have a happy day with my family. No crying or thinking about death. Just pure happiness.

A few hours later, our family sat around the living room, sipping coffee. I looked at eight sets of sleepy eyes and different styles of bedhead. Vance started a crackling fire, then read the Christmas story from the Bible. We took turns holding Alice and opening gifts.

Jazmin handed me a thin, beautifully wrapped gift. I tore off the paper. Inside was a book of photos she'd put together from their wedding day. A tear escaped my eye and rolled down my cheek. I walked to the sectional where she snuggled beside Eythan and gave them each a hug. I would cherish this for years to come.

Jazmin had also bought all of us girls and herself matching one-piece zip-up pajamas. We immediately dispersed to bedrooms and came back modeling our new pj's. We posed in front of the fireplace for a photo, our arms wrapped around one another.

The day was wonderful. Music played, lights twinkled, our bellies were full, and a sweet baby rested in Jazmin's arms. She was in her happy place, being with people she loved on one of her favorite holidays.

I had worried so much about becoming a grandmother, especially with Kyle living at home. I'd also worried about whether Jazmin would ever hold Alice. But in the end, God made a way.

What do you worry about? Do you believe God can manage your situation? Ask Him to work a miracle in your life and let the cares of this world go.

Lord,

Help us to lean into You when we are
overwhelmed by unique and difficult situations.
Make a way where there is no way.

Amen.

CHAPTER TWENTY-ONE

New Beginnings

*We have been so blessed to be able to stay with my in-laws
during this time, but we were so excited to finally
have our own place again!
Our new home is small and old
but adorable.*

—JAZMIN HENSON

January 2019

A NINJA GYM WAS OPENING up in our city, and the owner knew Eythan from a gym they had worked at the year before. He needed someone to be the manager since he was a full-time teacher. He offered Eythan his dream job.

He and Jazmin would live close by, and our family was delighted.

On the weekend they came to look for apartments, Jazmin and I sat at my kitchen table, chatting and sipping on hot coffee that cold winter morning.

I smoothed out the teal-and-white checkered tablecloth. "Are you excited for the big move?" I looked at my daughter-in-law with her auburn hair in a ponytail.

Jazmin had her feet up on the chair in front of her and her knees against her chest. She took another sip. "I get lonely being in our house by myself when Eythan is at work. If we move here, I'll have lots of company. I love having people around."

I couldn't say I agreed with her. Sometimes I wished I could have an hour to myself in our house. With Kyle's staff constantly rotating in and out, sometimes eight different people in a week, and Kyle bouncing around in his room above the kitchen, our home was always noisy. Doesn't every woman crave a quiet house, at least once in a while? The only way I could accomplish that was to rise at four in the morning.

But Jazmin seemed to have too much alone time. Too much time to think about her health.

"I'm hoping Eythan and I will connect with some of the young families in your church. It would be fun to hang out with other married couples!" Jazmin's eyes lit up. Then she grew quiet. "And Eythan will need his family when I'm gone."

Her eyelashes lowered as she fiddled with the handle of her mug. Gosh, these conversations came out of nowhere, and I was never prepared for them. *How do I respond to this?* "I agree, Jazmin. Eythan can move back in with us when that happens so he won't be alone." Such heavy thoughts.

Having Jazmin and Eythan move to our city would also give me a better opportunity to be more involved in Jazmin's care as the cancer progressed.

She shifted, trying to get comfortable. "That makes me feel so much better. My family loves him, but it's not the same as having your own parents and siblings nearby. That's why I encouraged Eythan to get a job here."

I hadn't planned on talking about death when we sat down at the table. But how do you plan such deep conversations ahead of time? These moments were best if they happened when Jazmin brought them up.

I was getting good at keeping my tears in check when I was around her. I didn't want her thinking I would fall apart every time she needed to have a hard conversation with me. It wasn't her job to worry about my emotional state. She was the one dying, not me.

Jazmin was always thinking of others, and she had the most unselfish heart. I appreciated that she was willing to talk about the serious subjects.

She had made it clear to Eythan that she wanted him to remarry after she was gone. She also expressed this to me. Her desire to want what was best for her husband overrode any insecurities she felt. Jazmin didn't want any of us to make Eythan feel bad if he fell in love again. She also talked to her family about Eythan remarrying and made it clear that they were to be happy for him and give him their blessing.

For now we would take one step at a time and think about them finding a house.

They found a small two-bedroom bungalow on a busy street. Vance and I went with them to see the house after they agreed to rent the space. I was concerned about the neighborhood. The motel across the street looked shady, and people went in and out all hours of the night. There were rumors it was used for prostitution.

The back entrance of the little house led into a kitchen, which had an L shape of white upper and lower cupboards. A big window facing the neighbor shone light across the dark-green and black flooring.

We walked through to the living room, which had beautiful hardwood floors and dark walls. Off the living room was a good-size master bedroom with a bathroom between it and the tiny second bedroom.

The house needed some tender loving care. But I tried to be positive and look at the possibilities of this house in a shady neighborhood only fifty feet in front of a railway track.

Jazmin was delighted to turn the bungalow into her new cozy nest, and she and I spent a week painting the whole interior. Her health was stable during this time, and the two of us blasted Christian music as we sipped coffee and ate doughnuts from our favorite bakery.

We painted the five rooms a bright white to bring more light into the home. Jazmin turned the tiny house into an adorable home. I had a wonderful time with her that week. Vance and the kids took turns bringing us food, and we stopped to visit when they came.

By the end of the week, I began to see potential in the bungalow.

Jazmin picked a forest-green color for an accent wall in their living room. When we finished painting the room, she stood back and admired her work. She smiled from ear to ear. "I just love this color. It makes me so happy!"

My heart joined her happiness. She was like Michelangelo looking at her beautiful painting. Jazmin loved beautiful things. They pulled joy into her soul.

As she transformed the dreary bungalow into a homey space, Jazmin shared her dreams with me. "I've always wanted to have babies." She stood on a chair, painting the wall in their master bedroom. "If I have a boy, I'd like to name him Aaron, after my dad."

I couldn't see her face as she rolled the paint. Her tall skinny frame balanced on the chair, and her jogging pants sagged since her body couldn't fill them out.

Lord, what do I say?

My mind filled with redheaded grandbabies running toward me. I grabbed a pink scarf from my hope-suitcase and wrapped it around my neck. I pictured those little ones I would love with all my heart. But I couldn't encourage Jazmin to hold on to false hopes.

I dipped my brush in paint as tears burned my eyes. I would never see those sweet babies. They were only a figment of my imagination. I took off the scarf. There was no sense wishing for something that could never happen.

I went home that night and looked up the meaning of the name Aaron. The first definition that came up was "miracle." I gasped and held my hand over my heart. Was this a sign? Would God heal Jazmin?

Okay, Cindy, this is stupid. Just stop it! Jazmin is not having babies. My self-talk helped me get a grip.

One day, as we painted, Jazmin turned to me with her roller held up in front of her to keep it from dripping and said, "More than anything, I want to be a good wife to Eythan."

"Jazmin, you are a wonderful wife!" I put down my paintbrush and placed my hands on my hips.

"Eythan deserves a wife who can give him a beautiful home. There's so much I can't do when I'm feeling sick. I want to be able to do those things for him to show my appreciation."

I wanted to sit on the floor and hold Jazmin in my arms and cry. How could this dear, sweet girl think she was not a good wife?

"Jazmin, Eythan knows you love him. He doesn't doubt that."

She shifted to her other leg, and her hip dropped a bit. "I know. But on the days when I can't get out of bed, Eythan has to make meals, get groceries, do laundry, and take care of me."

"Jazmin, you can't help being sick. Eythan knows that. You're being the best wife you can be."

Jazmin turned back to her task. I wanted to take away all her doubt and show her how much Eythan cherished her just for being herself.

The devil lurked when Jazmin was the most vulnerable, and I wanted to punch him in the nose.

At the end of the week, we were tired and happy—Jazmin because she had made something beautiful for Eythan and me because I had grown closer to my sweet bonus daughter.

They settled into their new house, and Eythan loved his job at the Ninja gym. Jazmin was content in her new surroundings. She spent her days cooking Eythan his favorite meals and desserts. She seemed grateful to have a husband, a dog, and a home, and we knew she didn't take these things for granted.

Jazmin's prayers were answered, and she felt ready for whatever was ahead.

I'm amazed at how God can give us the desires of our hearts. Jazmin's prayers were unselfish and focused on the needs of other people. God granted her those loving requests.

Are you, too, asking God to meet the needs of your loved ones? He delights in providing for His children and showing them how He cares about their needs—no matter how trivial they may seem.

Lord,

Help us to desire what You want and help us to pray unselfishly. Take care of our loved ones in a way that shows them You truly love and care for them.

Amen.

CHAPTER TWENTY-TWO

Only a Mother Would Do

God uses tough times to draw us closer to Him, to learn to trust Him and depend on Him, and to recognize that we can't go through this life without Him. I have no idea what I would do without Christ.

—JAZMIN HENSON

February 2019

MY PHONE CHIMED ONE afternoon. I put down my dish towel and the pot I was drying, picked up the phone, and read the message from Jazmin.

"Hi, Mom. I need some pain meds, and they're ready at the pharmacy, but Eythan is at work. Can you pick them up for me?"

I was alone with Kyle, so I couldn't leave the house. I texted Devyn, and he said he could get them. Devyn was always willing to lend a hand wherever he could.

An hour later, I got a text from Devyn. "Mom, Jazmin looks really sick, and the house is a mess."

Dread flooded me. "Thanks for letting me know. I'll check on her as soon as Kyle's staff arrives."

An hour later, I climbed the four stairs into Jazmin's kitchen and was shocked to see the counters and table covered in dirty dishes and bowls with leftover food.

I walked through the kitchen and into her bedroom. The room was dark, and the blinds were drawn. Her tiny frame was hard to see under the pile of covers.

"Hi, Jazmin. How are you doing?" I stepped closer to the bed. How long had she been in bed? Could she walk? Would she have lain here all day if I hadn't come along?

"I'm in a lot of pain." She winced.

I looked at her pale face. "Have you taken your pain meds?"

"Yes. But I think I need more. Can you grab me my morphine pills?" She pointed to the dresser, which was out of her reach.

I grabbed one and tried to read the tiny print on the label, but the room was too dark.

"No, not that one, the one to the left of it." Jazmin pointed.

I opened the bottle, handed her a pill, and moved her medications closer to her bed.

"Mom, could you get me some water, please? And heat up my beanbag?" She took it out from under her back and handed it to me. It was room temperature.

"Sure." I grabbed the water bottle from her side table. "Do you want anything to eat?"

"No. I'm nauseous from the pain. Maybe later. But thank you."

Lacey jumped off the bed, wagging her tail at me, wanting to be petted. I tucked the beanbag and the water bottle under my arm, reached down, and gave her ears a good rub. Lacey's tail wagged faster and she circled my legs, leaning up against me.

"Can you let Lacey out to go pee?" Jazmin tried to move to a more comfortable position.

I left the room, popped the bag in the microwave, filled the water bottle, and let Lacey outside. A couple of minutes later, I brought the beanbag back to Jazmin with her water and helped her to the bathroom. She could barely walk. She used my arm to support herself as she walked, hunched over from the pain. I closed the door behind me and went to the kitchen to start cleaning up.

"Mom, I'm done," Jazmin called. I helped her back to bed and grabbed more meds for her to take.

"Jazmin, how many days have you been like this?" Her hair looked like she had been in bed for days.

"About a week." She shifted and readjusted her beanbag.

"Why didn't you call me?"

"I didn't want to bother anyone. You all have responsibilities." Jazmin's voice was strained.

It broke my heart to realize Jazmin thought she was a burden.

"I would gladly spend my days with you, Jazmin." I grabbed her hand and squeezed it.

She looked up at me and gave me a weak smile.

Within an hour her pain had settled down a bit, and she fell asleep. I cleaned the kitchen, went to the basement, and did a couple of loads of laundry.

Later in the day, I slipped into her room and found Jazmin on the floor in a T-shirt and underwear, trying to pull herself up to her bed, but she fell back to the floor. I rushed into the room. "Here, Jazmin, let me help you!" I grabbed her under her bony armpits and lifted her into bed. "How long have you been sitting on the floor?" I pulled the covers over her legs.

"Ten minutes. I was calling you, but you didn't hear me." She leaned back on her elbow and tried to move herself up closer to her pillow.

I'd had music playing quietly in the kitchen and hadn't heard a peep. "You could have texted me." I helped pull the covers up to her chin and grabbed her empty water bottle.

"My phone was on the bed, and I couldn't reach it." Tears filled her eyes.

"Jazmin, from now on, I'm coming here every day. You can't be left on your own or you might end up on the floor all day." I looked down at her lying in bed with her hair splayed about her. Her room was dark, and clothes covered the floor.

"Mom, you can't come every day. You have your own home and Vance and Kyle to cook and clean for." Her lip quivered.

"Vance would rather have me here caring for you than worrying that you might be sitting on the floor by yourself."

Eythan worked twelve-hour shifts. He spent evenings and mornings taking care of Jazmin, getting groceries, and cooking meals. But he couldn't be at the house full time.

I was surprised Eythan hadn't let me know how bad Jazmin was. Knowing her, she didn't want to burden anyone. She probably told Eythan she was fine by herself.

I stepped outside and called Vance. "I'm going to stay the rest of the day. Could you be home in time to relieve Kyle's staff?"

"I will. Stay as long as you need." Vance's voice was laced with concern.

Birds sang in the trees behind the garage. I closed my eyes and took in a deep breath so I wouldn't cry. "Thank you, honey." I said goodbye and stepped back inside.

At eight fifteen in the evening, Eythan arrived. "Hi, Mom. Why are you still here?" He glanced around the neat and tidy kitchen, and I could tell he was happy to see it clean.

"I came over to check on Jazmin. She can't be on her own anymore. I'm going to come and stay with her every day when you go to work."

"That would be great. Thank you." He looked as if he carried the weight of the world on his shoulders.

"I made you some supper.."

Eythan looked toward the stove, where a pot of stew simmered. He lift the lid off the pot and inhaled the aroma. "I'm so hungry!" He got a bowl out of the cupboard, scooped himself some stew, and sat at the table. "Jazmin never wants me to call anyone to take care of her." He blew on his hot supper.

"I realize that. But at this point, she has no choice. She needs care. If I hadn't come to check on her, she would have sat on the floor until you got home. Her cell phone was out of her reach."

Eythan didn't like talking about Jazmin's frailty. It made him feel vulnerable, and I knew he was trying to keep his emotions in check. "That would really help a lot." He grabbed a glass out of the cupboard and filled it with water.

"Text me your grocery list each morning. I'll get whatever you need on my way over."

"Thanks, Mom!" He smiled, clearly relieved for the help.

I drove home heavyhearted. My son was too young to be taking care of a dying wife by himself. I cried on the drive home as I thought about their delicate situation.

I walked in my front door feeling exhausted mentally and physically. Vance sat at the table. I joined him and filled him in on my day.

I cried as I described finding Jazmin on the bedroom floor. Vance reached for my hand and squeezed. Tears glistened in his eyes. "Cindy, I can handle everything here. You just concentrate on Jazmin."

I loved this man. God had given him a servant's heart.

Over the next four weeks, I cared for Jazmin. She apologized a few times for me having to do things for her.

Having been Kyle's caregiver for almost thirty years, this role came naturally to me. "Jazmin," I said, folding a load of towels, "you're a delight to care for, and you're certainly not a burden. I consider it a great honor that God has placed you in my life, and you are never a wrench in my plans."

After a month, cooking and cleaning for both homes did become a challenge. I grew weary, and anxiety crept in. I slept restlessly, concerned for Jazmin's health.

One day I decided to pry a bit. "Does your family know your health is declining?"

"No. Only you and Eythan know." Jazmin shook her head slightly as she lay in bed.

I knew she would never ask anyone to come every day. She didn't want to pull her mom away from her work. Sherie had already lost a lot of wages over the years when Jazmin went through bad spells and needed a caregiver. But I could tell her mom was the one she wanted to take care of her.

I texted Sherie and let her know of Jazmin's health change, even though I felt like I was betraying my daughter-in-law.

Sherie was shocked that Jazmin hadn't said anything to her.

She dropped everything and came two days later. She stayed for three months with Jazmin and Eythan. There are some things only a mother can do for her daughter, and there's no bond quite like the one between a mother and daughter.

Once or twice a week, I dropped in to check on Jazmin and visit with her and Sherie. I wanted to stop by every day, but I didn't want Sherie to think I was overbearing or intrusive.

Sherie loved babies, and on Jazmin's better days Charity and I went over for a visit, bringing Alice along. Sherie held the baby and made the cutest noises. Alice responded with giggles and coos and was fascinated by Sherie's pretty-colored fingernails.

The four of us women sat around sipping coffee and talking about news, fashion, travel, cooking, and family.

The more I got to know Sherie, the more I liked her. She spoke her mind, and I never had to guess what she was thinking. Jazmin was so much happier with her mom taking care of her while Eythan was at work. And I knew Eythan was grateful for Sherie's help.

After three months, the school year was over, and Aaron joined Sherie to help care for Jazmin when Eythan was at work.

Jazmin did feel a bit better. But that could flip any day. Jazmin couldn't be alone if her health plummeted. I tried to figure out how I could care for two homes again. Vance and I discussed multiple plans, but we couldn't seem to figure out what would be best for Jazmin.

Would I have to move in with them? If so, for how long? These questions overwhelmed me.

God was going to have to come through for Jazmin, and we needed Him to come through for us too. He was our only hope.

Lord,

When our plans fail, light the way for us so we have clarity and know You are the one guiding us in the right direction.

Amen.

CHAPTER TWENTY-THREE

Change in Plans

*None of the pain meds were working,
and I was ready to take a knife and carve my kidney out
myself. That may sound crazy, but the brain often tries
to solve problems in weird ways.*

—JAZMIN HENSON

June 2019

JAZMIN HAD NOT PLANNED to do radiation, but desperation called for a change of plans. The cancer grew, filling her lungs, and her breathing became louder as she tried to take in oxygen with the very little space left for air. Jazmin decided to try radiation, hoping to relieve some of the pain from the tumor on her kidney.

I went with Jazmin to her initial radiology appointment, and I was nervous. I had never been in the cancer treatment department at the hospital. We were escorted to a small alcove with four chairs and sat down.

Jazmin picked up a magazine off the side table and leafed through it while I anxiously bounced my leg, waiting for someone to come get us. Ten minutes later, we were directed to a small room with no windows and sat side by side in two chairs.

A friendly nurse sat across from us and explained the treatment plan. Jazmin nodded as the nurse discussed possible side effects. My anxiety grew.

She said Jazmin could start radiation in a week.

"That will work with our schedule," she said, her hands tucked under her legs.

The nurse penciled it into her book, then looked up at Jazmin. "Actually, we have an opening right now. We could do your first radiation today. How does that sound?"

I'm sure my eyes bulged out, and my hand instinctively wanted to reach protectively for Jazmin like a mother does when she slams on the car brakes, reaches over to the passenger seat where her kid is sitting, and places her hand on his chest.

"That's fine," Jazmin said confidently, her ponytail bouncing as she nodded.

I tried to make eye contact with her to let her know we needed to talk in private before she agreed. But she was acting like she had just ordered a hamburger and fries, not radiation that could burn parts of her body.

I wasn't mentally prepared for her to have radiation that day and wanted to scream, "Nooo!"

The nurse looked at her schedule. "Oh, I made a mistake. We can't fit you in today after all. Sorry!"

Relief spread through me. I wanted out of there as fast as Jazmin's skinny legs could keep up with mine.

Jazmin and I talked about the radiation on the way to the car. She was determined to go through with it, and it wasn't my decision to make. She had been feeling better, and she was able to stay on her own for longer periods of time.

I dropped her off at her house and then drove home, heavyhearted. I hated cancer. It robbed people of life and love.

Jazmin and I returned the next week and entered the sterile hospital environment. After taking our seats, Jazmin looked at her phone while I bounced my legs.

"Jazmin Henson." A tall husky Black man stood in the doorway, smiling.

I smiled back. "I know you. You went to my husband's gym. Sam, right?"

"Yes. But I don't recognize you."

"I'm Vance's wife."

His eyebrows shot up. "I remember him!"

Everyone remembered Vance. How could they not? At six feet, three inches tall and 260 pounds, he was memorable. I sometimes teased Vance that no one ever remembered me because his presence was so much more obvious than mine.

Sam commented about what a nice guy Vance was. We chatted a bit longer, then he motioned for Jazmin to follow him. I felt better knowing Jazmin was with a kind Christian man who had a lovely wife and children.

Still, as I sat in the waiting room sending fervent prayers up to God, I had to will tears from spilling onto my lap at the thought of Jazmin being zapped in another room. Would it hurt? Would she have burn marks?

After a few minutes, Jazmin came out and stood in front of me, looking the same as when she left. "I'm done. We can go now." Her voice sounded nonchalant.

My stiff shoulders turned to putty when I saw her peaceful face.

As I pulled out of the parking lot, I asked, "What's radiation like?"

"It's like getting an X-ray." Jazmin gazed out the window as we drove past the thick trees lining the driveway leading away from the hospital.

"I was picturing a big, loud machine that burned you, like it was zapping the cancer." I glanced at her quickly as I drove.

She laughed. "No, it was no big deal. Honestly, it was easy. They put some tattoos the size of a freckle on my torso so they can radiate the same place each time. Then they pressed a button, I heard a little noise, and it was over." She pulled the visor down to shade her eyes from the bright sun.

Jazmin had a good sense of humor and could talk about cancer like other people talk about making supper.

I laughed at how I'd worked myself into a frenzy.

We stopped for coffee on the way home to celebrate. As we stood in line, I looked around at everyone coming and going. No one in that café knew that the thin girl I stood beside had just had radiation at the hospital and handled it like she had gone through a drive-through to get fast food.

The nurse had explained that Jazmin's radiation wouldn't be aggressive since it couldn't cure the cancer. The goal was simply to relieve the pain and make her more comfortable.

Radiation did help a bit with the pain, but Jazmin had the strange side effect of a really sore lower back and not being able to walk upright for a few months. The radiation also made her sick, tired, and listless. She had to use a walker in her tiny home, and it was difficult for her to get around. If she wanted to leave the house, she had to be carried down the stairs and to the vehicle.

It also heated up her body. When we hugged her, it was like hugging someone who had just come out of a sauna.

Vance stayed home from work on the days I needed to take Jazmin to an appointment. Sometimes Eythan took the day off or went to work late after he cared for his wife. Between the three of us, we managed to be her entourage of caregivers. We fell into a manageable schedule. We rolled with new plans and tried to accept that we were in a temporary stage of life.

But Jazmin's situation wasn't temporary. She couldn't escape the fact that she might be permanently crippled. We hoped the side effects of the radiation would dissipate and she would once again get around without a walker. She kept her hopes up and tried to believe her situation could improve.

> If we hope for what we do not yet have,
> we wait for it patiently.
> *(Romans 8:25)*

CHAPTER TWENTY-FOUR

Hospital Shenanigans

*You can't plan out your life! You can have goals,
and goals are important. But to sit down and plan exactly
how your life will turn out is a waste of time and thought.
Plans change.*

—JAZMIN HENSON

July 2019

AZMIN'S GRANDPARENTS OWNED A lodge on Onaping Lake with cottages they rented out each summer. Sherie and Aaron's cottage was on the property next to the resort. Jazmin had told me about times as a teenager when she woke up in the morning, grabbed a mug of coffee, and walked to the dock to watch the sunrise. She sat in her comfy pajamas with her dog, Sadie, snuggled under her arm.

Since Sherie and Aaron were teachers, they had summers off, and Jazmin and Vangie grew up on the lake. Once a year they had "cousins week." Jazmin and her cousins spent seven days swimming, waterskiing, and roasting marshmallows over campfires.

Jazmin's parents invited her to visit the family's camp and hopefully stay for a few weeks. She was excited about the trip and talked about it for days. Jazmin's fondest childhood memories were of trips to Onaping Lake.

While Jazmin was at camp, Eythan could enjoy a week of sleeping through the night and catching up on some much-needed rest.

After being at the camp for a week, Jazmin awoke one night and threw up. A massive amount of blood pooled on the floor. Panic ensued. Her parents called 911, and an ambulance was sent from forty-five minutes away. Eythan drove to Sudbury to be with Jazmin in the hospital. A few days later, Jazmin was flown to our city by air ambulance, and Eythan drove back to meet her at the hospital.

When I got the call, I thought, *This is it. This will be the end of our Jazmin!* Hope faded like a wilted flower. My hope-suitcase seemed empty.

When I walked into the hospital room, Eythan sat on a vinyl couch under the window, his face drawn and tired. Jazmin held a cardboard bowl on her lap, throwing up into it repeatedly. Her eyes were droopy and bloodshot, and she appeared exhausted.

How was she still alive?

My heart broke seeing her suffering. But I willed my face to not betray my emotions. I sat in a chair across from Eythan and waited until Jazmin finished throwing up, which seemed to take forever. I acted like this was something I'd done a thousand times before—as routine as doing a load of laundry.

"How often is she throwing up?"

Eythan leaned forward with his elbows on his knees. "Several times a day. She can't keep any food down."

I glanced at Jazmin. The head of her bed was raised, and she leaned over her container with her eyes closed, taking deep breaths. Finally, she leaned back against her bed, exhausted and pale.

"Do the doctors know why this is happening?"

"They don't have any answers." He propped his arm on the windowsill, sitting sideways on the couch, and looked at Jazmin.

As a mother, whenever my kids were sick, I considered it my job to figure out why. I disliked relying on a medical community for answers and long-awaited doctor's appointments to solve problems.

When Charity became very ill at sixteen, we had many doctor visits but no answers. I finally went to Google. After months of reading, I realized she had celiac disease. Eventually we persuaded our doctor to send Charity to a gastrologist, who, sure enough, diagnosed her with celiac disease. It changed her life, and she recovered her health.

This mama had no time to wait for slow answers. I asked Eythan all sorts of questions. Once Jazmin was done throwing up and had drunk some water, she looked at me with heavily hooded eyes. "Hi, Mom," she said weakly and tried to give me a little smile.

I walked to her bed and rubbed her arm. "How are you feeling, Jazzy?"

"I'm okay."

We chatted for a few minutes about what had happened at camp, then she lay back in the bed and fell asleep. Her kneecaps nearly protruded though her skin, and I knew she had lost weight again.

I felt bad that her visit to camp had ended early with a medical emergency. There were very few things left in life for her to enjoy.

Eythan took time off work and stayed in her hospital room for seven days. He tenderly cared for his wife, helping her to shower, sit, and walk. He was so patient and gentle with Jazmin. When she panicked, he stayed calm. Never in my life had I been prouder of my son.

I went in at night so he could go home and sleep, so he would be well rested and a better caregiver during the day.

Jazmin slept fitfully and woke often, asking for ice, water, or cold cloths. The drugs caused her to forget how long she had slept and when she had asked for something last. Sometimes her requests were five minutes to an hour or two apart.

Jazmin developed severe diarrhea along with the upset stomach. As I dozed in the chair one night, she yelled, "Mom, I have to use the bathroom!"

I jumped out of the chair, knowing she only had seconds. I sat her up, then quickly settled her into the wheelchair. As I circled her chair, I got caught in her tubing and panicked. Finally I untangled myself and pushed her toward the bathroom.

"Mom, my container—grab it quick!" Her face was green.

I saw the container on the other side of her bed. I leaped across her chair, landing on my stomach on the bed, and grabbed the container just in time to slip it under her chin.

"Hurry, Mom!"

I ran behind her chair and whizzed her into the bathroom, then lifted her out of the chair and onto the toilet.

Exiting the bathroom and sitting in the recliner to catch my breath, I started to laugh. I couldn't help myself. The whole situation was tragic and funny at the same time.

When I went to retrieve Jazmin from the bathroom, I still had the giggles. She laughed too. Once she was settled in her bed and I was back in my chair, we started laughing again.

"Mom, you don't need to panic when I'm going to throw up or have diarrhea."

"When you're yelling at me to hurry, how am I supposed to not panic?"

These moments collected in my heart—moments of bonding as I shared hardships with Jazmin through the trials of cancer.

> These moments collected in my heart— moments of bonding as I shared hardships with Jazmin through the trials of cancer.

Some nights Jazmin lay in bed reading on her cell phone. She closed her eyes for long periods, and I thought she was sleeping, but her hands were still holding up her phone. A few minutes later, she opened her eyes.

I finally realized she was praying.

For five days, Jazmin didn't eat and couldn't hold down any liquids. Since the diarrhea was emptying any nutrition left in her body, she looked severely ill. Her face became gaunt, her teeth prominent, and her legs the size of my wrists.

Jazmin was slipping away. I wasn't ready for her to die. My son wasn't ready. Her parents weren't ready. We needed more time. *Please, Lord, more time.*

> Jazmin was slipping away. I wasn't ready for her to die. My son wasn't ready. Her parents weren't ready. We needed more time. *Please, Lord, more time.*

But death seemed to be waiting outside her hospital door. We told our kids this was likely the end for Jazmin and she wasn't going to get out of the hospital.

There was no way she would make a turnaround. Unless God intervened. *Lord, Jazmin needs You. You're all she has. Please come through for her.*

One day, Eythan heard Jazmin crying in her sleep as he sat beside her hospital bed. He gently woke her and asked why she was crying.

"I had a dream. I was in a concentration camp with other people, and they were being treated badly. I was scared. My husband put his hand on my shoulder and said, 'Just breathe, Jazmin. Breathe.'"

When she told me about the dream, I knew the husband Jazmin referred to wasn't Eythan but a representation of a husband. I thought maybe it had been God telling her she was going to be okay. Often in the Bible, God refers to His children as the bride of Christ, and He talks of loving the church as a husband loves his wife.

Jazmin often experienced loneliness because she was the only one in her close circle of friends and family suffering from cancer. Even when her family surrounded her, she often retreated into a private space with God. She prayed a lot while I was in the hospital with her. Prayer helped her feel close to God when she felt afraid of dying.

One night she closed her eyes as she held her phone above her chest, her elbows on the bed. I watched her for a while, then went back to reading my book.

I heard a thud.

"Ow!" Jazmin rubbed her bony chest. "I must have fallen asleep and dropped my phone."

"Are you okay?" I walked over to her bedside.

"I have no fat, so my phone hit hard on my bones." She giggled.

I smiled at the little waif of a girl. How she laughed when life was so hard was beyond my comprehension.

> Stepping into the bright hallway was, at times, a thirty-second break from the death lingering in the room.

I grabbed her water jug, took it out to the hall, and refilled it with ice. Stepping into the bright hallway was, at times, a thirty-second break from the death lingering in the room.

When I returned, Jazmin looked sleepy. Her phone rested on her belly. I sat back in my recliner with a smile. We both fell asleep.

On Saturday, I planned to help decorate for my niece Kayla's wedding. I told Eythan I was going to sleep at home the night before so I could be rested for the big day.

On Friday night, I had a good, deep sleep. When I woke, I decided to go to the hospital and stay with Jazmin and Eythan for the morning instead of decorating but hoped to head home for an hour to get ready before the wedding.

When I walked into her room, I saw Eythan asleep on the couch, his legs hanging over the arm. Jazmin was lying in her bed with her arms crossed over her midsection. I watched them for a moment. This was love—in sickness and in health.

Eythan knew Jazmin was sick when he started dating her. I don't think he had a clue what he was about to go through. But he was still here, taking care of his wife. Some men might have disappeared, unable to handle caring for a dying woman.

> Eythan knew Jazmin was sick when he started dating her. I don't think he had a clue what he was about to go through. But he was still here, taking care of his wife.

I took out my phone and snapped a picture of them, capturing the precious moment, one of many I had secretly taken when they weren't looking. I had felt a strong pull to capture their cancer journey together.

> I took out my phone and snapped a picture of them, capturing the precious moment, one of many I had secretly taken when they weren't looking.

I dropped my purse beside the chair and sat down, then quietly read on my phone until they woke.

Jazmin said she felt much better and wanted to go for a walk in the hallway. Eythan and I managed to push her wheelchair and two towers of IV bags on wheels as Jazmin slowly walked the long bright hallway lined with floor-to-ceiling windows.

"Oh, I forgot my phone," Jazmin said.

"I'll get it." I ran back to the room. As I came back and turned the corner, I saw them walking, the sun casting soft rays across them.

A young couple, him standing strong and watchful, she rail thin and barely alive.

True love.

I snapped another photo.

"Can we go outside?" Jazmin asked.

Eythan wheeled her outside. As I held the door open, Jazmin turned to me and gasped. "Kayla and Austin's wedding is today! Did you miss it?" Her eyes were big with worry.

I smiled. "I still have half an hour until I need to leave."

"Oh, good. I wouldn't want you to miss the wedding because of me."

Jazmin relaxed and took in a deep breath of warm summer air. She closed her eyes and lifted her face to the sun. We enjoyed a half hour on the cobblestone terrace.

A woman strolled by with a small dog on a leash.

"Aww. Here, puppy!" Jazmin made a kissing noise with her lips and held her hand out to the dog.

The woman stopped for Jazmin to pet the little critter.

He wagged his tail, and Jazmin rubbed behind his ears. She smiled and talked to the gray dog.

If Jazmin could still smile, she hadn't given up on living. My imaginary suitcase opened a tiny bit. I grabbed a beaded necklace, pulled it over my head and around my neck, and held it tightly in my hands.

Jazmin basked in the sunshine and swayed slightly from side to side, as though she were dancing in a ballroom.

People tried not to stare at us. But they couldn't help it. Jazmin was just a waif and hooked up to all sorts of equipment. It was obvious she was young and dying. But Jazmin didn't let it bother her. She was always genuine and felt free to be herself, even if her appearance bothered people. Jazzy had let go of worrying about what people thought of her.

When my time was up, I left the hospital, raced home, went into the house, and threw on a dress I had bought off a discount rack but hadn't tried on beforehand. It was too big. But it was my only option. I pinned the back of the dress, threw on a white belt, and draped a white denim jacket over the top to cover the pinned-up back. My naturally curly hair was a mess, but there was no time to worry about my appearance.

Vance and I drove to the wedding. On the way, my suitcase-necklace of hope had broken, and all the beads sat on the floor of the car. I felt so tired and depressed I didn't think I would make it through the day. Coffee had sustained me in the past week, but exhaustion was hard to mask in a crowd of people I hadn't seen in quite some time. We were supposed to show enthusiasm and happiness when we saw them. But I didn't want to visit with anyone—I just wanted to go to bed for a month.

Sadness overwhelmed me. At any moment I could fall into a puddle of tears. I prayed God would help me keep my composure together at the wedding. Today was a happy day! My niece was marrying the man she loved.

I turned to Vance. "I'm not feeling up to going to a wedding today."

"Me neither."

My eyes teared up. "But I want to be happy for Kayla and Austin and celebrate their special day." I grabbed a tissue and wiped my eyes.

Vance grabbed my hand and squeezed it. "Eythan is taking care of Jazmin today, so let's enjoy the day!"

I nodded. He was right. We needed to live in the moment.

As we sat waiting for the wedding party to enter the room, I thought of how today marked the beginning of a new life for Kayla and Austin. I wondered what my niece and her husband would go through to test their love for each other. I hoped it would never be the journey Jazmin and Eythan were traveling.

Kayla looked beautiful. Her long dark hair had been curled to perfection, and her smile said it all as her eyes fell on Austin at the front of the aisle.

Kayla and Austin were married on a large interior balcony that wrapped around the reception area of a beautiful old stone building.

After the ceremony, the guests stood in the reception area with little sparklers in our hands and loudly cheered the bride and groom as they entered the hall. The joy and happiness from the crowd spread to me, and I had a moment when I forgot about cancer and felt giddy. We ate an abundance of delicious food, and people danced the evening away.

I looked at my phone quite often for texts from Eythan. Thankfully, Jazmin's day had been uneventful.

Vance and I went home early and right to bed. I was too tired to go relieve Eythan so he could sleep.

A few days later, Jazmin's doctors discovered a large ulcer in her stomach that was bleeding profusely. They gave her medication to heal it.

We thought Jazmin was going to die in the hospital. So we called her friends and family to say goodbye. But after five days of meds, she made a shocking turnaround.

Jazmin was discharged from the hospital a few days later. She didn't return to camp. But having her friends and family surrounding her and covering her in prayer bolstered her spirits.

She had turned a corner, and we all breathed a sigh of relief. We rejoiced as we realized God had answered our prayers and given Jazmin more time.

How many times would He answer that prayer? Could we keep Jazmin alive by praying?

Dear God,

Please help us to call on You when we need You most. Show us how You determine our days and that our life is in Your hands. Help us to trust in Your perfect timing.

Amen.

CHAPTER TWENTY-FIVE

Blended Family

*I'm so thankful to have a husband who also strives
to lead our family in the direction of Christ daily.
I am truly thankful that I get to have him by my side.
I love him more than words can express.*

—JAZMIN HENSON

August 2019

AZMIN MADE IT TO their two-year wedding anniversary. Vance and I thanked God for this unexpected gift. If they had been given a year together, we would have thought it was incredible.

Jazmin needed constant care, so she was staying in Sudbury.

At night, Sherie and Aaron were her caregivers. Eythan worked four days a week and traveled to Sudbury each weekend to spend three days with Jazmin.

Jazmin and Eythan gave up their bungalow. If by some miracle God healed her, they would find another apartment or house to move into.

I doubted that would happen. But the new setup gave me a measure of peace, knowing we could be with Eythan to support him through the mourning he might face shortly.

But how would the separation affect their marriage?

In September 2019, Charity started talking to Eythan and texting Jazmin about that. Jazmin said she wanted to be with her husband, and Eythan felt the same way about her. We invited Jazmin to move into our home. At first, she was hesitant because she didn't want to burden us.

We reassured her that we wanted to be her caregivers along with Eythan. Jazmin agreed to try the arrangement for a week, and if she didn't feel comfortable living with her in-laws, she would return to her parents' home.

Eythan was ecstatic. The day of her arrival, he ran around the house getting everything set up. It was important to him that Jazmin's stay go perfectly. He missed his wife and didn't ever want to part with her again.

We gave them our master bedroom on the main floor since Jazmin struggled to climb stairs. Vance and I set up their new room to be a cozy retreat. Our bed could be raised on either side, so Jazmin could sit up. She was still throwing up every day and sometimes didn't have the strength to sit up quickly, so she could prop herself up when she slept.

Our spacious master bathroom was easy to navigate for a person with special needs. It had a walk-in shower and a walk-through closet that linked the bathroom and bedroom.

It seemed as though God had planned the setup for Jazmin fourteen years before, when we had our home built.

Our kids were happy to have Jazmin nearby again. They had missed her. They came over for dinner on the weekends. Jazmin was happiest when everyone was together. She loved the chitter-chatter of our big family.

On her good days, Jazmin sat at the counter or table and helped chop vegetables. She loved cooking and was passionate about food. When we girls were in the kitchen together, we often laughed over some dramatic story Jazmin told us. On those days her eyes grew brighter as she spoke of something she was excited about. Her hunched spine straightened and her hands flew with her unfolding story. We all cherished these moments together.

Jazmin enjoyed her stay with us so much that she decided to make it permanent. Vance and I knew this would be the best setup for their marriage to continue to thrive. We told her parents they could come visit Jazmin whenever they wanted—our home was their home.

We settled into a new routine of taking care of Jazmin while Eythan was at work. Vance adjusted his work hours so he was home whenever Kyle didn't have support staff.

We watched Eythan take care of Jazmin each morning and late evening. He grew tired from the demands. But Jazmin was happier, and being with her husband helped her thrive emotionally, which made Eythan happy too.

After visiting our home, her parents felt good about the new arrangements. That made us happy since we didn't want her family worrying about her care.

We adopted her parents and sister as our new family. We were Team Jazmin.

We started a new chapter of our life—one that would challenge us and cause us to grow spiritually. It became one of the most dramatic chapters of our lives. Together we learned more about God than we ever thought possible, and our love for Jazmin grew and deepened.

If you remain in me and my words remain in you,
ask whatever you wish, and it will be done for you.

(John 15:7)

CHAPTER TWENTY-SIX

Jazmin and Alice

In Sudbury, we were near my parents, but my sister had moved to Windsor and most of our friends had moved away. This move meant we can be near Eythan's whole family as well as a church community we love. Eythan and I speak daily about the abundant blessings God has provided for us.

—JAZMIN HENSON

October 2019

ALICE'S BIRTH WAS TIMED perfectly in our family's journey. Jazzy loved our granddaughter, and her face lit up whenever Charity and Dan walked in the door with her. "Hello, sweetie!"

Alice scampered across the sectional cushions and onto Jazmin's lap, grabbing the oxygen tubing under her nose.

Jazmin kissed Alice's chubby cheeks and smiled.

On Jazmin's good days, she played with Alice and cuddled with her. We saw an abundance of smiles from Jazmin and heard cute cooing noises from Alice.

But on the days filled with pain, Jazmin couldn't stand any noise, and it was a struggle for her to interact with Alice or hear her chatter. Jazmin retreated to her bedroom to try to manage her pain in a quiet environment.

We tried to time the visits so the baby could see Jazmin on her better days. We were thankful God had blessed us with our granddaughter during a time of sadness.

Jazmin loved babies and was a huge defender of the unborn. Her desire to be a doula came from out of a heart for a baby's care from conception until birth and after. Jazmin sat at our table in a comfy chair and studied her textbooks and typed her assignments on her laptop.

She talked of her plans after God gave her a miracle, how she would assist women when they gave birth. Sometimes she pulled me into her dreams, and I pulled a pair of socks out of my hope-suitcase and got ready for the journey.

There were times when Jazmin didn't show any interest in Alice. We weren't sure why this dramatic change happened.

Months later, Jazmin told us she couldn't bear the thought of dying and missing out on seeing Alice grow up. She had determined to not get too attached so it wouldn't hurt so much when she died.

One day when she was praying, God encouraged Jazmin to love Alice and not protect her own heart from getting hurt. That pulled her out of the sadness that had enveloped her.

Jazmin shared this message of hope at church one Sunday morning. She was teary-eyed when she talked about not wanting to miss out on Alice's life. Our family sat in the back row crying.

Jazmin painted four adorable animal pictures for Alice's bedroom. Charity hung them in Alice's room and promised to tell Alice as she grew up about Auntie Jaz and how much she loved and cherished her.

Do you protect yourself from getting too close to people in case they leave you or you have to leave them? God wants us to give our love to others and trust Him to help us through the hard feelings of loss or abandonment. This is what Jazmin learned.

Dear God,

We are humans who get hurt easily. Help us to love like You love and be willing to risk feeling pain, to do what is best for others.

Amen.

CHAPTER TWENTY-SEVEN

Friends and Family Equal Happiness

He said to me, "My grace is sufficient for you, for my power is made perfect in weakness." Therefore I will boast all the more gladly about my weaknesses, so that Christ's power may rest on me. That is why, for Christ's sake, I delight in weaknesses, in insults, in hardships, in persecutions, in difficulties. For when I am weak, then I am strong.

(2 CORINTHIANS 12:9–10)

October 2019

ᴇᴀʀʟʏ ᴏɴ ᴀ Sᴀᴛᴜʀᴅᴀʏ morning, I came out of my office and saw Eythan asleep on the couch. His bedroom door was open, and Vance sat on the edge of Jazmin's bed. Jazmin's nurse, Dawn, was hooking up her IV.

I slipped into the bedroom.

Dawn packed up her supplies. "Hi, Cindy." Her bright smile was always warm and her long black hair and pretty face refreshing to see.

"Good morning." I stepped around Vance and close to the bed. Jazmin appeared pale and lifeless. "How are you feeling today, Jazmin?"

"Not good. I'm having a lot of pain." Her face looked distressed, and her eyes were heavy.

Vance continued to talk with Jazmin. She loved it when Vance sat and chatted with her. Their brains were very similar, and they had long conversations that left me confused. Vance was good at getting Jazmin to express how she was feeling.

I asked Dawn what we could do for Jazmin.

She picked up her bag of supplies and swung them over her shoulder. "She could alternate some of her pain meds so they overlap. And she can increase her morphine if the current dose isn't working."

We were not allowed to administer the drugs. If Jazmin was in horrendous pain, we were supposed to call Dawn to come give the injection. In the laundry room we had a large gold envelope labeled "Emergency Stash" that Jazmin's doctor had given to us. I was comforted knowing we had a backup plan.

Dawn looked at Jazmin. "Don't try to ride out the pain, because it may get worse, and then it's hard to get it back under control." She zipped her hoodie over her nurse's scrubs.

"I'm going to try to stay on top of it better." Jazmin grabbed her beanbag from under her back and asked Vance to heat it up.

I followed Dawn out to the porch and closed the door behind us. "Can I ask you a question? I want you to be honest with me."

She took in a deep breath, then exhaled. "Sure."

"How much longer does Jazmin have left?" I pulled my sweater tight around my torso and crossed my arms over my chest.

"At the rate she is increasing the morphine for pain, it won't be long now. Maybe a week or two." Her voice was quiet, and she looked at me with tenderness.

My heart sank as I swallowed the lump in my throat. Tears threatened to fall. Dawn kept a steady gaze on my face.

"Can we keep Jazmin here until she dies?" More swallowing and shifting as I worked to keep my composure.

"Yes," Dawn said softly.

"What if her pain meds don't work anymore?" Anxiety piled up as I thought of the possibilities.

"We will hook up a morphine pump, and you can administer the drugs when she needs them. The pump controls the pain better than pills." Her calm words brought a measure of peace.

"What if she needs a ventilator?" I needed to know all the options before we made final decisions.

"She doesn't want to be resuscitated, so she won't need a ventilator."

I couldn't believe I was having this conversation on my front porch. You would have thought we were standing in the halls of a hospital, not on a veranda in an eight-acre wood. I wished I were Tigger, bouncing away on my tail into the Hundred Acre Wood, where daughters didn't suffer or die and childhood dreams were filled with wonder and happiness.

My biggest fear was that we would watch Jazmin struggle to breathe and she would suffocate. How was I supposed to prepare myself to watch my daughter-in-law die? The thought

> You would have thought we were standing in the halls of a hospital, not on a veranda in an eight-acre wood. I wished I were Tigger, bouncing away on my tail into the Hundred Acre Wood, where daughters didn't suffer or die and childhood dreams were filled with wonder and happiness.

> My biggest fear was that we would watch Jazmin struggle to breathe and she would suffocate. How was I supposed to prepare myself to watch my daughter-in-law die?

terrified me. I had been with other people when they died, but they were elderly, not twenty-two years old and a beloved daughter-in-law.

Keeping Jazmin at home until the end was the plan, because that was what she wanted. Originally, I had wanted her to go into hospice so we wouldn't have to feel panicked if she was struggling and suffering.

But I doubted that I could stay calm if Jazmin was in distress. This was way too heavy for me.

God, please carry this for me.

Jazmin hated it when people panicked, and we were less likely to lose our composure if a nurse was by Jazmin's bedside around the clock.

So far, with God's help and nursing care, we were managing Jazmin's health care beautifully. I would have to take each day moment by moment. There was no sense in borrowing worry from tomorrow. I had to leave this in God's hands.

> I would have to take each day moment by moment. There was no sense in borrowing worry from tomorrow. I had to leave this in God's hands.

Dawn pressed the remote start on her key chain and looked at me. "I'm not sure how much time Jazmin has left. I'll ask Rita, our supervisor and palliative nurse practitioner, to come and do an assessment. You should let Jazmin's family know."

A small breath caught in my throat. "Sherie thinks Jazmin is getting a miracle. How do I tell her that her daughter is going to die soon?" I hoped Dawn could pull out the right words.

"Jazmin and Sherie have talked to me many times about getting a miracle. Their faith is inspiring. But you need to tell Sherie to come."

I thanked Dawn for her kind words, and she walked down the four steps of our porch. I swallowed hard. Gained my composure. And opened our front door.

Lord, give me strength, and help me not to cry.

I called Jazmin's parents with the news. Sherie was flabbergasted.

I told her Rita was coming the next day, and I would call her after I talked to Rita and confirmed that she and Dawn were on the same page.

The next day, with fog lingering close to the earth and frost covering the grass in our large front yard, Rita and I stepped onto the porch after she assessed Jazmin.

"Rita, how much time does Jazmin have left?" I looked into her eyes for any sign of hope.

Rita's shoulders rose and fell as she took in a deep breath. "I don't like to give anyone a timeline because everyone is different."

"If you could give us an estimate, that would help us decide whether to tell friends and family." I wrapped my sweater tight around me and glanced at the sunrise coming up behind Rita.

"Days, maybe a week—two weeks at the most." Rita's eyes never left mine. Her honesty was shocking, and it wasn't what I wanted to hear. But I needed to know the truth.

Rita and I had the same conversation I'd had with Dawn, and she encouraged me to tell Jazmin's parents to come.

I called Sherie again and told her what Rita had said. She, Aaron, and Vangie arrived the next day. We all hugged at the front door, and I saw concern in Sherie's and Aaron's eyes. We were growing to love these three people more and more with every visit.

Jazmin's friend Emily had been messaging me. She and Serena suspected that Jazmin was near the end whenever they talked with her on the phone. Emily asked if they could come for a visit.

"We would love to have you here," I texted Emily.

We didn't mention how much time Jazmin had left. The three girls had been best friends almost their whole lives. Emily and Serena had been amazing, supportive girlfriends from the day Jazmin told them she had cancer. I didn't want to worry them in case by some miracle Jazmin didn't die that week.

Jazmin told Sherie at the beginning of her cancer journey to never tell her how much time she had left. "God decides when I die, not a doctor or nurse." So we didn't say anything to Jazmin and kept all conversations about death private.

I embraced the girls when they arrived from different parts of Canada. Serena, a pretty brunette with a bright smile, was the quieter of the two. Emily was a tall adorable blonde with a big personality. They found Jazmin in her bedroom, and loud voices and nonstop chatter ensued.

When Jazmin's friends and family were around, her spirits rose. The happiness of having her favorite people near her touched her heart tremendously. We were heading into a week of uncertainty, and only God knew what was about to happen.

Have you received overwhelming news recently? Maybe you want to fight. Or run away. Fight or flight are the brain's psychological responses to trauma or fear.

Sometimes all we can do is pray and wait for God to take our hands in His and lead us where we need to go.

Scared, I called on God. *Please don't take our Jazzy. Give her more time.*

Peace I leave with you; my peace I give you.
I do not give to you as the world gives.
Do not let your hearts be troubled and do not be afraid.

(John 14:27)

CHAPTER TWENTY-EIGHT

Hope Rises

Be strong and take heart, all you who hope in the Lord.

(PSALM 31: 24)

OUR CHILDREN CAME FOR dinner most nights that week, making fourteen of us. The girls usually took their plates to Jazmin's room, and the rest of us ate around the table.

On the nights she felt better, Jazmin joined us at the dinner table. We had a camping chair with cushions piled high for her to sit on. She kept her plate on her lap and reclined as she ate. She often grabbed her bucket and threw everything up after. Despite the side effects from drugs, we had some wonderful evenings with Jazmin. Our thankfulness grew.

Vance and I took care of Jazmin from three thirty to eight thirty each evening while Eythan was at work. He reduced his hours so he could spend more time with his wife. Vance and I had many heartfelt, meaningful conversations with Jazmin in the evenings, and we got to know her in a deeper way. The more we cared for her, the more we fell in love with her.

Since her loved ones were staying in our home, we needed to share Jazmin with them. There was no room for selfishness or self-pity; everything was about giving Jazmin the best life we could for her final few weeks.

Eythan generously let friends and family take as much time as they needed with Jazmin. The two of them had no privacy with the nurses around and loved ones in and out of their bedroom at all hours of the day or night.

Having family and friends around to keep Jazmin company was a huge relief to Eythan. Her emotional state weighed heavy on him since he didn't know what to say to his wife to bring her comfort.

While the girls entertained Jazmin, Sherie took over her primary care along with Eythan. Jazmin was very particular about how her food tasted, and I'm not a gifted cook. But Sherie was incredible. I appreciated how Sherie doted on Jazmin and tried to meet her every need, including showering her. I was grateful I didn't need to bathe her—it seemed like I would be crossing a line most mothers-in-law don't step over.

Although that week was one of the hardest we'd ever had to face, a beautiful peace fell over our home. God's presence filled the house, and He seemed to be in every nook and cranny.

Emily, Serena, and Vangie piled onto Jazmin's bed every day, and they giggled and reminisced together. The peals of laughter I heard from the bedroom soothed my soul. Was the close fellowship of friends and family sustaining her, or was God? I couldn't be sure.

We also saw Serena and Emily cry. The girls instinctively knew Jazmin was slipping from them. The three would defend one another to the bitter end if anyone dared hurt their best friend. They had been in one another's weddings when all three were married within a one-year period.

While Eythan snoozed on the couch after Dawn left, Vance and I entered Jazmin's room.

"I want my people to pray for me today. Can we do that?" Jazmin's lips trembled as she lay in the recliner, hooked up to oxygen. Now half the weight she had been four years ago, she struggled to stay alive while her body failed her.

How could she live much longer?

We didn't know where to start. How could we bang on heaven's doors for someone who was thinly veiled between life and death?

Eythan, her parents, Vangie, Emily, Serena, Vance, and I surrounded Jazmin and prayed one by one, asking God if He would heal Jazmin's body.

But I couldn't pray that prayer. I knew in my heart that our Jazzy was leaving us. Instead I prayed that God would give her peace.

With sacred prayers, we were cocooned with the Holy Spirit as He wove His presence of peace through our hearts.

Jazmin looked up. "I'm tired. I don't want to live like this anymore. If God isn't going to heal me, I want to go to heaven."

I felt bittersweet emotions. We needed to hear that she was ready.

We sat around her chair for ten minutes, encouraging her. Emily and Serena sat cross-legged on the floor beside the recliner, endless tears streaming down their cheeks. Eythan was quiet and his face was drawn as he leaned forward with his elbows on his knees.

My heart filled with gratitude for these beautiful people.

Jazmin asked, "Are we ready to watch the movie?"

The six of us girls disappeared and came back in our pajamas. We plopped on the couches in the great room with popcorn and snacks and turned on the new *Lion King* movie.

The girls snuggled under blankets together.

I wept as I listened to the first song: "The Circle of Life." Jazmin's closest and dearest people were around her—and yet her circle of life was coming to an end.

I soaked in this heartfelt moment, imprinting it in my mind to cherish for a lifetime. My hope-suitcase had turned a corner, closed, and locked tight. It was the kindest thing I could do for Jazmin and myself—to accept that she was going to die in the next few days.

We planned a spa day for the following day, Saturday. Vance and I hired a woman who owned a local spa to come and pamper the girls. We preordered a big meal from a local restaurant. We prayed Jazmin would feel well enough to join us in the living room for her last girls' day.

Hope. Something that had been lacking in my life for many years. Hope that God would give Kyle and Jazmin miracles.

From day one, Jazmin had told us she was holding out for a miracle from God. But it seemed like a flitting butterfly she could never catch. Jazmin came close—then it disappeared again. She always looked for the butterfly, and when it appeared, her hopes rose that maybe today would be the day she'd capture it in her hands.

I wanted to grab my suitcase and smash that butterfly with it.

> **I wanted to grab my suitcase and smash that butterfly with it.**

I found watching Jazmin's hopes rise and fall hard to watch. I didn't want to go back to that place of hoping only to have my hopes smashed into a thousand pieces. I also didn't want Jazmin to fall into the deep pit of bitterness and anger I had fallen into years before if she didn't get her miracle.

I made it my mission to try to help Jazmin come to grips with her idea of getting a miracle. I wasn't straightforward with her; I just said subtle things to help her grasp that there was a possibility she might never get a miracle. I thought this was the kindest thing I could do for a dying girl whom I loved.

But Jazmin didn't waver in her faith in God or in His power to heal her.

Each time Jazmin neared death's door, she relentlessly said, "God could heal me." Three times Jazmin rose from the ashes. Her courage was unbelievable, and God's power was unmistakable.

Could it possibly happen again? She looked a bit better today. Or was that just a figment of my imagination?

I wanted to hope, I really did. But I was going to get hurt if the miracle butterfly flitted away again.

And if Jazmin never received a miracle . . .

I struggled to pull the tiniest bottle of perfume out of my hope-suitcase.

> And if Jazmin never received a miracle . . . I struggled to pull the tiniest bottle of perfume out of my hope-suitcase.

I went to bed that Friday night with a prayer on my lips.

Please, God,

Let Jazmin live through tomorrow. Give her this one last day with her family. You can take her to heaven on Sunday.

CHAPTER TWENTY-NINE

Heavenly Spa

You have made my days a mere handbreadth;
the span of my years is as nothing before you.
Everyone is but a breath, even those who seem secure.

(PSALM 39:5)

SATURDAY MORNING ARRIVED. SPA day. I woke up and saw Jazmin's oxygen outside her bedroom door, making a swooshing noise.

Jazmin was still with us!

When Eythan got up, I asked how Jazmin was doing.

"Good, I think," he said, grabbing a frying pan.

Thank You, God, for letting her live until today.

Jazmin spent the morning getting ready with her mom's help. Putting on clean pajamas exhausted her, let alone doing her hair and makeup.

Charity arrived early and helped me get the living room and kitchen ready. Three nail stylists arrived with arms full of nail kits, foot baths, towels, and other accessories. They set up the living room and kitchen into different spa areas. Two footbaths in the living room had everything needed for pedicures. The kitchen table was strewn with bottles of nail polish for manicures.

Our friend Christina, who was a couple of years older than Jazmin, had arranged the spa day and even brought face masks for us to try. She had explained to Roberta, the owner of the spa, that Jazmin was dying, and it was the last time she would do anything with her friends and family.

Jazmin came out of her bedroom, slowly pushing her walker, looking rail thin but adorable. She had put on a pair of black yoga pants and a white T-shirt with a brown cardigan over it. Her leopard-print hat covered her short, thin hair.

Sherie helped her lower into the recliner, and Jazmin pressed the remote to raise her feet.

We turned on soothing music, sipped on coffee and tea, and relaxed as the three women pampered us. Happiness filled our home.

In the middle of the spa day, a lovely surprise happened. Sherie's friend Kathy had texted me the day before, asking if she could come for the day and surprise Sherie.

I knew this was exactly what Sherie needed. She had been looking like she was trying to hold it together all week, but I guessed she was feeling like a glass doll ready to shatter. So was I.

"Yes, please come!" I had texted back.

Kathy made the four-hour drive to our home. When she came in and Sherie saw her beautiful friend, her face lit up. She grabbed Kathy in a hug as tears streamed down her face.

We spent four hours visiting, laughing, eating, and being pampered. The day was wonderful, and Jazmin was able to lie in her recliner and have her feet massaged and her toenails painted.

We had prayed Jazmin would make it through this day. I thought for sure this was going to be her last.

But in case she was still around the next day, I asked everyone if they wanted to have Sunday morning church in our living room. The vote was unanimous.

Before going to bed, I hugged Jazmin, holding back tears. As I walked out of the room, I wondered if that was our last goodbye.

Dear God,

Thank You for the beautiful day You gave Jazmin.
If You are going to take her tonight,
please don't let her suffer.
Let her slip away
in her sleep.

Amen.

CHAPTER THIRTY

Flabbergasted Hope

Lately I've been thinking about time. Not in a super-deep, philosophical way or anything, just that time goes by so differently for everyone.

—JAZMIN HENSON

Sunday

*J*AZMIN WOKE UP THE next day.

After breakfast we brought the dining room chairs into the living room. Some of us grabbed mugs of coffee, and others plunked on the couches or found a chair. Jazmin sat in her recliner. Charity and Dan arrived with Alice, and they led us in worship music as Dan played the guitar.

Peace fell on the room in waves.

Vance gave us a beautiful message on God being able to meet each person's needs.

Then we had communion. The presence of the Lord filled the house. There were fourteen of us in the living room, and we all felt honored to be a part of this sacred moment.

We prayed for Jazmin.

And we waited on the Lord.

And she had another fairly good day.

We held our breath.

Monday morning Jazmin woke up looking better than the day before. She had improved every day for four days. She ate, she laughed, she colored in her adult coloring book, and she stayed in her recliner for hours without asking to be moved to her bed.

Dawn came to change her IV. Afterward, I stepped out onto the porch with her. "Jazmin seems to be getting better, not worse. Do you know what's happening?"

She glanced out over the lawn. "I'm not sure if this is a final rally of Jazmin's body before she passes on or if Jazmin had a strange virus and it's finally gone." So I wasn't the only one confused by this change of events.

Oh, God, please, yes, let it be a virus!

Dawn collected her thoughts. "Let's watch her for the next few days and see what happens. I'll be back tomorrow. But call me if Jazmin's health changes."

"Thank you. We'll keep a close eye on her."

Jazmin stayed awake most of the day. We hadn't seen that in months.

On Monday I told Sherie what Dawn had told me, and we just stared at each other.

Thoughts swirled between us. Did we dare say the impossible— that God had given Jazmin more time?

"Well," Sherie said as she leaned on the kitchen island. "God can still do a miracle."

I nodded. I wasn't about to pop her miracle-bubble now.

For the first time in a long time, the smallest bit of hope escaped my suitcase and wrapped around my heart like a warm sweater. Did

God still perform miracles? Would I dare venture to step my toe over the line and cross over to the side that Jazmin and Sherie had been standing on for five and a half years?

I would wait a few more days and see what transpired.

On Tuesday morning, Jazmin didn't feel well. The afternoon was better, and in the evening the girls watched a movie with her.

Still alive.

Still here.

She had made it through another day.

On Wednesday morning, Eythan came into the kitchen around seven thirty. He looked tired, and his eyes were puffy. He'd probably cried in the shower, like I did every morning. With a house full of people, there was nowhere else to get alone with our emotions.

"How's Jazmin today?" I stood beside him at the counter while he opened a loaf of gluten-free bread, took out two slices, and popped them into the toaster.

"I think she's good." Eythan grabbed a frying pan and turned on the burner.

My brain tried to do a waltz and a polka at the same time. This was so befuddling. What on earth was happening?

At eight o'clock, Kyle's staff and Jazmin's nurses let themselves in. At that point, I never knew who was coming or going throughout the day. I'm sure a burglar could have sneaked in and no one in our group of fourteen would ask who they were.

When I saw Dawn walk past the kitchen and head for Jazmin's bedroom, I followed her.

"How did the night go?" Dawn asked Jazmin.

"Good. I slept straight through from one till seven a.m. I didn't even wake up to take my pain meds."

What? I looked between Jazmin's tiny frame lying in the bed and Dawn, with her beautiful white smile.

"I'm glad you had a good night's sleep. What's your pain level at right now?" Dawn collected supplies to get Jazmin's IV going.

"It's between one and two."

"That's great!" Dawn put her bag on the floor.

I stepped closer to the bed. "That's amazing, Jazmin. You haven't been below three in months!"

Jazmin looked proud of herself, and a sweet smile lifted her cheeks.

My brain felt upside down and confused. I didn't know if I should sit on top of that hope-suitcase or open it and let hope loose, wild and free.

As Dawn hooked up her IV for hydration, I told them I was going to slip out for a bit. I liked to leave Jazmin alone with her nurse for a few minutes, in case she wanted to confide in her with no one present.

When Dawn came out of Jazmin's room, we stepped out onto the porch. "What do you think, Dawn? Is Jazmin over the worst?"

"I'm not sure what's happening, but I think she's turned a corner—for now. Her family and friends can leave if they want."

"This isn't her body rallying at the end?" I held my breath.

"If she'd had two good days, I'd say yes. But this is six fairly good days, and she keeps improving. It's more than a rally."

My breath released, and a shiver went down my neck and through my spine. I wanted to grab Dawn's hands and jump up and down like a contestant on a game show who's just won the big prize.

> I breathed in the most wonderful lungful of cool morning air and looked across the yard as golden rays turned frosty grass into icy diamonds. The world looked beautiful!

"Thank you, Dawn!"

I breathed in the most wonderful lungful of cool morning air and looked across the yard as golden rays turned frosty grass into icy diamonds. The world looked beautiful!

Excitement and relief filled my being, and hope streamed into my heart. My feet danced to the front door, and I opened it with hope on my wings as I became an angel of good news.

I found Vangie and told her Jazmin had turned the corner.

She let out a big breath. "That's a huge relief!"

Emily came down the stairs and joined us. I shared the message of hope with her. She smiled, and tears pooled in her eyes.

Vangie ran upstairs to tell Serena, and I went into the kitchen to tell Eythan.

"Good!" he said, processing the information as he continued making breakfast for Jazmin. Eythan had to keep a solid countenance in these life-or-death moments so he wouldn't become unglued.

He rarely expressed emotions. They were there, very close to the surface, but he kept them hidden.

As a child he'd always shared his feelings with great exuberance and drama. Temper tantrums on the floor happened every day. For which I had very little tolerance, since we were also dealing with Kyle's constant extremes.

Teaching Eythan to control his emotions might not have been easy when he was small, but it had been a gift to his wife when everyone else around her felt unglued.

I went into Jazmin's room. She still didn't know that Rita had told us jus one week earlier that she had been close to death.

"Dawn says you're over the worst of it, and it looks like you've turned the corner!" My exuberance filled the room.

"I was thinking I had made it through this bad spell." Her face looked peaceful, and she spoke as though she had just taken a walk in a park. No big deal. Just another blip on the cancer radar.

Jazmin, seventy pounds of bones, full of fight and determination —hoping she was still going to get a miracle.

I told Vance the good news when he came upstairs. He smiled calmly. Vance is a lot like Eythan in crisis situations. But I could tell he felt the joy of hearing Jazmin had turned the corner. Death had not won this time.

An energy filled our house as laughter and a release of tension spread a huge sigh throughout every room. We could relax, breathe, and let down our guard.

I ran next door to my mother-in-law's house, where Sherie and Aaron slept each night. The sun had peeked up above the treetops, and its orange glow seemed to be smiling down on me. I traveled the beaten path between our houses and through the old fence gate, its hinges barely hanging on. I climbed the five steps to the front door, gave a light knock, and stepped inside. My rosy cheeks warmed immediately as the warm air welcomed me.

Mom stood at the counter in her blue velvet zip-up housecoat, cooking breakfast. "Oh, hi, Cindy. You're up early."

"Hi, Mom. I wanted to share some good news with Sherie and Aaron. Are they awake?" I took off my boots and stood at the island.

"I think they're still sleeping." Mom flipped the eggs she was cooking. The aroma made my stomach growl.

"I don't want to wake them." I proceeded to share Jazmin's news. Mom listened teary-eyed.

"You should text Sherie and wake her up." Mom grabbed a plate and flipped the eggs onto it.

"I might scare her with a text, and she may think the worst." I looked toward the stairs going up to the second story.

"Tell her it's good news!"

I texted Sherie, and within a minute, she rushed down the stairs. She had sleep lines on her face, and her curly hair had loosened itself out of its ponytail.

"Jazmin has turned the corner!" My words tumbled out quickly. "Dawn said she won't be dying this week—she has more time."

Sherie rubbed her face and eyes. "Well, I've been praying for a miracle from day one. Some of my friends and family think I'm crazy; I can see it in their eyes. But Jazzy and I have always believed she would get a miracle!"

Aaron entered the kitchen. We shared the news with him. He didn't know what to think as he paced the small room, running his hands through his hair.

I sat at the counter. "We need to keep praying for Jazmin every day. Whoever is around should lay hands on her and pray."

Our faith was bolstered like an army as we marched onward into the spiritual battle ground of cancer. We hoped that with God's help, we could fight off the demons of fear, anxiety, and death.

> Our faith was bolstered like an army as we marched onward into the spiritual battle ground of cancer.

Team Jazmin would go forward, praying with intensity and expectancy. Every moment she was awake, one of her prayer warriors would spend time encouraging her, praying for her, or being with her.

When I ran back home, Jazmin was in her recliner with food on her end table and a coloring book in hand. The three girls, still in their pajamas, giggled on the couch.

Our home was filled with joy.

Tonight we would celebrate!

Gayle's parents, Charlene and Jason Katzenback, were supposed to be coming for one final goodbye to Jazmin before going back to their home in Texas.

I messaged them the good news. Charlene was so excited!

Jazmin got all dolled up for the evening. Before Jason and Charlene arrived, Jazmin, Eythan, and the girls took pictures on our front porch. We joined them, wrapping Jazmin's bony body in our arms, and posed for our celebratory photos.

Sherie, Aaron, Vangie, Jazmin, and Eythan snuggled together for a family photo. My heart wrapped in the biggest hug as thankfulness flooded my soul.

The evening was amazing as we enjoyed friends and family around our table and living room.

Jazmin was tuckered out from her incredible day and went to bed early.

I was still teetering . . . still waiting to see what exactly was happening to Jazmin's body.

Hope was there, but it was in the background. I didn't dare say Jazmin had received a miracle. This might just be a momentary gift from God. A few more months with our daughter. But for now we had a reprieve from despair. Watching Jazmin live in her fountain of hope, I soaked up every drop of happiness I could squeeze.

Jazmin wasn't surprised when God pulled her out of the clutches of death. That was how much she trusted and believed He could do the impossible. Her faith was incredible. Had she finally captured the butterfly?

The butterfly showed up at the most unexpected times. And every time, it took my breath away. I prayed again and again that no matter what, God would prepare Jazzy for the future.

> He replied, "Because you have so little faith. Truly I tell you, if you have faith as small as a mustard seed, you can say to this mountain, 'Move from here to there,' and it will move. Nothing will be impossible for you."
>
> *(Matthew 17:20)*

CHAPTER THIRTY-ONE

The Sisterhood

I'm the most nostalgic person out there. Reminiscing with my
two best friends, Serena and Emily, is my favorite thing to do.
We three have been best friends since, well, forever.
Emily is my cousin, and Serena has been in my life
since I was three. I love them both so much.

—JAZMIN HENSON

November 6, 2019

EMILY DECIDED TO STAY longer. She knew if everyone left at once, it would be hard on Jazmin. She had taken time off work as a nanny, and her husband, Mattias, had told Emily to stay as long as she needed. He was a gem.

Jazmin and I chatted while Emily cooked dinner. I stood beside Emily at the counter, and Jazzy sat in the corner of the sectional.

I looked at Jazmin. "That was a close one this time. It's amazing you made such a big turnaround."

Jazmin played with the sleeves of her beige hoodie. "The Sunday before my family came, I thought I was going to die that day. And I didn't want to be left alone in case I passed away."

I was shocked. "Why didn't you tell us?"

She shrugged, letting me know she didn't want to discuss it further, and fiddled with a thread hanging from the hole in the seam of the couch.

But I knew the answer. She didn't want to burden anyone.

"Jazmin, if you ever feel like that again, please tell us. We don't want you to be alone if you're dying." Emotions passed over me in that moment. I saw her as a little girl in need of a mother lifting her onto her lap and wrapping her in a warm hug. But God had carried her through until her family and friends had arrived to pray for her.

Jazmin's resilience was incredible.

Later that day, Emily and I drove downtown so she could run some errands.

I asked her, "If Jazmin thought she was going to die the one Sunday, why wouldn't she tell us?"

Emily's long blond hair reflected the sunlight. "She's been this way from the time she was little, long before she had cancer. She never wanted to be a burden to anyone."

My heart sank to hear Emily say this. I understood why God paired Eythan and Jazmin together. Jazmin loved Eythan's quiet strength. It helped calm her and made her feel like the world wasn't falling apart.

Back at home, Emily stood at the counter, chopping sweet potatoes. Jazmin sat in the corner of the sectional in the living room. She leaned her elbow up on the back of the couch and watched Emily prepare supper. "I've been so nauseous lately. But I love your sweet potatoes. I hope I can keep them down tonight."

"Hey, Jazmin, maybe you're pregnant!" Emily blurted out.

Pretending to look mortified and joining in on Emily's fun, Jazmin straightened her spine and raised her neck about three inches. "Don't say that. We can't afford a child, and I'm dying."

"That was my attempt at being funny. Soooooo not funny!" Emily nervously chopped the sweet potato faster.

I burst out into deep belly laughs.

Jazmin grinned.

"Okay, I'm going to stop trying to be funny," Emily said.

Emily definitely knew how to lighten the mood when it got serious. And Jazmin needed laughter. Her life was dull and boring. Other than walking our driveway on two of her best days, she had been cooped up in the house for months.

Jazmin loved socializing with people her age. Without Emily staying for the extra weeks, I believe Jazmin would have declined quicker. She had been a gift to Jazmin in her time of need. She was bubbly and happy and could lift a discouraged spirit off the floor with her joyful energy. Once again God had brought Jazmin exactly what she needed. It touched my heart deeply, and I saw the value of having godly girlfriends who would move heaven and earth for a dying girl.

Dear God,

When we are down and feeling discouraged,
send us a friend who will stick closer than a sister
and help lift our spirits.

Amen.

CHAPTER THIRTY-TWO

Retail Therapy

It's funny how life changes and crazy how fast we grow up!
I keep seeing this meme that says, "At some point in your
childhood, you and your friends went outside to play for
the last time, and none of you knew it." Thinking about
this makes me sad. My friends and I used to play outside
all the time. Even in our midteens, we ran around playing
Mantracker and had campfires and built snow forts.

—JAZMIN HENSON

AZMIN HAD TWO REALLY bad days in a row. Her lungs hurt, and her breathing was more difficult. Her nurse told us this might be the end.

There seemed to be a battle going on for her mind. I wasn't sure what was worse, watching her struggle with physical pain or witnessing her mental sadness.

On Thursday night, Vance, Emily, and I gathered around Jazmin's bed. We prayed that God would give her a big leap in her health so she would know she was getting better.

Jazmin didn't get out of bed on Friday. Sherie and Aaron arrived around suppertime. We were happy to see them again.

Sherie hugged me. "It feels like we're coming home after a week at work." Her words gave my heart a warm squeeze. We loved that they enjoyed being here. But I heard weariness in her voice.

"We feel the same way. You two are like family." Vance hugged Sherie, then he gave Aaron a man-hug, complete with that weird pounding-each-other-on-the-back thing men do.

After we chatted for a minute or two, they made their way into the bedroom to check on Jazmin. They looked forlorn when they came out. Everyone went to bed heavyhearted.

On Saturday, I woke up first. Jazmin's oxygen tank was still swooshing loudly outside her bedroom door. Relief spread through me.

A few hours later, Vance joined me for coffee in my office, away from the main part of the house. We agreed Jazmin needed a shopping trip. But how was that possible? We discussed giving her an online shopping spree. She and Emily could use Jazmin's laptop to shop from Jazmin's bed.

We hoped this would help lift her spirits, at least for the day. Then we might have her with us a bit longer.

While we sat around the table eating breakfast, Jazmin said, "I want to go to the mall today. Is it possible to do that?"

Did she have supersonic hearing and heard us praying on the other side of the house?

"Yes, we can do that. Are you feeling well enough?" Sherie asked.

"I feel really good today. I woke up with hardly any pain, and I'm breathing better."

Vance and I smiled, our souls warmed by the possibility that Jazmin had turned the corner again.

Sherie helped Jazmin get ready, then she, Emily, and Eythan took Jazmin to the mall.

While they were out, Emily got a text from Serena. "Today I've been praying Jazmin will feel well enough to get out of the house and do something."

Serena had no clue what had transpired that morning. But God had heard her prayer.

Jazmin had an incredible day. She used a wheelchair to get around the mall. She came home happy and energetic and did a modeling show for me with everything she bought. A new toque, winter coat, and boots.

I sat in the recliner, grinning at Jazmin as she ran her hands down the front of her coat, admiring the sleek black fabric. Her dancing eyes told me she had thoroughly enjoyed her shopping trip.

"That coat looks beautiful on you!"

Jazmin struck a model pose, lifted her chin, and fluttered her eyelashes.

I laughed.

I was amazed at her turnaround! Jazmin went from being in bed the past two days to this energetic, happy girl. What was happening?

That evening our kids came for dinner. Aaron brought the outdoor deep fryer he used for camping and cooked supper in the snowbank in our front yard. He came in with batches of food, his loud voice declaring he had another gift for us as he walked into the kitchen, stomping with his heavy winter boots.

We played board games and ate homemade french fries and battered fish. It was an evening of perfection. Supper was delicious, there was lots of laughter, and a spirit of peace and joy lingered.

After the kids went home, we sat around the table in the evening.

Jazmin grew serious. "What if this is my day of rallying before I die?"

She always caught me off guard with these blunt thoughts.

After a wonderful day of feeling normal, she didn't want to leave the people she loved.

Team Jazmin took turns going to battle for her once again. Our little group surrounded her and laid our hands on her body. We prayed that God would protect Jazmin from the devil's attacks and that God would give her peace as she slept.

And again we asked God to heal her of cancer.

I went to bed with a prayer on my lips that this wouldn't be a day of rallying but instead a miraculous turnaround and answer to our prayer from Thursday night. I prayed for God to give Jazmin a huge leap in her health, as a sign that she was getting better.

My prayers were changing as I began to ask God more and more to heal Jazmin. I kept my suitcase of hope nearby and glanced inside it each day to see if there was something I could grab on to.

Without my sweet Jesus, I don't think I could have gone this far in Jazmin's journey with cancer.

My love for Jazmin grew daily, and it was getting harder to let go of her.

My relationship with God was also changing. I clung to Him each morning as I cried my heart out and pleaded on Jazmin's behalf. God met me daily, held me close to His heart, and let me unload all my sadness and grief.

Without my sweet Jesus, I don't think I could have gone this far in Jazmin's journey with cancer.

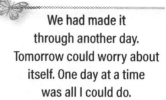

We had made it through another day. Tomorrow could worry about itself. One day at a time was all I could do.

We had made it through another day. Tomorrow could worry about itself. One day at a time was all I could do.

He said to me, "My grace is sufficient for you, for my power is made perfect in weakness." Therefore I will boast all the more gladly about my weaknesses, so that Christ's power may rest on me.

(2 Corinthians 12:9)

CHAPTER THIRTY-THREE

Alive and Fairly Well

*I know God has a plan, and I'm happy I get to leave my life
in His capable hands. For now I am enjoying life.
I live life day by day. Each day may be amazing or terrible,
but my husband and I are enjoying every second
we have together, now, just in case.*

—JAZMIN HENSON

ARLY SUNDAY MORNING, VANCE and I had coffee together in the living room and prayed God would give Jazmin a wonderful day. The night before, she had expressed a strong desire to go to church. She hadn't been to church in quite some time. But today was Alice's baby dedication service.

Swoosh, swoosh, swoosh. I heard the noise as I climbed the basement stairs. *Thank You, God.*

A few hours later, Jazmin came shuffling into the living room.

"How are you feeling this morning?" Vance asked.

"Pretty good." She lowered herself to the cream-colored recliner.

"That's amazing!" I said, sitting on a couch perpendicular to the recliner.

"I want to eat breakfast and get ready to go to church." Jazmin crossed her ankles. She had on a pair of beaded moccasin slippers Charlene had bought her the Christmas before. She loved those slippers. "When my mom is ready, she's going to come over and get me dressed and do my hair."

Excitement filled me. "That's wonderful, Jazmin!"

Vance and I left to pick up my mom. Eythan would bring Jazmin to church. Sherie and Aaron were coming in another vehicle.

We were chatting with friends before the service when Jazmin walked into the sanctuary. She was rail thin, wearing baggy jogging pants and a green sweater. Eythan followed with her oxygen tank. Jazmin sat in a chair we had brought for her so she wouldn't have to sit on the hard plastic church chairs.

The congregation whispered to one another, and excitement filled the air. We had been giving our church family updates, and they were all ecstatic to see Jazmin.

This was truly a miracle.

Jazmin having gone from death's door to sitting in church worshipping could only be explained as a transformation from God.

Jazmin had a good day. She still thought two good days might be a rally. So we prayed before bed that she would have a third good day. We knew heaven still wasn't ready for her.

On Monday, Jazmin was still alive—and very well!

We sat around the living room, chatting in our pajamas and having coffee.

Vance and I were getting used to being home a lot. We rarely went anywhere unless we absolutely had to. We wanted to spend every moment with Jazmin and didn't want to miss out on her good days. Coffee in the morning with Jazmin feeling good was better than any outing.

But I felt like I'd been neglecting my family and friends as we made life about living every moment with Jazmin.

She hung out in the living room and kitchen most of the day. We noticed improvements. Her voice was stronger. She was gaining some weight. Her coloring looked better every day.

Jazmin felt the large tumor in her abdomen and told us she thought it was smaller.

My heart was hopeful. Would we witness another miracle?

Maybe I would hold the redheaded grandbabies I had dreamed of having from Jazmin and Eythan. Oh, how I wanted a little grandbaby running toward me and wrapping its chubby little arms around my neck.

I saw the butterfly flitting close to Jazmin—oh so close.

Lord,

Remind us of how powerful prayer can be. Oftentimes we forget that You hold the power to heal, to restore, and to make new. Build our faith in Your ability to answer our prayers.

Amen.

CHAPTER THIRTY-FOUR

Christmas Decorating

When I was a kid, winter was my favorite season.
I loved everything the winter months had to offer.
Going to camp in the winter with my family
was so much fun!

—JAZMIN HENSON

November 27, 2019

As VANCE AND I prayed with Jazmin in the morning, she joined in with her own prayer. She asked God to give her a good Christmas. She told Him she wanted to participate in all the events surrounding the holiday and not be in bed the whole time.

My heart went out to her. Her prayers weren't asking for much. Just the simple things in life we all take for granted.

The next day, Jazmin and I stayed in our pajamas and planned an indoor winter day. Vance had started a fire in the fireplace before he headed for work, and it gave a good crackle and a warm orange glow to our rustic living room.

Jazmin picked some Christmas music for us to listen to.

I went to the basement and hauled out boxes of decorations. Jazmin absolutely loved Christmas and decorating. The two together were her dream team of happiness.

I emptied the boxes so she could see the thirty-year stash I had collected. I held up tinsel, garland, ornaments, wreaths, miniature lights, and an assortment of knickknacks.

While Jazmin looked over the possibilities, I grabbed a mug of tea for her and coffee for me. I plunked onto the sectional and sipped my drink. "Do you see anything you like?"

She held her mug with two hands, letting it warm her palms. I heard a little snicker. "Well, this is kind of a mismatch of stuff. Do you have any Christmas throws or pillows to decorate the great room with?"

"What do you mean?" I asked, not sure what she was looking for.

"You need forest-green and red or plaid pillows and a blanket in Christmas colors."

I looked at the floral pillows on my couch and realized they clashed with the collection on the floor.

"I'll tell you what. When Vance gets home, I'll run to Winners and get some things." If this was her last Christmas, I wanted it to be special. I also hoped this new improvement meant we'd have many more with her.

Jazmin put her mug on the end table and pushed the remote on her chair to put her feet up.

I grabbed the garland, which was wrapped in mini twinkle lights, and attached it to the timber mantel above the fireplace. Jazmin directed me on how to center the loops. She was pretty particular about where home décor was placed.

I was happy to have this special moment with Jazmin as her face was filled with contentment and peace.

Being intentional with my daughter-in-law was important to me. I wanted to make sure Jazmin always felt loved and accepted. Today I wanted her to know I cared about what made her happy.

In the afternoon, I went shopping and bought a red knitted blanket, green plaid decorative pillows, and some red-and-black checkered ones. I came home and put it on the couch.

When she saw the new Christmas décor, she said with a big smile, "Oh, it looks so Christmassy now!" Jazmin let out a sweet-sounding sigh as she closed her eyes and slipped into childhood happiness and memories of the wintertime she cherished.

> Jazmin let out a sweet-sounding sigh as she closed her eyes and slipped into childhood happiness and memories of the wintertime she cherished.

Jazmin loved reminiscing about her childhood winters with Vangie. "We loved sliding! We had a few GTs, some crazy carpets, and two 'good' sleds that we hauled around with us as we went off looking for a hill to slide down. Once we got older, all the hills we used to frequent seemed lame, so we tied the GT or flat sled to one of the snowmobiles and took turns pulling each other behind it on the ice. It was so fun! We competed to see who could send the other flying off the sled the most times. We whipped each other around so much!"

I hung onto Jazmin's every word.

"One day, Vangie was driving the snowmobile and managed to send me flying off the sled every fifteen seconds! I was so frustrated, but of course Vangie thought it was absolutely hilarious to watch me roll on the frozen lake like a rag doll. It made for some good laughs!"

Moments like these were rare and precious. I thanked God for this one. I knew I would cherish it for the rest of my life.

Little answers to prayers reminded me that prayer can move mountains.

In the morning, LORD, you hear my voice;
in the morning I lay my requests before you
and wait expectantly.

(Psalm 5:3)

CHAPTER THIRTY-FIVE

Donkey Clouds
and Dark Waters

*My life is not that bad at all. I have a great life, actually.
I have family who love me unconditionally. They don't love
me because of my life's successes. I have friends who support
me and care about me. I have a husband who continually
displays his true love for me. And most importantly, I have a
Father in heaven who loves me more than I can comprehend.*

—JAZMIN HENSON

*God sees all of my hurt and pain and frustration, and He tells
me to trust Him. Trust that His plan is perfect and that
He will use me and my experiences to glorify His name.
Wow! I feel completely useless to everyone on this earth,
but God doesn't think I'm useless. He loves me so much,
and He knows I have purpose.*

—JAZMIN HENSON

December 2019

Jazmin went through a few days of stomach pain and nausea. Her weight dropped again. I didn't think she had any more weight on her.

Fears of her dying resurfaced. Vance and I talked about it in the mornings when we sat in my office having coffee. Tears came easily to both of us.

I sank into a donkey cloud of discouragement. Between Kyle not sleeping at night and Jazmin being so sick, I was exhausted, and depression began to overwhelm me as I fell into premourning. My brain was filled with fog. My energy was depleted. I was just putting one foot in front of the other, dragging my suitcase along.

One day, I backed into the plumber's shiny new black van in our driveway, causing three thousand dollars in damage. Another day I blew through a stop sign.

Watching someone die ever so slowly and struggle every day to stay away from death's door is one of the hardest things I have ever experienced.

I felt old. There was rarely a moment of being lighthearted. I wanted Funny Jazmin to spend time with us, yet she seemed to be lost in pain with her head in a bucket. She used to be able to control her pain with medical marijuana. Heavy narcotics altered her personality.

Marijuana had made her hilarious. A year before, when Jazmin first started taking medical marijuana for pain, she was a hoot! One morning she woke Eythan up when he was in the middle of a deep sleep. "Eythan! Eythan!" He rolled over, and Jazmin was sitting on her heels on the bed, looking at him. "Your dad is my best friend!"

"Oh, really? Why?" He knew she was high but thought he would find out what Silly Jazmin was up to.

She raised her arms above her head. "He's so big, and I'm so little!" She sighed and put her hands on her knees, her face in a dreamy state.

Eythan laughed as Jazmin sat on the bed thinking of her big best friend.

Sometimes she hallucinated, and Eythan had to calm her down. Other times she made up hilarious inventions in her head that made sense to her but sounded so outrageous to Eythan he chuckled.

"I'm going to write them down because no one would ever believe I came up with these genius ideas!" Jazmin ran out of the room to find her journal so she wouldn't miss out on the millions of dollars she was going to make. When she came off her high and read about her inventions, she laughed and laughed.

When Vance and I felt sad about the way she was now, we shared stories with each other of Happy Jazmin or Silly Jazmin. We had to hang on to the girl we once knew and continue to remember her on the days when Drugged-and-Cranky Jazmin showed up.

Leaving the house for quick trips to the grocery store helped clear my sad thoughts. I used to dread going to the store, but now I looked forward to it.

As I parked my car, I'd say a prayer. "Please, God, don't let me see anyone I know." If someone asked me how Jazmin was doing, I would dissolve into a puddle of tears on the floor.

I was in the grocery store one day when Jazmin texted me. "Mom, can you pick me up adult diapers?"

I started crying right there in aisle three. *Cindy, pull yourself together.*

I wiped tears with my sleeve as I looked through the sizes. Jazmin was too tiny for the smallest size and could have easily worn toddler pullups. She had about sixty pounds on her five-foot-seven-inch frame.

With wet eyes, streaked black mascara, and a snotty nose, I was a hot mess! I had no tissue. I pulled my shirt over my nose and blew, then zipped up my jacket to hide the mess. If you own a grocery store, can you please stock aisle three with tissue?

I went home with the pullups. My donkey cloud seemed to follow me everywhere. I couldn't shake it off. I talked to God daily and cried out to Him on behalf of our sweet Jazzy. It wasn't her fault that drugs were altering her personality and causing the Jazzy we knew to slip through our fingers.

My hope was completely gone, and I couldn't seem to muster it no matter how hard I tried. I put my suitcase in the basement, the farthest corner of our house. I wasn't angry with God, but I bounced between begging Him to take Jazzy and pleading with Him to take her cancer away.

I have no clue why I asked for a miracle when I didn't believe she was going to get one. Maybe it was denial. Maybe it was a survival response.

Vance and I sat at the table having dinner with Jazmin one night while Eythan was at work.

"I wish I could help out more," Jazmin stated.

Help out more?

We felt honored to be caregivers to this precious soul, as if we were on sacred ground, doing the smallest things for her.

I looked at Jazmin, and her face was forlorn. "If you're trying each day just to get through *that* day, you're doing enough."

"Sometimes I feel useless." She looked down at her dinner plate.

Oh, how the devil is relentless in making people feel like they aren't doing enough.

We tried to make Jazmin feel useful by asking her opinion on everything. What we cooked for dinner. What color our new couch should be. How we could arrange the furniture.

I missed the lighthearted, easygoing girl who loved to laugh. But we had grown to love the new Jazmin deeply. Hardly ever did she smile, since she was in constant discomfort. And the days that she did made us feel like we were walking on a cloud. Those days gave us hope that underneath the drugs and the cancer, our dear Jazzy was still there.

Hope is a funny thing. For some people, circumstances can cause hope to fade. But Jazmin had a hope that was more powerful than the circumstances that crushed her frail body.

Some weeks she grew extremely weary of the fight. She dreamed of God taking her from the deep, dark water that cancer was threatening to drown her in and up into heaven. But beneath the surface a small bubble of hope still bobbed.

We believed the prayers of Christians around the world kept Jazmin above the thin ice she was walking on. When it seemed like the ice was cracking all around her and she was going to fall into the freezing waters of death, someone told us they were praying. She walked on solid ice once again.

There were days when the darkness threatened to overwhelm me. I closed my eyes and dreamed I was standing by the railing of a cruise ship overlooking the ocean. The warm breeze blew my hair as I inhaled the salty ocean air, listening to the waves slap against the boat.

And I prayed. "God, help me get through this. I feel like I'm drowning in sadness."

Vance and I loved vacationing on cruise ships. We often escaped to Deck Four, a long wooden deck lined with lounge chairs. I sat and read a book, listened to the waves splash against the boat, and enjoyed the warm air across my skin.

But for now we were far from this dreamy state.

We tried not to talk to anyone about our emotions. We didn't want our sad feelings to get back to Jazmin. Our marriage strengthened as we leaned into each other for support. We knew this wasn't about us. This was about serving God with a willing heart and doing what was best for Jazmin.

> We knew this wasn't about us. This was about serving God with a willing heart and doing what was best for Jazmin.

If Jazmin knew we were overwhelmed, she would feel like a burden. We didn't want that. This was just the reality of someone dying from cancer. We knew God was going to carry us through the unknown and the impossible until Jazmin was healed or in heaven.

Jazmin had a few stable weeks. Her pain was being managed fairly well with the drugs. We began to prepare for Christmas, and I wondered if she'd make it through Christmas Day. That was her prayer—to have a wonderful Christmas. I wanted God to grant her this wish.

I also wanted Him to help us encourage Jazmin more and to make her feel useful so she wouldn't feel like a burden. What could we do? What weren't we doing? Was there something we hadn't thought of? Questions swirled in our heads as we tried to make Jazmin's life more meaningful.

Dear God,

Help us to make the ones we love feel cherished
and wanted. If there's something we can do
to show our love better, show us the way.

Amen.

CHAPTER THIRTY-SIX

Praying for a Christmas Miracle

*I trust that God has a plan for me and that He will heal me.
God's timing is perfect. He has allowed me to suffer (a little)
for His plan and His kingdom, and I'm happy to do so.
But I'm only human, and I do get discouraged and weary and
doubtful. I try my hardest to put on a happy face all the time,
but it is really hard sometimes, and that's okay.*

—JAZMIN HENSON

*I know my body can't go on like this for much longer.
The cancer is growing and taking over my lungs. I know that
soon I will be in heaven with my Lord or cancer free and
sharing with everyone I know the story of how God gave me
a miracle and healed me. I want to be here. I want to have
kids and a career and get to celebrate my fiftieth wedding
anniversary with Eythan. But if it's not His plan, then I'm
happy to know I didn't let cancer define who I am.
My identity is found in Jesus, and I want to go to Him
and know that I never lost my identity.*

—JAZMIN HENSON

December 17, 2019

*I*N THE EARLY-MORNING HOURS, Vance and I discussed Jazmin's declining health over coffee.

"She needs a Christmas miracle." Tears streamed down my face.

Sadness filled my husband's eyes as he wiped his own tears with tissue.

We both agreed that a miracle was all we had left. If Jazmin didn't get one soon, she would be gone.

That afternoon, Charity and Aryanna came over to do Christmas baking. Jazmin felt well enough to sit in her special camping chair at the table. She was weak and could barely walk. She used her walker, and we walked behind her to make sure she didn't trip on her oxygen tubing.

We had a lovely time, the four of us. Alice crawled around the kitchen.

"I can understand why people take their own lives near the end," Jazmin said. "I'm so weary of this battle."

I was ready to burn my suitcase in the fireplace. Words like these stole any ounce of hope I had left that Jazmin would come out the other side of cancer.

I struggled for words. "It's perfectly normal to feel that way. You've fought long and hard, and you're tired."

Jazmin talked about how she felt with her body racked with cancer and pain. We all tried to lend her our strength.

Charity suggested we update her prayer group on Facebook.

Jazmin nodded. "Tell them to pray I get a Christmas miracle. That God takes me or heals me, but either way that it happens quickly."

No, God, please don't take her quickly. I'm not ready to let her go.

Early the next morning, which was Kyle's thirtieth birthday, I posted an update in Jazmin's Facebook group. I asked people to pray that Jazmin would get her miracle quickly—an entrance into heaven or a miracle on earth.

That morning, Jazmin shut us all out. She wouldn't talk to us other than a yes or no. A battle was going on in her mind, and I wasn't sure what it was about. Was she reacting to seeing her prayer request written in words and the finality of her situation? Or was she shutting down emotionally because this was the end?

We planned a birthday supper for Kyle. Today was his first day out with his staff in many weeks, and he didn't want to come back into the house. His staff brought his birthday supper out to the van and took him for another drive.

Jazmin was quiet at dinner. She ate half of her supper and then asked for her bucket and threw up at the table. After that, she was exhausted and didn't have the strength to get back to her bedroom. She asked Vance to help her.

He lifted her out of her chair and carried her like she was a small child. Oh, how I loved this man. I had watched him tenderly care for Jazmin and sit on the side of her bed and hold her hand or speak words of encouragement to her. If Jazmin had asked for the moon, Vance would have figured out a way to get it for her.

Jazmin had said the day before how much she admired Vance and his love for God and his family. Vance and Jazmin had a special bond that was priceless. She looked up to him as a strong father figure.

I texted Sheri that I thought Jazmin was declining again.

That night, I went into her room and prayed for her to have a peaceful sleep. I hugged her tightly.

I went to bed and cried, my heart heavy. We'd received messages all day from friends and family who said they were praying. But my heart didn't want to say goodbye to my dear, sweet daughter-in-law.

I was exhausted. Emotionally drained. My hope-suitcase dragged, bumping against the backs of my shoes. I could barely wait for eight o'clock each night so I could hop into bed.

We were expecting a lot of company over the holidays, and I prayed God would get me through. We loved having everyone here. But the stress of watching someone die was taking its toll on me.

My body ached every morning as I rolled out of bed. I felt a lot older than fifty.

Mourning someone before they die is a terrible feeling. Although they are living right in front of you, you know they will leave soon, and you prepare yourself so the pain won't be unbearable when the time comes.

It reminded me of a CrossFit competition I had participated in with my family. The six of us took turns carrying a weird object a long distance.

One young man carried a huge yoga ball half filled with water. His face strained as the weight of the water in the ball constantly shifted. His arms and legs grew weary, and he began to stumble. His beet-red face looked like he was in utter agony. The shifting weight was too heavy for him to bear, and his team lost the race due to his inability to carry the object.

I felt this way as I watched Jazmin die. I couldn't carry cancer much longer or I would fall apart. I knew a miracle was unlikely. My burden of sorrow would become even heavier as we headed into the Christmas season. I desperately needed God's help to carry this heaviness.

On December 19, I woke up at three thirty in the morning with heaviness weighing my heart. I rolled out of bed and hopped into the shower. The tears came immediately. I prayed as I shampooed my hair, "Please don't take our daughter, God."

Millions of parents have prayed that prayer, and one in a million get the answer they want. If God was planning on taking Jazmin, I hoped He would change His mind.

Vance saw Jazmin's bedroom door open after Dawn left and went in to check on her. "Why were you so quiet yesterday? What was bothering you?"

"After Cindy posted the update, people wrote me saying goodbye. Everyone thinks I'm going to die, but I wanted them to pray for a miracle." Her lower lip trembled.

Vance tried to encourage her not to focus on the goodbyes but to keep hoping for a miracle.

But the goodbyes caused her to feel down, and she began to decline. Her nurses thought she might have a week left.

My heart sank.

Later in the day, Jazmin's nurse and I started chatting. Dawn said she and Rita, the palliative nurse practitioner, had talked. Jazmin was declining again, and they didn't think it would be long. Dawn and Rita had seen hundreds of people die and knew the signs of someone being close to death.

I was tired of calling the family to come back. I was sure they were going to think I was crying wolf.

I was done with this stupid roller coaster and ready to put my suitcase of squashed hope on the ride and press the "eject into overdrive" button.

God, please help us! We're tired. Jazmin's tired. This battle is too hard. Please do something—anything.

God answered my prayer in an unusual way.

No longer able to sit on the couches or recliner, Jazmin was stuck in her bed most days. One day she confessed, "Being in the bedroom is comfortable, but it makes me feel isolated from the rest of my family."

The next day, the medical equipment team delivered a bed and set it up in our living room, as close to the kitchen as possible so Jazmin could watch us cook or be part of the conversation when we were at the dinner table or in the living room.

Jazmin felt immediate happiness. When joy lifted her spirits, hope grew.

Now she spent her days in the living room and only slept in her bedroom at night. Jazmin felt like she was part of the busyness of our home and was able to chat with anyone who came in the front door.

Slowly we watched Jazmin scamper away from death yet again. This quick transformation helped me realize how much a person's mental state affects their physical health.

God cared.

He moved.

We breathed.

Jazmin sighed.

God's faithfulness was constant, and our thankfulness was a never-ending fountain. I opened my suitcase, took out a safety pin, and clasped a tiny bit of hope over my heart. I sent up a prayer.

God,

Please let Jazmin live through the Christmas holidays.

CHAPTER THIRTY-SEVEN

The Last Christmas

Mom, you can't put up a fake tree.
It's just not Christmas unless you have a real one.

—JAZMIN HENSON

HEN CHRISTMAS EVE CAME around, Sherie and Aaron had dinner with our family. We had a lovely evening together. Aaron shared funny stories that had most of us laughing. Jazmin grinned as she watched our families grow into a blended one.

On Christmas morning, I woke up early, like usual, and climbed the basement stairs to the main floor.

Swoosh, swoosh, swoosh.

I let out a big sigh. *Thank You, God!*

I poured myself a big mug of coffee and turned on the Christmas tree lights. Thoughts swirled in my head as I stared at the tree. I wanted to be happy since this was undoubtedly Jazmin's last Christmas. It was important that the day be special. I was determined to find some joy, even if it was fake, and plaster it on my face.

A prayer escaped my lips, the same one I'd prayed over twenty-five years on Christmas Day: *Lord, heal my son,* and I added, *Please give Jazmin a miracle.* A tear dropped from my eye, and I caught it with my fingers. *I can't cry today. Lord, give me the strength to get through today, and please uplift my spirits.*

I went down the hall to my office to write.

Vance joined me for coffee a few hours later.

We were both tired and feeling sad.

A half hour later, Charity came up the stairs with Alice in her arms, and I snuggled with my granddaughter on my lap. Alice could dissipate any sadness I felt with one giggle or the touch of her chubby hand against my cheek.

Devyn came upstairs, and we chatted for a bit with the kids. We all had puffy eyes. We hadn't been sleeping. There had been too many close calls. Everyone was on edge every time we laid our heads on our pillows.

But on this morning, having our children with us brought peace.

My phone buzzed with a text at 7:19. It was from Jazmin. "Wanna come help me up? Please."

My heart leaped with joy. Jazmin had lived until Christmas Day! Today was going to be wonderful! I could feel it in my spirit as I bounded down the stairs.

I quietly stepped to Jazmin's side of the bed. "How are you feeling this morning?" I whispered so I wouldn't wake Eythan.

"Good! Can you help me to the bathroom? Then I want to come out to the living room." Jazmin reached for my hands, and I pulled her up into a sitting position.

"I'm so glad you're feeling well today." I put my arms under her armpits and around her back while she held my neck, and I lifted her up. Jazmin grabbed the handles of her walker and slowly wheeled to the bathroom. Five minutes later, Vance had her comfortable in her hospital bed in the living room.

We could tell right away that Jazmin was feeling stronger, and her breathing was better.

A little spark of hope belted itself around my tummy.

Sheri and Aaron had slept at my mother-in-law's house next door, and I sent them a text. "Jazmin is up, and she is excited to get the day started!"

Sherie and Aaron came in the door a half hour later, and we all wished one another a Merry Christmas with hugs.

Aryanna arrived at eight forty-five. By then Eythan was up. We had our Christmas hugs and greetings as cheer spread throughout our home.

We ate waffles and ham and drank steaming coffee in the crowded kitchen. Jazmin moved to her chair piled with soft pillows at one end of the table, and she surprised us with a chatty voice as we enjoyed our meal. Joy filled the room as we laughed and ate together.

Kyle felt less anxious that day, and we told his staff he could be part of the celebration. Vance spent most of his time shadowing Kyle to make sure he wouldn't throw anything that might harm Alice or Jazmin.

Jazmin liked seeing him too, and it cheered her up knowing Kyle was having a good day. She empathized with Kyle because she understood what it felt like to be isolated, unable to participate in events.

For over an hour, we had a wonderful time opening presents. Jazmin sat in the recliner. A fire crackled in the fireplace. An enormous tree twinkled in the corner. The room felt cozy and nostalgic.

I had planned on putting up our artificial tree because I didn't want Alice to get needles in her hands or knees. But Jazmin had insisted a real tree was needed. Vance had found us an enormous one.

Piles of Christmas paper were strewn about the living room, and mugs of coffee were refilled as family members tried out their new toys or clothes. A perfect Christmas.

My family arrived for lunch, and we stuffed ourselves with potatoes, turkey, dressing, vegetables, and salads. Pumpkin pie and at least five other desserts followed. After lunch, our kids pulled out board games and spent the afternoon having fun. We made homemade pizza for supper—not that anyone was hungry.

Vangie arrived from southern Ontario around eight. She always called Jazmin Slim Jim and hadn't seen her sister in two months. Jazmin had lost even more weight, and now she really lived up to the nickname.

Jazmin had her family together. We knew this made her happy. Her day had been really good, and we praised God for the beautiful gift He gave us—one more Christmas with Jazmin. He had granted Jazmin a Christmas wish, and she was tickled pink.

I didn't fake my happiness. God made it easy to for me to be genuinely joyful on Christmas Day.

Lord,

When we are joyless, please help us over the hurdle
of sadness. Show us You are present and near.
Help us to overcome our grief
when our family needs us to support them.

Amen.

CHAPTER THIRTY-EIGHT

One Day at a Time

*The waters closed over my head, and I thought I was about
to perish. I called on your name, Lord, from the depths of the
pit. You heard my plea: "Do not close your ears to my cry for
relief." You came near when I called you, and you said,
"Do not fear." You, Lord, took up my case;
you redeemed my life.*

(LAMENTATIONS 3:54–58)

*Trust in the Lord with all your heart and lean not on your
own understanding; in all your ways submit to him,
and he will make your paths straight.*

(PROVERBS 3:5–6)

December 28, 2019

JAZMIN WOKE UP FEELING fairly well, but within a few hours,
she became weak and exhausted. Her parents came for coffee,
but Jazmin didn't have the energy to visit with them.

Eythan took her to the bedroom and tucked her into bed. He
made sure she had everything she needed.

While Jazmin rested, Sherie and Aaron went to visit relatives. Vance took a drive with Kyle. I took down all the Christmas decorations while the house was quiet. I wanted the Christmas memorabilia gone. If Jazmin was going to pass away, I didn't want anything related to Christmas around the house. Having a loved one die over the holidays can create many sad memories connected to Christmas. We would move on today and start the new year early.

When Jazmin woke from her nap, she rolled her walker into the living room and glanced at the tree. Her face sank. "You took it all down?" Sadness filled her voice.

"We need the extra space for people to sit. And since the tree was coming down, I thought I'd put away all the decorations too." I hoped she would fall for my excuse.

Jazmin shrugged it off and was over the disappointment within a few minutes.

That evening she felt better, and she, Eythan, Vance, and I sat around the dinner table.

Jazmin leaned forward in her chair, putting her elbows on the table. "Lately I can really sense God's presence, and I feel led to pray for the ministry I'll have when God heals me of cancer. I believe with all my heart God is going to give me a miracle. But I know He is going to let me stay in this poor state for a little while longer."

The three of us felt encouraged to hear Jazmin talking positively and with so much peace in her voice. I nodded and smiled. Even though I knew she was going to die, I didn't want to discourage her.

Vance sat across from her at the other end of the table. "Jazmin, if you get a miracle, I'm taking the whole family to Florida for a vacation."

Eythan and Jazmin smiled at each other. They loved that idea. A warm, happy vacation sounded good to all of us!

I hoped with all my heart that I was wrong. I wanted to sit on a beach and watch my family swim in the ocean and know that was a gift from God.

Only God could give us this miracle. The medical community had nothing they could do for Jazmin because this type of cancer doesn't go into remission.

If Jazmin lived, it would be a miracle, and trying to muster any hope was nearly impossible. I just had to look at the skeleton of a girl in front of me to know we were running out of time.

> If Jazmin lived,
> it would be a miracle,
> and trying to muster any hope
> was nearly impossible. I just
> had to look at the skeleton of a
> girl in front of me
> to know we were running
> out of time.

I was exhausted beyond belief from the sadness I'd been dealing with for months. I felt like I was in a deep state of mourning and depression. It was getting more difficult to remain cheerful and upbeat in front of Jazmin, then walk downstairs to my bedroom, shed some tears, and come back up with a smile.

I loved the kind of tears that spilled when I laughed. They were cherished. But I couldn't remember the last time I had belly laughed. Like I-can-barely-catch-my-breath type of laughing. I sometimes brought up old memories to cheer myself up.

I recalled a day with my kids ten years before when we went shopping on a cold winter day. As we left Walmart, I yelled, "Race you to the car! Last one there is a rotten egg!"

We took off running, and I made it to the van in fourth place. Aryanna, who was ten, was running at full speed. As she neared us, she tried to slow down, but the icy parking lot was too slippery, and she did a full body slam up against the van. The impact knocked her to the ground, and she lay sprawled out in the perfect position to do a snow angel. We all stared at her.

When I realized she was okay, I burst out laughing. Not just a giggle. A snorting and crying and slapping-my-knees kind of laugh. I'm such an empathetic mother.

Devyn helped Aryanna up. I drove us home while tears streamed down my face. I kept looking in the rearview mirror at Aryanna with her arms crossed over her chest and a glare on her face as I laughed some more.

Now that Aryanna's an adult, she and I giggle together over this memory. Of course, I still snort and cry.

But now I felt the way Aryanna had that day—slapped up against cancer and flat on my back with the devil laughing down at me. He was working hard to defeat me, and I felt like he was winning.

I wanted to have one of those days of laughing until it hurt because at this moment, with cancer pulling me in a million directions, I didn't know what to feel. I just knew I was tired of being sad.

Our situation wasn't about me. It was about Jazmin and making sure she was well taken care of while she was dying. Our children could feel my sorrow and knew I was putting on a smile to help keep her spirits up. They saw beyond my surface feelings and knew I was struggling to remain happy on the outside.

Having the Christmas decorations stored away made me feel better. That chapter was over. By God's grace, we had squeezed Christmas in, and we were thankful. But there was a niggling feeling that Jazmin wouldn't see another Christmas.

I continued to put one foot in front of the other. It was all I could do.

On December 30, our power went out at five thirty in the evening. I had just finished making supper. Thankfully, we had a generator—Vance had bought one several weeks before—so Jazmin wouldn't be without oxygen.

Within a minute, Eythan had Jazmin hooked up to her new portable oxygen tank. Vance went outside and got the generator going. We quickly had Jazmin's large electrical oxygen tank, our fridge, her microwave beside her bed, and her electric bed plugged into power.

We ate our dinner by candlelight in the dining room. The only lights hooked to the generator were the ones in the living room, which were open to the kitchen.

We went to bed in a warm home, with Jazmin's oxygen going and a microwave beside her bed so she could heat her bean bag up in the night.

We had everything we needed. God had prepared us for this power outage. Perfect timing on His part.

Vance spent twenty-four hours taking care of our family as he kept the generator going. He didn't sleep well that night due to wanting to be awake if the generator shut off. He was tired the next day. But Vance could roll along easily with changing circumstances in an emergency, and I loved that about him.

Our kids came over New Year's Eve. We plugged in a griddle and electric pot and made tacos and tortillas. Jazmin sat at the table making salsa and guacamole. We ate our last meal of 2019 by candlelight.

The power came back on just as we finished dinner. It had been out for twenty-four hours. I went to bed incredibly thankful that God had gotten us through one of the hardest years of our lives and that Jazmin had lived another year that none of us thought she would.

Jazmin and I prayed together before bed. We prayed that 2020 would be a year of healing for her. Not that I believed she was going to get a miracle. But I knew my prayer would give her peace before she went to sleep.

As I walked out of Jazmin and Eythan's room, I wondered what 2020 held for all of us, and especially for Jazmin.

Dear Lord,

When the world around us is falling apart and we are tempted to panic, pull us close and shelter us from worry and anxiety.

Amen.

CHAPTER THIRTY-NINE

Stepping Over the Line

*May the God of hope fill you with all joy and peace as you
trust in him, so that you may overflow with hope by the
power of the Holy Spirit.*

(ROMANS 15:13)

January 2020

CHARITY AND I HEADED across the bridge that connects our
city with the US to do some shopping. As I drove, I told her I
had come to a point where I realized I'd been living in a state
of mourning for the past couple of months.

"I know, Mom. You were really depressed."

My kids weren't used to seeing me depressed. But I did have
situational depression when I was sleep deprived.

I swallowed the lump in my throat. "I was preparing myself for
Jazmin's death. But a few days ago, I realized I can't live every day
thinking she is going to die. She may live in this state for another
year."

Charity looked at me. "God showed me the same thing—that I
need to live with hope."

We talked about the power of hope and what it had done in our lives. I glimpsed at my hope-suitcase again, but differently this time. When a person loses hope, she also loses her joy and happiness. I had lost my hope in Jazmin getting a miracle from God. I'd been preparing for my child's death, and it was killing me.

I shared with Charity what had happened a few days earlier when God and I had a special moment together. As I sat in the recliner in my office, with my face in my hands, weeping uncontrollably, I heard His still small voice.

Cindy, I'm in control of Jazmin's life. I want you to stop mourning and live each day as though she is going to get a miracle. I need you to be one of her biggest cheerleaders and cheer her on so she can run this race with hope. I don't want Jazmin to live out her last days feeling hopeless. Please, Cindy, surrender your mourning to Me, and let it go.

Who was I to give up? Why would I number my daughter's days and get ready for the worst? I was protecting myself from getting hurt if Jazmin left us. But Jazmin needed me to hang on to hope with her, and Sherie needed us to do the same. They couldn't do this alone.

For the past few months, Vance had seen my depression every morning. He had tried to encourage me to hang on to hope and not give up. "Cindy, it's okay for us to live in both worlds. We can acknowledge that Jazmin is dying, and we can also embrace the hope that she might get a miracle. You can't live like this, mourning all the time. It's affecting your health and sleep."

So I stepped over the line and hopped onto Jazmin's hope-train.

> In a glorious instant, God filled me with an incredible amount of joy. My suitcase flapped open, and God grabbed everything in it and dressed me in every article of clothing that flew out. I looked ridiculous but felt incredibly peaceful. I felt the wind in my hair as I rode Jazmin's hope-train at full speed.

In a glorious instant, God filled me with an incredible amount of joy. My suitcase flapped open, and God grabbed everything in it and dressed me in every article of clothing that flew out. I looked ridiculous but felt incredibly peaceful. I felt the wind in my hair as I rode Jazmin's hope-train at full speed.

The deep, dark sadness dissipated, and I felt the warmth of the joy that my newfound hope gave me.

If we are children of God, our lives shouldn't be so wrapped up in our loved ones that if we lose them, we lose ourselves too. God wants our joy to be tied to Him so if we lose everyone dear to us, we still have Him.

> If we are children of God, our lives shouldn't be so wrapped up in our loved ones that if we lose them, we lose ourselves too. God wants our joy to be tied to Him so if we lose everyone dear to us, we still have Him.

Hope is beautiful because it means we are trusting God. Joy and hope are tightly linked—these two treasures can help us overcome the most difficult circumstances.

God had numbered Jazmin's days before she was born. I couldn't change that. He knew how long her life was going to be, and no amount of mourning could add a single day to her life. Living each day with hope allowed me to experience joy and happiness despite the circumstances around me.

Jazmin stood a better chance of winning the lottery than getting a miracle. I had seen many people win the lottery, but I had never seen anyone get a physical healing from cancer. If Jazmin had decided there was no chance she would ever get better, she would have given up. Giving up is the quickest way to die.

Jazmin had survived six months of the worst possible life she could imagine, but every day she woke up with the beautiful thought that today could be the wonderful day she got the miracle she had hoped for—and captured the butterfly.

Lord,

When we are hopeless, be our hope.
Sustain us when we feel discouraged, uplift us,
and bring us back to trusting You to determine
how long we or our loved ones will live.
Give us joy.

Amen.

CHAPTER FORTY

Pain Free

Having faith means that I believe what I ask from the Lord will be delivered to me. When I pray to be healed from cancer, I pray with expectation that it will happen. If God can do it—and there is no thing that God cannot do—then who I am I to doubt God?

—JAZMIN HENSON

I HAD A NEW PURPOSE. Every day I was going to be a hope giver. I began to start sentences with "When you get better . . ."

There was no more mourning or thinking of her dying. I placed Jazmin in God's hands and lived each day with joy so I could be a wonderful caregiver for her. Instead of plastering on a fake smile when I was mourning inside, I now had genuine happiness. I felt like I had transformed from Eeyore, the depressed donkey, to Tigger, the bouncing ball of joy. The donkey cloud had lifted, and I wanted to bounce through each day.

One evening, as Jazmin ate in her comfy chair at the end of the table, she said to me, "You and Vance should get away for a break. You could go on a cruise."

"We don't want a break, Jazmin. We want to be near you."

"I know you do, but my grandma and grandpa could come stay with me so you two could get away. You could use some rest."

I hated it when she worried about us. We weren't the ones who were sick. "Jazmin, we would not relax knowing you are so ill. Once you're better, we'll go on a trip."

We wanted Jazmin to live. If that meant a year of no vacations, it was worth every last minute seeing her recover and get a miracle. (At the time, we didn't realize Canadians would soon be under a travel ban. We thought we had lots of years to go on vacation. But this might be our last year with Jazmin, and we didn't want to miss any moments with her.)

Early in January 2020, I slipped into Jazmin's room at eight o'clock. She said she felt good but wanted to sleep longer, and when she got up, she wanted to get ready for church.

I stepped back out of her room with a spring in my step, smiling. I found Vance at the table and told him what Jazmin said.

"I doubt she'll have the energy to go to church." Vance was always logical.

"You're probably right. But let's get ourselves ready early in case she does." I went downstairs to change out of my pajamas and into jeans and a pretty top.

Around nine o'clock, Eythan came out of their room, looking tired but happy. "Jazmin is using the bathroom, and then she wants to get ready for church."

Vance and I grinned from ear to ear. Eythan got breakfast ready for him and Jazmin while I gathered Jazmin's meds and pillows and

Vance collected her oxygen bottles. We placed everything by the front door.

An hour and a half later, Eythan carried Jazmin into church and lowered her into her camping chair. The building filled with joy, and the worship team led us in music. The congregation had been praying for months for Jazmin and knew she had almost died many times. My heart was bursting with happiness as I saw their smiling faces. To have her in church was truly a miracle.

Jazmin made it through the morning feeling comfortable. When the service ended, church members came over to greet her.

When it was time for Eythan to lift Jazmin back out of her chair and take her home, I walked up to her. "How did it feel to be in church today?"

She laid her head back against her chair, smiled at me, and sighed. "It felt wonderful!" She smiled as if she had just eaten the most delicious seven-course gourmet meal and was completely satisfied.

The morning had worn Jazmin out, and she went home and took a nap.

Later that evening, she asked Eythan to shower her, and he gently guided her to their room. Once she was in clean pajamas, Eythan brought her to the living room and laid her in her bed, looking completely happy and peaceful.

Jazmin had had her first day free of pain, nausea, and throwing up in many months. Usually she experienced at least one of these three symptoms, or all of them, every day.

Around Christmastime, our pastor, Wendell, had anointed her with oil and, with his wife, Lila, prayed for her at our house. I wondered if it was possible that God had started a miracle on that day.

Tonight we could tell she was overjoyed. And we thanked God for this day. Vance and I prayed for Jazmin before she fell asleep. Then I reached down and hugged her.

"I love you, Mom," she whispered in my ear as her boney arms circled my neck.

"I love you too, Jazzy." I kissed her cheek.

When Vance bent to hug her, she expressed the same sentiments to him. We closed her bedroom door and went to bed happy and thankful.

On January 6, Jazmin woke up with some pain in her kidney area. She stayed in bed for a little while, then Eythan got her up.

She was a bit more drugged than usual, due to going off Tylenol 3 with codeine and having upped her morphine. "Maybe it's the Tylenol, but I hope it's from yesterday's going to church and moving around," she said. "I'd rather be drugged and tired with a bit of pain than pain free with lots of nausea and throwing up."

Jazmin cooked dinner for us. I was her hands and eyes, and from her bed in the living room she directed me on how to cook our meal of marinated sirloin steaks, roasted sweet potatoes, salad, and broccoli. She had the head of her bed raised and could see me at the island to give me specific instructions. She held her phone and read me every detail of each recipe.

I'm a bit of a creative mess in the kitchen since I like to throw things together. When Jazmin watched me cook, I sometimes saw a look of mortification on her face if my measuring cup had a tiny bit more flour or liquid in it than was called for. Sometimes I purposely overfilled the measuring cup just to see her eyes grow big like saucers. It cracked me up every time!

Once, when I made oatmeal squares, I was tossing ingredients in my big mixing bowl without carefully measuring. I felt Jazmin's eyes on me. When the squares came out too soft and falling apart, Jazmin commented with a flat, annoyed voice, "It's because you didn't measure the oatmeal."

I tried not to snicker.

Jazmin was definitely the better cook of the two of us, and I didn't mind letting her make dinner while I listened to her instructions and followed each step carefully.

At dinnertime, when everyone commented on how delicious the meal was, I piped up, "Jazmin cooked everything."

She was about to take a bite of food, but she lowered the fork and stared at me. "Mom, you always give me way too much credit."

I laughed. I knew the meal wouldn't have tasted this good if I'd been in charge.

After dinner, we sat around the table, chatting. Jazmin again mentioned her future ministry. We dreamed with her about what that would be like—a book or maybe a movie. Her life would make an amazing movie, that's for sure, with people wondering how the story was going to end.

"Jazmin, maybe you'll travel the world speaking." Vance's voice sounded upbeat.

I raised my hand. "I'll be your travel companion." I dreamed of all the fun we would have going to exotic places.

"I'm not crazy about traveling. Whenever I've flown, I've always been in pain or discomfort." Jazmin reached for her glass of water and drank from the straw.

Eythan munched down his food while listening to the three of us dreaming.

I felt happy, and the transformation was amazing. I sang and danced in the kitchen (when no one was watching). I laughed and felt joyful.

I was my old self again after taking a break from feeling so sad. Yet my circumstances hadn't really changed. Jazmin was still very close to death. Kyle still had severe autism. But I no longer carried the burden suitcase of their illnesses. God was carrying that big, bulky box, and I was living in His beautiful presence each day with the hope He had gifted me. I was learning. Why pray if you're going to worry? Why worry when you can pray?

Since God had helped me do a 180-degree turn in my hope and faith during that month, I returned to my live videos at six thirty each morning.

I was my old self again after taking a break from feeling so sad. Yet my circumstances hadn't really changed. Jazmin was still very close to death. Kyle still had severe autism. But I no longer carried the burden suitcase of their illnesses. God was carrying that big, bulky box, and I was living in His beautiful presence each day with the hope He had gifted me. I was learning. Why pray if you're going to worry? Why worry when you can pray?

I lift up my eyes to the mountains—
where does my help come from?
My help comes from the LORD,
the Maker of heaven
and earth.

(Psalm 121:1-2)

CHAPTER FORTY-ONE

Million-Dollar Question

*Who am I to say that cancer is too big for God? It isn't.
If He wanted to, He could say the word and all the cancer
in my body would go away in an instant.*

—JAZMIN HENSON

January 7, 2020

AZMIN WOKE UP FEELING well. Eythan helped her come out to the table, and the four of us chatted before dinner.

We talked about random stuff, and something Eythan said caused me to say, "I wonder how many people became rich out of the blue under crazy circumstances."

Eythan came up with a funny story. "How about this? A YouTuber contacts you and asks you if you want to be in a contest. You have to stand on a rope suspended in the air and hold on to another rope over your head. It's you against the other people he asked to be in the contest. If you hang on the longest, you win one million dollars."

The situation sounded too far-fetched. "Did that really happen?"

"Yes!" He smiled as he got up to make his tuna sandwich.

"How long did the winner hold on for?"

Eythan laid four slices of bread on the counter. "Sixteen hours."

"Wow. Who would want to do such a crazy thing for a million dollars?"

"I would!" came a muffled voice to my right.

I glanced toward Jazmin, whose mouth was full of cereal.

Vance and I burst into laughter.

I chuckled. "Jazmin, if you're even thinking of doing anything that requires energy, you are definitely feeling good today!"

How did the girl who needed her hubby to practically carry her to the table this morning even think of hanging from a rope for sixteen hours?

Hope.

Jazmin had come close to death again and again, yet she kept trudging up the down escalator of death, fighting against this rare cancer, believing God was going to heal her.

Most of us, maybe all of us, would have given up long ago.

Jazmin had done what most people could not. She had stood on the unstable cancer death rope for six years, with nothing to hold on to except her dear Savior. Every time she felt like giving up, God sent people into her life to pray for her, encourage her, and help her to hold on a little longer.

When Jazmin wanted to pass through the thin veil between earth and heaven . . . when she was throwing up everything she ate . . . when she looked like a skeleton with sunken eyes and cheeks, pale skin, and every bone in her body protruding . . . God picked her up and carried her, and she clung to Jesus with all her being.

Our waif of a girl was clinging to her sweet Jesus. He was sustaining her day by day.

> I wait for the Lord, my whole being waits,
> and in his word I put my hope.
>
> *(Psalm 130:5)*

CHAPTER FORTY-TWO

Jazzy Does the Jazz

My full name is Jazmin Faith Henson.
My middle name, Faith, was given to me
because my parents felt that God's plan for my life
would heavily involve faith in Him.
Boy, were they right.

—JAZMIN HENSON

January 10, 2020

RYANNA AND HER BOYFRIEND, Daniel, came over around four.

Jazmin asked to be moved to the table to eat snacks with us as we played Monopoly before dinner. She was energetic and talkative.

"Will you turn off the music?" someone asked, referring to the jazz music I had playing in the background.

I bemoaned the fact that I was the only one in my family who had great taste in music.

But Jazmin agreed with my family and started imitating my music. Her lips came together in a tight, thin line, and she made saxophone noises while playing her imaginary instrument. Her fingers flew up and down the keys and her head tossed back as she tipped her invisible saxophone.

Aryanna, Daniel, and I burst into laughter.

We hadn't seen Jazmin be carefree and silly like that in a long time. Our Jazzy was slowly coming back to herself. My hope soared to heights I had never known. It had been three months since the nurses thought Jazmin might pass away and her family and friends had come to say goodbye. She had lived a quarter of a year since then.

After supper, Sherie and Aaron arrived from Sudbury. The last time they had seen Jazmin was seventeen days before, and she wasn't doing well then. They were ecstatic to see her improving.

"Sweetheart, you look wonderful!" Aaron gave Jazmin a hug.

"Hi, Dad!" Jazmin's voice had a little pep in it.

Sherie gave Jazmin a hug and stood next to her, softly running her hands over Jazmin's short, thin hair. "It's so good to see you feeling better!"

Joy filled the room as we all smiled at one another.

Sherie and I chatted in the kitchen while Vance and Aaron watched a hockey game on our TV in the living room. Vance had persuaded me to buy it for him as a Christmas gift, but I didn't like its New York City size.

It wasn't unusual for Aaron to jump out of his chair and shout if the game got intense. He and Vance were opposite personalities, and Vance got a kick out of Aaron's enthusiasm.

I leaned toward Sherie and spoke quietly, glad Aaron's loud cheers were a barrier from anyone listening in on our conversation. "Jazmin is getting better and improving every day!"

"I can see that!" Sherie looked confused but ecstatic.

"Her body desperately wants food. If a person is dying, it's the opposite. Jazmin is even waking up hungry in the night."

Sherie's smile grew bigger as we talked.

"Vangie and I have both had dreams recently of Jazmin being healthy," Sherie said, looking at me with watery eyes.

Had God finally given Jazmin her miracle? We moms agreed He had. We needed to cling to hope, whether we saw dips in Jazmin's health or saw her having a good day.

The next night, the kids came for dinner, and we ordered from a restaurant to have a belated New Year's party with Sherie and Aaron.

Eythan and I drove to the restaurant to pick up the food. While we waited for the waitress to bring our order, we talked about the new TV. "Your dad installed this app to my and his phones, and we can control the TV from it."

"That's cool!" Eythan glanced up, then looked back down to send a text to Jazmin.

I showed Eythan my phone. "If we lose the remote, I can turn the TV on and off with the app." Kyle sometimes stole the remotes and threw them over the balcony until they broke. "I wonder if I could turn the TV off from here. Do you think I can?" My eyebrows raised as I chuckled.

"You should try it!" Eythan looked at my phone, and a big grin spread.

We stood for a minute, hitting the on and off button repeatedly, the two of us laughing.

My phone chimed. It was Vance. "Stop it!!!"

Eythan and I roared. Tears streamed down my face. Gosh, it felt so good to laugh hard.

When we got home, Aaron said, "Cindy, I had no clue you were such a prankster. I'm shocked!"

Each day seemed to bring us new blossoms of hope as we watched Jazmin continue to improve. The butterfly was flitting near her. Heaviness lifted on the good days, and we held our breath in wonder. What was God doing? Was Jazmin finally going to get her miracle?

> When times are good, be happy; but when times are bad,
> consider this: God has made the one as well as the other.
> Therefore, no one can discover anything about their future.
>
> *(Ecclesiastes 7:14)*

CHAPTER FORTY-THREE

Peachy Goodness

I'm an optimist in every aspect of life.
The glass is always half full in my eyes.

—JAZMIN HENSON

January 12, 2020

Two Sundays in a row, Jazmin went to church, which was incredibly uplifting.

The next day, Vance and I took Jazmin for a blood transfusion at the hospital.

Eythan offered to go with her, but he hadn't been feeling well for a week and needed to sleep.

Vance helped me get Jazmin into the hospital. We had brought her specialized air mattress to put on top of the stiff hospital bed so she would be comfortable. He ran back out to retrieve the mattress while she and I found the room. Once she was settled in, Vance left to get us some lunch and snacks.

A nurse wheeled a big scale into the room, then left to retrieve medical supplies.

"Jazmin, do you want to know how much you weigh?" I asked.

Up until this point, Jazmin didn't want to know because it discouraged her to see her weight dropping so drastically.

"I don't mind," she said, shrugging.

I hoped the number wouldn't discourage her. She had been doing so well.

When the nurse returned, we stood Jazmin up, one of us supporting her on each side, and helped her step onto the scale.

I looked at the digital number: 31.1 kg.

After we sat Jazmin back down in the vinyl chair in the corner near the head of the bed, the nurse left.

"I'm sixty-one pounds." She gasped. "That's crazy!" Her eyes widened so much her eyebrows disappeared into her hairline.

"No, 31.1 kilograms is 68.42 pounds."

"Oh, good!" She relaxed her spine and leaned back, letting out a slow, deep, happy sigh.

Her countenance had changed so quickly from shock to relief, I burst out laughing. Our girl was happy she was sixty-eight pounds instead of sixty-one.

The nurse came back and helped me transfer Jazmin to the bed. Jazzy and I had a lovely time together while we waited for the transfusion to slowly drip. We chatted about her future and how I wanted her to help me pick out things like flooring, paint colors, lighting, and design for the new house in a year and a half. We planned to build and design a house that suited Kyle's needs better. Vance and I proceeded as though Jazmin and Eythan were moving with us.

Her oncologist came into the room. Jazmin was sitting cross-legged on her bed with her Subway sandwich in front of her. She continued eating as the doctor talked.

"In my research, I found an animal antibiotic that was being tested on patients with the same cancer as you, and so far, one patient has had success with it."

Jazmin nodded and continued eating her sub.

"There's a very low-dose chemo pill that you've tried for a short period in the past, and I'm wondering if you'd like to try it again."

Jazmin tilted her head side to side, weighing her options. She didn't show any emotion.

"Let me know if you want to try those meds. You have my number." The doctor left.

"What do you think?" I asked.

She shrugged and finished her sandwich.

Jazmin had always believed her miracle was going to come from God. The treatments might have helped other cancer patients temporarily, but Jazmin believed God wanted to give her a miracle. There would be no doubt that He was the one who had healed her.

"I asked Dawn what she thought of my health improving, and she said it wasn't a rally."

I was surprised. "Well, it's been weeks of improving, not just a couple of days."

I didn't know what to think either. After each really good day, fear settled in. *What if this is her last day? Should I get my hopes up, or will they just fall flat again?*

I had to choose hope. Otherwise, I'd be squashed by sadness-suitcase again!

Jazmin felt yucky for two days after her transfusion as her body tried to accept the donor's blood. But her coloring was great. She had gone from pasty white to a nice peachy color. And life felt peachy—sweet and full of goodness because she had a couple more good days after that.

Lord,

When we have big decisions to make, guide us.
You are the wise physician and know what is best for us.
Help us not to go by our feelings, but help us be guided
by Your Holy Spirit.

Amen.

CHAPTER FORTY-FOUR

I Was Hungry

*I'm a total foodie. I LOVE food. Since I've been sick,
I've had to eat a very strict diet, so I've learned to really
appreciate rich and fresh flavors. My sister, Vangie,
is an amazing cook, which makes her one of my
favorite people.*

—JAZMIN HENSON

January 17, 2020

AT ONE IN THE morning, I was in the middle of a rare night when I'd slept soundly when I heard a loud noise. *Crash! Thud.*

I sat up in bed, breathing fast. Had I dreamed that?

My first thought was that Kyle was in the kitchen and had thrown something. But the thud was louder than an object being thrown.

That couldn't be Jazmin, could it? She could barely walk!

I flew out of our basement bedroom and up the stairs.

Eythan came out of his bedroom looking concerned. "Where's Jazmin?"

I looked in the kitchen. She wasn't there.

Eythan checked their bedroom bathroom.

Then I noticed her oxygen line. My eyes followed it into the kitchen and around the island.

Jazmin lay on her back, still and lifeless.

I knelt beside her. "Jazmin, are you okay?" My legs shook.

Eythan found us and dropped down to the floor, placing one hand on either side of her.

Her hand moved slightly, and she moaned.

"I'm going to pick you up slowly, okay?" Eythan waited for a response.

Jazmin nodded.

Eythan and I eased her up. She leaned over the stove while we supported her. After a minute she became more oriented.

Eythan carried her to their bedroom. He looked up the signs of a concussion, checked her pupils, and read the symptoms.

Thankfully, she didn't have any of them.

"Does anything hurt?" Eythan put his phone in his pajama pants pocket.

"My head and my tailbone." Jazmin rubbed her head and let out a moan.

Eythan and I stepped closer to the bed. I laid my hands on her and asked God to take away all her symptoms from the fall.

Vance came into the room fully dressed. We relayed the information to him, and he looked concerned.

"Jazmin, why were you in the kitchen?" Eythan asked.

"I was hungry. But when I tried to lift the bowl with one hand and open the microwave door with the other hand, I lost my balance." She looked dejected, like she had gotten an F on a report card.

Empathy filled my heart. "Wow, just the fact that you had enough energy to get out of bed, walk to the kitchen with your walker, and get yourself food is impressive!"

"I'm so embarrassed." An impish grin pulled at the corner of her mouth.

We all laughed.

"Jazmin, we're just happy you're okay and that you had the strength to do all that." I squeezed her hand, reassuring her that no one was angry.

"I'm sorry I woke you up." She rested her hands across her tummy.

We would gladly get up every night with Jazmin for rest of our lives if it meant she was healthy, breathing, and alive. We reassured her that she could text us in the night to help her.

Eythan told her to give him a good swat in the night if he was sleeping heavily and she needed anything. He's like his dad—once they are in a deep sleep, it takes a bit to stir them. Jazmin and I had joked that we would fight off any burglars while the men slept.

Eythan slipped out of the room, found her food, heated it up for her, and brought it back. We said good night, and I walked out of the room, smiling. Drugged-Jazmin had sneaked out of her room. Maybe she was reliving her nights of sneaking food with Gayle. Food always tastes better when snatched and whisked to a bedroom without anyone noticing.

Through it all, Eythan was fairly calm and level headed. His ability to remain strong and steady when others panicked was incredible.

Jazmin woke up the next morning very sore in her torso and neck. But she had no bruising, which was incredible.

For the next few days, Jazmin felt uncomfortable and discouraged. Tears came easily. She was beginning to feel like giving up the battle again.

I reminded her of the dream I'd had on New Year's Eve.

Coming around the corner of the kitchen, I saw Jazmin climbing the outside of the open staircase, slowly inching up the railing. I gasped and yelled her name. She startled and fell fifteen feet to the concrete landing. I heard a loud thud, and I thought she had broken her bones. I screamed for Vance and Eythan. They came running. When they slid to a stop at the top of the staircase, Jazmin was walking up the stairs, perfectly fine. There wasn't a scratch or cut on her body.

"Jazmin," I said, "I think God is telling me that when you decline again, I don't need to worry, because He is going to heal you, and you are going to rise up out of this illness and be stronger than ever."

There was no other explanation for a dying girl who was only a skeleton to survive a bad fall. She had no muscle or fat to protect her bones. And to not have any permanent injuries or broken bones was a miracle.

"Thank you, Mom, for that reminder. I forgot about your dream. Let's hope I make a turnaround." Jazmin closed her eyes and tried to sleep.

God is capable of giving busy moms dreams in their sleep. It's hard for a mom to find a quiet place to hear God's voice. Our heavenly Father knows He can get a woman's attention while she sleeps. He can reveal to her things that are important for her to know. If you are a busy mom living in a noisy home, ask God to minister to you while you sleep.

"Call to me and I will answer you and tell you
great and unsearchable things you do not know."

(Jeremiah 33:3)

CHAPTER FORTY-FIVE

Something Has to Change

*Who am I to say cancer is too big for God? Because it isn't.
If He wants to, He can say the word and all the cancer in
my body would go away in an instant. But He has a plan,
and maybe that's not it. Or maybe just not right now. I don't
know. I don't understand exactly how God operates.*

—JAZMIN HENSON

WO DAYS LATER, JAZMIN woke up feeling much better. After breakfast she asked me if she could sit in the recliner. She hadn't done that since we decorated before Christmas. She read a book comfortably for a couple of hours.

I went out on a limb. "Jazmin, let's go for a drive."

"Okay!" Jazmin sounded enthusiastic.

"Really?" I wasn't expecting her to say yes.

"Yes. I feel good, and I would love to get out of the house." She sat forward in her recliner, anticipating what would happen next.

Eythan, Vance, and I scrambled to get the long list of things we would bring for Jazmin before she changed her mind. We scurried like a woman who's told unexpected company is arriving in ten minutes.

We took Jazmin for a one-hour drive, and she asked to go through two drive-throughs—McDonald's for a hamburger and french fries and Starbucks for an iced tea. She felt comfortable and happy. When we came home, Jazmin sat in her recliner and read for a couple more hours.

After dinner Jazmin stayed in her camping chair until bedtime. Vance and I sat on either side of her.

"Jazmin, do you still have hope?" Vance asked as we were about to do our evening prayer time.

"I am feeling discouraged. My body keeps going. But I live in this constant state of being bedridden and needing help to do everything. I just want something to change." She laid her head back against the chair and took in a big deep breath, then let it out slowly.

Vance leaned forward and rested his elbows on his knees. "We completely understand why you feel that way, and it's okay to be discouraged."

I grabbed her hand. "You are a living, breathing miracle! God still has a future planned for you. I believe we need to live each day as though we believe God has already healed you. We should try getting you out every day, even if it's just for a drive." God had really impressed this on my heart that morning when I was praying for Jazmin.

We had to get Jazmin out of her bed and out of the house more. In the past, pain had caused her to not be able to leave our home. But recently, her pain was well managed.

The next day, Jazmin woke feeling fairly good.

Her physiotherapist came after lunch for her first visit. She was a sweet lady and very encouraging.

The therapist was impressed as she watched Jazmin walk toward her unassisted. "Wow, Jazmin, I'm surprised you can walk at all since you've been in bed for most of the past three months." I was pretty sure the therapist was surprised that someone as underweight as Jazmin was upright at all.

Jazmin lowered herself into the recliner. "Other than walking to the bathroom or the table to eat, I haven't moved my legs much, and I've always needed assistance. But recently I've been feeling stronger."

The therapist gave Jazmin daily exercises. After she left, I asked Jazmin if she'd like to go for a drive.

"I'm going to lie down and rest for an hour, and then I want to get out of the house." Jazmin walked to the bedroom without any help.

An hour later Vance and I had her in the car. Eythan was at work, so we had her to ourselves. We grabbed some snacks and went for a long drive. We stayed out for two hours.

When we arrived home, Jazmin went to the recliner unassisted and sat there the rest of the evening.

She had sat eleven hours in a recliner or chair. A new record! It had been about six months since she stayed awake all day and sat up for most of it.

I had a feeling Jazmin was climbing toward a new life. Every day we would encourage her to live and focus on her new, bright future.

God had transformed me from a woman who was going to lovingly prepare Jazmin for death to a mother who was going to help her daughter-in-law live.

Life was changing, and Jazmin and I were living each day with new possibilities as our hope soared, along with Vance's and Eythan's.

On January 21, I texted Sherie to let her know Jazmin was improving dramatically since her fall in the kitchen. She was excited and texted back with happy emojis.

I dreamed of the future. Pretty soon she and I would be going out together every day while Eythan and Vance were working. I pictured the shopping trips to Winners and the coffee dates at Starbucks. Jazzy and I would have so much fun!

Vance took some time off since he had hired a new operator to run the logging equipment. The timing couldn't have been more perfect. With the winter weather, we needed someone strong to carry Jazmin down our slippery stairs and to the SUV.

While Vance stayed with Jazmin, I ran out to pick up her medical supply order. Her nurse was coming to give Jazmin her daily IV fluids for hydration, which she had been getting every day for months.

As I left the pharmacy, the heavy box in my hands, I prayed, *Lord, please let this be the last box of hydration I pick up.*

Our prayers were becoming more specific. Instead of *God, please heal Jazmin of cancer*, we prayed for the very thing we needed God to do for her. We were learning how to pray in new ways each day.

When I got back with the supplies, Jazmin looked at me from the recliner. "I'm going to skip hydration today since I'm urinating a lot and have swollen feet. My body has too much fluid."

I felt butterflies in my tummy. Jazmin not needing an IV bag hanging from her arm every day—this would be the first medical sign she was getting better! Thank You, Lord!

Jazmin felt a bit tired from all the extra activity. But she wanted to go for another drive and more treats. Many healthy foods didn't stay down, but she learned she could eat McDonald's chicken nuggets, a few fries, and her new favorite drink, a Starbucks vanilla bean frappuccino. Though broccoli might have been a healthier choice, Jazmin ate whatever wouldn't come back up—which sounded logical.

We stayed out for three hours. Vance and Jazmin chatted away in the front seats while I messaged Sheri updates and a photo of the two of them.

We stopped at the grocery store, and I quickly ran in. Vance and Jazmin talked while I was gone.

Vance pulled down the visor to shade his eyes. "You've been a patient for so long that you might find it hard to let go of people doting on you."

Jazmin sat with her elbow on the armrest and her fist supporting her head. "God and I have been chatting about that recently. I agree that I need to gain some independence."

We hoped we could encourage Jazmin to be as independent as her body allowed her to be. But we didn't want her to do it to make us happy.

We pulled into the driveway twenty minutes later.

Jazmin moved to her hospital bed for a bit and then lay down and had a nap before dinner.

We had a lovely meal, but Jazmin was still tired from her big day. She had kept down all the food she ate for forty-eight hours. Three good days in a row! We went to bed feeling hopeful.

Before I woke up the next morning, I had another dream.

Jazmin had gained weight quickly—so fast we were all surprised. Her parents came for a visit on Friday and noticed the difference. A few weeks later, Emily and Serena visited, and they bubbled with excitement over Jazmin's turnaround.

I woke up, hoping this was a dream from God and not just my subconscious wishing she would get better.

Jazmin's face had been hollow, with sunken cheeks and pronounced teeth. It would be wonderful to see her look like herself again. Jazmin wanted a big change to happen too. Sherie, Aaron, and

Vangie were coming on Friday. Jazmin had said while on our drive, "I wish I could feel more like myself when they come to visit."

"That's three days away. You might be yourself by then." I was open to any possibility. But I knew it would take a miracle, because the extremely large doses of morphine kept Jazmin in a constant dull and sedated state.

On Friday, Jazmin felt good and had very little pain. She was well enough to sit in a regular dining room chair instead of her soft camping chair.

Friday night, when her family arrived, they were surprised to see the camping chair missing. We sat around the table visiting with Sherie, Aaron, and Vangie. There was lots of laughing as Vangie and Aaron told funny, dramatic stories. Jazmin was talkative and laughed with the rest of us.

Aaron and Jazmin sat at opposite ends of the table, and he smiled at his daughter. "Sweetheart, I can't believe how good you look—and you're sitting in a regular chair!"

"I'm feeling much better, Dad." Jazmin smiled back.

A bubble of excitement spread, and I felt hope grow in the room.

When Sunday came around, Sherie and I chatted at the kitchen counter while Jazmin napped in the bedroom. She looked at me as she rearranged her curly ponytail. "Jazzy mentioned that she thinks she's ready to have us and her grandparents come less often."

"She did?" My heart leaped with joy. Jazmin was ready to start living a more normal life.

Sherie took in a deep breath and let it out. "I'm so happy Jazzy is doing well! Aaron and I are getting tired of working full time and traveling here every weekend. We need some rest."

Sherie had bags under her eyes, and I did too. We were all worn out. I didn't blame them; living out of suitcases and never having a day to unwind could exhaust anyone. It seemed we were all on the same page. We would step out in faith, believing Jazmin was getting better!

But when it came time to implement the plan, Jazmin changed her mind and wanted to go a little slower. Either way, we hoped all of us were heading toward more normalcy.

The next Tuesday, Sherie and I took Jazmin out for a drive while Eythan was at work.

Jazmin said, "I'm thinking I don't need my parents anymore, but I want you two to have freedom to come and go."

"We don't need help caring for you now that you're getting better. Vance is going to take time off so we can take turns running errands when Eythan is at work."

"Are you sure?" Doubt filled her voice.

"Absolutely!" we both chimed.

Going back to a normal life brought us hope that we were moving forward with Jazmin. I was thrilled that Jazmin was ready to embrace a new life!

We drove to the grocery store, and Jazmin went out in public for the first time in five months. She sat on two pillows in her wheelchair, with her portable oxygen purse hanging over the handle. Vance pushed her around the grocery store while I followed them, pushing the cart. People stared. We ignored them.

We saw Aryanna and Daniel.

"Jaz, you're out of the house!" Aryanna greeted her with excitement.

Daniel stood beside her, his blue eyes shining.

"I'm tired of sitting around. It's nice to see people—and food!" Jazmin laughed.

The three of us had so much fun shopping! Jazmin oohed and aahed over the different foods like a kid in a candy store. I scolded myself for grumbling in the past when going to the grocery store. I now saw this privilege through new eyes.

We headed back home after a very successful trip, and Jazmin sat in her recliner with a brush in hand, doing a paint-by-number vase of sunflowers I had bought her for Christmas.

We chatted as we ate supper, sharing with her the improvements we had seen in the past month. Jazmin talked of having a normal life again. She was dreaming of all the possibilities.

Our faith was growing, and our hope was flitting nearby! Maybe, just maybe, Jazmin would scoop up that butterfly.

Dear Lord,

Remind us daily that our lives are in Your hands.
You are the one with the ticking watch.
We are called to live life to its fullest
while putting our hope in You.
We praise You for the little miracles
You give us to bolster
our hope.

Amen.

CHAPTER FORTY-SIX

"I Saw Nothing!"

Although I'm a northern girl,
I'm also a total girly girl.
I love clothes and makeup and hair.
I love dressing up and looking fancy.

—JAZMIN HENSON

January 29, 2020

S WE ATE BREAKFAST, we decided it was time to update Jazmin's prayer group. We told them of all the improvements we had seen in her since Christmas as well as the things she still needed prayer for. People were encouraged by Jazmin's progress, and it was nice to give them good news.

In the afternoon, Jazmin went to the bathroom and then came back to the living room. Vance stood in front of her as she attempted to get down the step into our sunken great room. She leaned on the back of the couch for support. Jazmin was getting better at this as her arms got stronger each day. I walked behind her, ready to catch her if she stumbled.

As Jazmin walked to the recliner, a high-pitched, squeaky "Oops" came out of her mouth.

Vance's head, which had been down watching her feet closely, jerked up, and his eyes looked at mine. He raised his eyebrows.

I couldn't figure out what he was trying to silently communicate to me. Then he motioned his head toward Jazmin and cast his eyes downward quickly, trying to get me to look down.

Jazmin's pants were pooled around her feet.

I quickly bent down and pulled them up. My funny bone started poking me in the ribs. I burst into laughter. My sense of humor is embarrassing. I laugh at the most inappropriate times and should be ashamed of myself.

Jazmin laughed, too, as she sat in the recliner with Vance's help. I was no help at all—bent over at the waist, supporting myself by holding my knees, tears streaming down my face.

Vance grinned. "I was at eye level, and I saw nothing!"

Jazmin couldn't laugh hard because her lungs couldn't take in enough oxygen. So I made up for it by laughing loudly for ten minutes. I might have snorted a few times. Jazmin joined me with her tiny giggle that sounded like little hiccups.

When Charity came in the door a few hours later carrying a squirming Alice, Jazmin told her the story, but she started laughing before she finished. Charity joined us, and all four of us enjoyed recalling the comical theatrics of Jazmin-the-pants-dropper and Cindy-the-inappropriate-mom and Vance-the-liar.

Seeing Jazmin have a carefree moment was refreshing. I wanted to grab on to it and make it stay.

Jazzy told Charity about her trip to the grocery store. Her enthusiasm was contagious. If we could get Jazmin out more often, she could have more interesting conversations with people who visited. Jazmin's days were always the same, so it made it hard when people asked, "What did you do today?"

Jazmin had five good days. Then two bad ones.

A week later, Vance and I were tucking Jazmin into bed while Eythan was at work. The last few days hadn't been the best, with her lungs feeling tight and her breathing a bit more labored.

"Mom," she said, "ever since you did the update, my health has gotten worse. Do you remember when I did a live video with you in your Fresh Ground Faith with Cindy Facebook group, giving the women an update? I got much worse that day too." Jazmin had done an incredible job of sharing her faith with the women through a live video. As soon as the video was over, she stood up, and Vance carried her downstairs, with me following. She was in bed for days.

"Yes, I noticed you got worse after both of those updates. I think it's the devil." Why was Jazmin such a threat to him? What did he know that we didn't?

Jazmin and Vance agreed with me.

We laid our hands on Jazmin and prayed that God would protect her from the devil's attacks. She had gained a few pounds in the past couple of weeks. We wanted to stay encouraged and not let that low-down devil discourage us.

Amazingly, the oppression lifted, and Jazmin felt much better. Her spirits rose again. A few weeks went by, and Jazmin was still stable. Her relatives took a two-week break, and she still improved. More hope added to the collection we were gathering, and I didn't want to stop.

What would happen if we stopped? I didn't want to find out. We had to keep going. The momentum was encouraging!

Dear Lord,

When the devil tries to discourage us and bring us down,
remind us to call out to You for hope and encouragement.
You are the rock we need to cling to.
Hold us tight and don't let go.

Amen.

CHAPTER FORTY-SEVEN

Give God the Glory

*I believe in miracles, and I believe that God is capable
and willing to give me a miracle.*

—JAZMIN HENSON

February 15, 2020

*J*AZMIN'S REGULAR NURSE, DAWN, was off for a few days, and another nurse came instead. She hadn't seen Jazmin in months. The last time she saw her, Jazmin was bedridden.

Vance met her at the front door and invited her inside.

"I'll head to the bedroom to see Jazmin." She kicked off her sneakers.

"Oh, she's at the table eating lunch." Vance nodded toward the kitchen.

"What?" Her head popped up in surprise, and her voice rose an octave.

Vance smiled and headed to the kitchen. The nurse followed.

I looked up as she came into the room and said hello. Jaz was chowing down on her lunch. The nurse chatted as she hooked up Jazmin's IV pump. "The last time I was here, you were in bed and not doing well." She grabbed supplies and put them in her medical bag.

"I've been feeling much better." Jazmin had one elbow up on the table and her right arm straight with the IV sticking out of it.

"You haven't had any chemo treatment since I saw you last?" She looked at Jazmin, confused.

"No."

The nurse looked at Vance and me, hoping to get a logical explanation. "I wasn't expecting you to be doing this well."

Seeing the nurse's expressions and hearing her disbelief in how Jazmin could be doing so well confirmed that God was doing miracles in Jazmin's life. We weren't just dreaming up these good spells.

> Seeing the nurse's expressions and hearing her disbelief in how Jazmin could be doing so well confirmed that God was doing miracles in Jazmin's life. We weren't just dreaming up these good spells.

I gathered my and Jazmin's plates. "Her turnaround was due to prayer. She has a lot of people praying for her."

"Oh, I agree in the power of prayer!" The nurse smiled at me.

Hope was there, beautiful and bright.

We loved having conversations with people where we could give God all the glory. We hoped people would come to Jesus through Jazmin's miracle and testimony. That was the reason Jazmin kept believing in miracles. She was going to be the girl who loved Jesus even through suffering so others could know Him. We prayed she was coming out of the suffering and would soon be through the worst part of her life. We felt very close to the miracle.

Shout for joy, you heavens; rejoice, you earth; burst into song, you mountains! For the LORD comforts his people and will have compassion on his afflicted ones.

(Isaiah 49:13)

CHAPTER FORTY-EIGHT

The Walls Are Closing In on Me

Peace I leave with you; my peace I give you.
I do not give to you as the world gives.
Do not let your hearts be troubled
and do not be afraid.

(JOHN 14:27)

*V*ANCE AND I PRAYED that if God wanted us to get away for a vacation, He would provide a way. We asked Him to give us an answer that very day as a sign. We told no one of our prayer. By evening, we had no sign.

That night, after I went to bed, Vance stayed up with Jazmin and Eythan.

Jazmin said, "I want to go to my parents' camp when they're off from teaching, during the March break."

Sherie and Aaron had planned to spend their week off from teaching with Jazmin.

We had a small window of opportunity to fit in a vacation because Vance had agreed to take care of church responsibilities while our pastor and his wife were on vacation.

Jazmin's and Kyle's care was arranged by coordinating multiple people to help. Team Jazmin was Sherie and Aaron. Team Kyle was Charity, Dan, Devyn, and Kyle's day staff.

God pulled it off, and we booked a two-week vacation that included a seven-day cruise out of Miami. The COVID pandemic had just started. Ships were being held in the ocean, and we hoped we could have this trip without being stranded at sea under quarantine. Not that it would have bothered us. Vance and I could have easily sat in a stateroom for two weeks reading books and eating bread—well, I could have eaten just bread; Vance would have wanted a hamburger or two or ten. But we didn't want to leave Kyle and Jazmin for long.

We were ready for some rest and sleep.

My sleep had become very light since Jazmin's last fall in the kitchen. Yep, she tried again, that little stinker. Every night I woke around one o'clock and couldn't go back to sleep. I worried constantly about Jazmin during the night.

After Jazmin decided she wanted to go to her parents' camp for March break, she fell into a deep depression. The morphine was at a higher dose, and I was sure it was affecting her mind. She struggled to get out of bed each morning and began to lose her appetite.

Vance and I tried to stay above the cloud of heaviness. Jazmin needed us to stay upbeat.

I was determined to keep my suitcase empty. I still had on all the clothes, but some nights I eyed the hope-suitcase in the corner of our bedroom and was tempted to take off my scarf or sweater. I prayed more fervently and held on to my sweater for dear life.

When Sherie and Aaron came for the weekend, Jazmin was still in a deep pit of sadness. Sherie spent a day in her room, hanging out with her and watching movies.

"Jazzy, what can we do to lift this depression?" Sherie looked at Jazzy, who had been crying. "What if we went to camp earlier and you stayed longer?"

"Can we, Mom?" Jazzy asked, her face strewn with tears.

Sherie lay beside Jazmin, her heart heavy. "Of course we can!"

Jazmin smiled, and Sherie felt hopeful.

Jazmin and Sherie told Vance and me the news. I don't think we were ready for it. Jazmin had become our life. This was what we did every day. Now she was leaving for a month?

We cried as the news settled in. "Jazmin, we're happy for you. We know you need this break, but we are really going to miss you!" I grabbed a tissue, wiped my tears, and blew my nose.

Vance wiped away tears too.

Our emotions surprised us. We tried to keep them in check when we were around Jazmin. We didn't want to make her feel guilty for wanting to go to the one place that held her nearest and dearest memories. She would also get to have a long visit with her parents. Jazmin needed them and missed them tremendously.

Jazmin had Eythan, Vance, and me to care for her, but I could tell Eythan was struggling after work each night to go into their bedroom and visit with Jazmin when he was done with supper. He didn't know what to say to his dying wife to make her feel better and help lift the sadness. He felt helpless to cheer her up.

Eythan knew she needed this change. He agreed she would have a few weeks alone with her parents and said he would join her for one of the weeks.

We immediately saw a big improvement in Jazmin's spirits. She began eating, smiling, and even laughing.

She was going home.

Dear Lord,

When sadness fills our souls, be our comforter and draw us close so we can feel Your presence and be filled with Your peace.

Amen.

CHAPTER FORTY-NINE

Going Home

I'm sure if I was still in touch with the Sick Kids oncological team I had when I was sixteen, when I started this trek, they'd be shocked to find out I'm still here. Only by the grace of God does it make sense to me.

—JAZMIN HENSON

*V*ANCE AND I WERE ready to drive Jazmin to Sudbury, but the weather forecasted lots of snow and storms. We didn't think we were going to pull this off that day.

I texted Sherie, asking what the weather was like in Sudbury. She texted back, "Pretty good!"

Maybe God had cleared the way for us. Jazmin was feeling good that morning, and if we didn't go right away, we might not have another chance, which would devastate her.

We packed all her medicine, clothing, and medical supplies and loaded up our vehicle. There was so much stuff. We also had to carry six bottles of oxygen and change them every few hours. Her nursing care and the weekly meds her doctor ordered had to be transferred to Sudbury's facilities.

Our trip went better than we thought. At the halfway point, we stopped at a small indoor market.

An elderly man was asleep in a chair, and when he heard us, he lifted his head.

I stepped from behind Vance, the oxygen tank in my hands. "Do you mind if we use your bathroom?"

He jumped to his feet, happy to assist. I helped Jazmin into the tiny bathroom while Vance chatted with the elderly man. He asked Vance about Jazmin and was compassionate as he listened.

As we went out the door, we thanked the sweet man. We were grateful God had provided us a private setting for Jazmin to use a bathroom without a crowd staring at her.

We pulled into her parents' yard. Vance carried Jazmin into the house and laid her on the adjustable bed that friends had given Sherie.

The look of pure joy on Jazmin's face as she lay in the bed in her childhood home was worth the trip! She looked around, taking in every detail, and sighed as she sank farther into the bed.

Sherie and Aaron arrived home from work a half hour later. Jazmin's family was overjoyed that she was home.

We visited for a few minutes, and then it was time for us to say goodbye to Jazmin.

How do a mother and father say goodbye to a daughter who at any moment could die of a flu bug, pneumonia, or tumors in her lungs? This young woman had filled every nook and cranny of our life for six months. We had grown close to Jazmin and loved her deeply.

Jazmin looked up at us. "Can you guys pray for me?"

"Yes!"

Vance sat on the edge of her bed, and I knelt near her head and took her bony hand in mine. Vance and I prayed for her, as we had done every day.

When we finished, we looked at Jazmin, and tears immediately sprang from my eyes. "Jazmin, we love you, and we will be praying for you every night and every morning!"

Jazmin didn't cry anymore unless she was in terrible pain. Her emotions were dulled by her medications. But we saw sincerity in her eyes. She reached for me, and I bent over the bed and hugged her.

"I love you, Mom!" she whispered.

"I love you too!" I kissed her cheek.

My tears fell on her face. I stepped away and let Vance and Jazmin hug, telling each other they loved each other.

Would this be our last goodbye?

I cried as I hugged Sherie. "We'll feel lost without Jazmin."

"We can switch roles now, Cindy. You can rest, and we'll care for Jazmin."

"If she declines, text me, and we'll take the first flight home." I looked at Sherie, her blue eyes pooling with tears. "We'll come get Jazmin after we get back from vacation."

That was the plan, and everyone was good with it.

Vance and I drove out of the yard of the home where we had left our daughter. Some parents might feel the girl their son marries is someone they should keep at arm's length, but we wanted to keep the kids added to our family where we kept our own children—close to our hearts.

We felt like we were abandoning Jazmin. The feelings were conflicting and confusing. But this had been Jazmin's choice, and we knew this decision would bring her joy.

When you lie down, you will not be afraid;

when you lie down, your sleep will be sweet.

(Proverbs 3:24)

CHAPTER FIFTY

Can We Visit?

*My flesh and my heart may fail, but God is the strength
of my heart and my portion forever.*

(PSALM 73:26)

WE HAD TWO RESTFUL weeks at home and then headed
to Miami for vacation. Five days into our holiday,
we had to come back home since our government
said the border might close due to the pandemic. We quarantined for
a few weeks to make sure we didn't pass COVID on to anyone.

Jazmin's parents had managed to get her to camp two weeks
before the government canceled camp-going.

Eythan came home from visiting Jazmin. He looked pale and
sick and had lost weight, having eaten gluten. Within four days of
almost constant sleep, he started to improve. Eythan had become
exhausted and could barely take care of himself, let alone his wife.

He told us Jazmin was doing well. That was good to hear.

Three weeks into self-isolation, while Vance, Eythan, and I sat at
our kitchen table, I got a text from Sherie. "Hey, Cindy . . . Jazmin
asked me to text you for prayer. She's been struggling lately. She told

me this morning that she's done. Her body is rejecting food. She's very tired and weak and says she feels terrible. We've been praying for her, multiple times every day, and believing for her miracle. I've prayed for wisdom for next steps. Please pray for wisdom to know what to do."

My heart sank. "Sherie said Jazmin is done."

"Really?" Vance asked in a whisper.

Eythan's Adam's apple went up and down. "She has lots of bad days. I didn't realize it was *that* bad."

Heaviness set in. Emotions passed over Eythan's face. He was barely holding it together.

Jazmin's best friend, Emily, had flown in from British Columbia to be with her. After the required quarantine period, she moved in with Jazmin's family. This brought us comfort. Emily was such a sweetheart.

I texted Emily, asking for an update on Jazmin.

"She and I were sitting on the deck today," Emily texted back, "and she said, 'Thank you for being here with me. It means a lot.'"

I didn't know whether Jazmin would have made it this long without Emily and Serena, as they had messaged her nearly every day since she was diagnosed.

Eythan wasn't sure what to do. Should he stay or go back to see Jazmin and possibly infect her with COVID? He was asymptomatic. But the tension over COVID in Ontario was intense. No one wanted Jazmin to get it. She couldn't come back with Eythan, because we no longer had staff to care for Kyle, and our house had become a germ-filled place. We couldn't protect Jazmin if Kyle was roaming the house.

Eythan was caught between a rock and a hard place.

I stood at the kitchen sink doing dishes, my back to the men and my eyes filled with tears. My heart ached for Eythan and Jazmin. I did

286

the same thing I had done thousands of times in the past two and a half years—I prayed.

We messaged the rest of our kids and some of our close friends and asked them all to pray.

Then I called Sherie. "How's Jazmin doing?"

"We're going to have to take her somewhere for oxygen." Her voice was filled with worry. "She's not getting enough, and she's struggling to breathe. Her home oxygen tanks only go up to five C, and the hospital tank goes up to ten."

My heart went out to Sherie. I knew this was hard on her. "What if you called hospice to see if you can take her there? Then she can avoid the germs at the hospital."

"That's a great idea. I'll give them a call."

Was this the final hour? Would Jazmin make it through this rough patch?

"We're praying for Jazmin and for you and Aaron. Keep me updated."

A few hours later, Sherie messaged me. "We've got Jazmin's breathing back under control, and she's resting."

I breathed a sigh of relief. Thank You, God!

We felt helpless being so far away and not being able to help with Jazmin or pray for or encourage her in person.

Sherie messaged me later that an oxygen machine had been delivered to their camp that could go much higher. Sherie had called after the oxygen company closed, and someone answered the phone and said they would still deliver the tank in an hour.

God had performed an amazing feat. We breathed a sigh of relief.

On April 14, Jazmin messaged me early in the morning. "It's really humid here today. Please pray for my lungs, but more so, could you pray for my weariness?"

Tears stung my eyes.

I messaged her back, encouraging her and telling her I was praying. We missed her tremendously and didn't know what to do. Sherie and Aaron hadn't said anything about us coming for a visit, and we weren't supposed to leave our district, because of COVID guidelines. More than anything, we wanted to see Jazmin.

Jazmin had lost a lot of strength in the past few weeks and could no longer use her walker. I wondered how much worse it could get. Would her parents have to spoon-feed her and change diapers? We hoped it wouldn't get that bad.

That afternoon, I asked Eythan if he had heard from Jazmin. He said, "She's had a really bad day. Last night she had a dream that she was completely healed. It was so vivid that when she woke, she went to hop out of bed to go tell her parents that she was healed, but her body couldn't get up. That discouraged her, and I think it's contributing to her not feeling good today."

My heart went out to her.

We knew her miracle would be soon. The miracle of being healed of cancer or the miracle of being in the presence of Jesus.

These were the final hours. We had no idea which direction Jazmin's miracle would go. All we could do was pray—so we prayed. Fervently.

Lord,

Hear our pleas as we cry out to You.
Answer our prayers so we can know that You are listening
and that You love us. Help us to accept Your answer
no matter what You decide.
We love You.

Amen.

CHAPTER FIFTY-ONE

Hospice

The Lord is a refuge for the oppressed,
a stronghold in times of trouble.
Those who know your name trust in you,
for you, Lord, have never forsaken those who seek you.

(PSALM 9:9–10)

*T*WO DAYS LATER, EYTHAN told me, "Jazmin decided she wants to go to hospice because she isn't comfortable with just homecare anymore."

Her decision hit me like a half-ton truck.

Hospice?

This was it.

I went to my office to do my live video with the women in my Facebook group. My hope for a miracle was still alive, but barely. Although I had put most of my clothes back in my suitcase, I clung to a handkerchief with fine embroidery around the edges.

When her parents called hospice, they were informed that only one family member could be with Jazmin for the duration of her life. Jazmin didn't like that idea and declined the offer. Hospice agreed to take everything Jasmin needed to Sherie and Aaron's house, and nurses would come twice a day for visits.

On April 17, Sherie called to let me know Jazmin was settled at their home. She had a catheter so she could sleep at night. The nurse had installed a morphine pump to control her pain. Jazmin had resisted getting one for six months. She knew once a pump was installed, she wouldn't have long, but we never told Sherie that.

While Sherie was on the phone with me, I heard Jazmin calling out to her.

"Jazmin wants to know if you and Vance are coming for a visit."

My heart leaped with joy. "We were worried that you didn't want us there due to COVID. We don't want to infect Jazmin if we have it."

"At this point, it doesn't matter." Jazmin's voice sounded sad.

"We'll be there tomorrow!" I hung up and made arrangements. Devyn agreed to come stay with Kyle. What a godsend he was.

We could hardly wait to see Jazmin!

Vance and I got on the road the next day. Eythan planned to join us the following day and stay until Jazmin passed away or got a miracle.

When we arrived, everyone spilled out of the house to hug us with tears in their eyes. We hadn't seen Jazmin's parents, her grandparents, or Emily and Serena since October, when they all spent weeks with us at our house. We were glad to be back with Team Jazmin.

We went into the house and found Jazmin lying in her bed in the living room. The bone structure in her face was even more prominent than before. Her knee bones looked enormous. But our beautiful Jazzy was still there.

I bent over her, and she hugged me for a long time. Vance and I had missed our sweet girl. We sat by her bed for at least an hour, just chatting. She had a hard time talking because she didn't have the lung capacity to take in deep breaths.

We had a wonderful visit, then Jazmin closed her eyes and rested for a bit while we reconnected with everyone else.

Before we left, I sat on the edge of Jazmin's bed, Vance sat next to her in a chair, and we prayed for our daughter. We asked God once more to give Jazmin a miracle.

We hugged her again and told her we loved her. She told us she loved us too. Was this our last goodbye? *Please, God, more time.* I hugged her longer and memorized the smell of her hair and the bones of her shoulder blades beneath my hands.

> I hugged her longer and memorized the smell of her hair and the bones of her shoulder blades beneath my hands.

We said goodbye to everyone else and drove the four hours back home.

Eythan left the next morning to be with his wife. He texted me each day with updates on how Jazmin was doing. Whenever I woke in the night, I checked my phone to make sure Sherie or Eythan hadn't called to tell us Jazmin had passed away.

We planned another visit for the following Friday. Charity wanted to come with us. Devyn agreed to watch Kyle.

The night before we were to visit, I went to bed around eight o'clock. I awoke at eleven thirty and saw that Jazmin had texted me at ten.

"I don't know if you're still up or not, but I'm just letting you and Dad know that I'm feeling different tonight. Anxious but peaceful, overwhelmed but still calm. I can't help thinking back to my brief dream and the possibility of something happening sooner than I think. I don't know, but prayers for peace and mercy would be appreciated. I love you."

I racked my brain to remember the dream she referred to. Had she told me about it?

Regardless, she obviously realized she could die in the next twenty-four hours.

I went to the living room and prayed throughout the night between dozing on the couch. I hoped Jazmin would make it until we saw her the next day. Unless she got her miracle, we'd be saying our final goodbye until we saw her in heaven.

How was I going to do that without falling apart?

Let everything that has breath praise the LORD.

Praise the Lord.

(Psalm 150:6)

CHAPTER FIFTY-TWO

Prayer in the Night

Hear my prayer, Lord, listen to my cry for help.

(PSALM 39:12)

HE NEXT DAY, VANCE and I left for Sudbury. Charity went with us. She hadn't seen Jazmin in a couple of months. We walked into the house and gave everyone a hug. It was so good to see Eythan, but he looked tired and pale.

I stepped into the living room, where Jazzy lay on her bed. She was in a drugged state and even thinner than the week before. Her mouth and teeth protruded. I tried to swallow the lump in my throat.

Sherie told us we could wake her, but we let her sleep. We chatted with everyone else for an hour. I told them about the text Jazmin had sent me the night before, and they were surprised. They said she'd been too drugged to really communicate a whole lot, let alone think clearly enough to message someone.

Vangie confessed that she was having a hard time not showing her feelings on her face when she looked at Jazmin. "If I walk into the room, sometimes she asks me to leave. I can't hide that I think she's dying."

We understood how hard it was to keep a neutral expression. Vangie loved her little sister and would do anything for her. But how do you not show sadness when a loved one is dying?

Sherie held her phone, hands shaking. "Jazmin told me last night that she might not wake up in the morning and wanted me to be prepared."

My heart went out to Sherie. Watching her daughter die was emotionally breaking her down.

Sherie woke Jazmin, and it took her a good half hour to come out of her drugged state. When she was finally awake, she apologized for sleeping through part of our visit. We told her she never needed to apologize when her body needed rest.

She sat in the rocking chair and attempted to eat a bowl of soup, but it came back up. Sherie made her a smoothie, and Jazmin sipped on her drink as we chatted with her. Her head bobbed occasionally as she tried to visit, and she dozed off again.

When Jazmin woke, she looked at Charity. "So what's new with you?"

Charity smiled, and the two of them had a lovely conversation.

Every once in a while, Aaron said something funny, and we all laughed. The group of us had a nice conversation with Jazmin about life in isolation during the pandemic. The best thing for Jazmin was knowing the people around her were living a normal life. She loved to hear everyone chatter and laugh.

Before we left, we asked Jazmin if we could pray for her. We agreed as a group that God still wanted us to stand in the gap for her. Sherie said God had told her, "Having done everything to stand, continue to stand!" Vance and Charity said they had been getting the same impression from God.

Since Jazmin believed she was going to get a miracle, the best thing I could do was continue to encourage her to not give up and to keep expecting her miracle—it would have to be soon.

Eythan sat beside her as we prayed, rubbing the thin piece of skin spanning across the inside of her elbow. He had always loved to squeeze her cheeks. But she didn't have any flesh left, just skin and bones.

Eythan never acted like Jazmin was dying, and Jazmin loved that about her husband.

Was she going to get it? From looking at her physical state, I would say no. But based on her determination to live, to keep trusting in God, and to not give up—I would say a hearty yes.

I had no clue what was going to happen next, but I wanted her to get this miracle she had kept believing in for over six years. It was time for her to capture the butterfly.

> I wanted her to get this miracle she had kept believing in for over six years. It was time for her to capture the butterfly.

We said goodbye, trying not to appear as though we thought it was our last visit. We hugged our dear daughter-in-law's broken, sick body, and my heart tried to fill up on this memory.

We walked away feeling encouraged, which was the strangest feeling. We felt hopeful because of how strong Jazmin's spirit was.

Everyone stepped out into the mudroom to say goodbye. As Sherie and I hugged, she choked up. "I'm so thankful God gave your family to Jazmin."

"We feel honored God picked us to be Jazmin's bonus family. She has been a blessing to everyone and a wonderful wife to Eythan." I squeezed Sherie's shoulders.

Charity asked Eythan, "When you married Jazmin, did you ever think she would get this sick?"

He said he always thought Jazmin would get her miracle.

I had the sickening feeling a mom gets when she can't fix something that is broken for her child. I couldn't make Eythan's wife better, and I knew it hurt him to watch her die a little more each day.

Vance and I gave Eythan a big hug, then got in our truck and drove home.

We hoped that the next time we saw Jazzy, she would be walking, talking, and breathing normally, that we'd have our girl back and Eythan could live a wonderful life with his loving wife.

Would we have a next time?

Lord,

You can do the impossible. Nothing is too hard for You.
Give us the faith to believe in You when the world around
us is falling apart.

Amen.

CHAPTER FIFTY-THREE

Fighting for Life

I know God has a plan, and I am happy that I get to leave my life in His capable hands. I have no clue what the next little while will bring, but I trust that God knows and will help me and my family through whatever it is.

—JAZMIN HENSON

April 26, 2020

*V*ANCE AND I PRAYED for Jazmin in the morning over coffee. As my husband prayed, I had a vision.

Jesus was carrying Jazmin into a baptismal tank. She looked lifeless and wasn't moving. He submerged her under the water, and when she came up, she was completely healed and normal, looking like she did before she got cancer. Full of life, she smiled at Jesus.

I texted Sherie and told her what I'd seen, saying that I didn't know what it meant but I hoped it would bring her peace. She messaged me back, thanking me for sharing with her.

Sherie told us Jazmin wasn't waking up. I tried messaging Eythan but found out later that he was beside her bed, holding her hand. He got her to squeeze his hand a few times, but she seemed to be in a semiconscious state.

We messaged some close family and friends, telling them Jazmin was in her last few hours and asked them to pray.

Vance and I sat at our kitchen table, crying. We couldn't go to Sudbury because hotels were all closed to the public. We watched our phones for any news.

We planned to leave the next morning, get to Sudbury by two in the afternoon, and try to get back home before dark. We would have three or four hours to visit, and we hoped Jazmin would still be alive when we got there.

Emily messaged me, saying they were able to wake Jazmin. She was sitting up and had eaten pudding, bone broth, and cereal. She was also talking a bit.

What a fighter. Jazmin was not going down without a battle!

We admired her fighting spirit, even though it put us on such a dreadful emotional roller coaster.

I messaged friends and family again, telling them Jazmin was awake, eating, and talking. Sometimes I wondered if I should just wait until Jazmin went to heaven or was healed to give any news to loved ones.

Due to pandemic mandates, only ten people could attend Jazmin's funeral. So we decided to have our own gathering. We had a wonderful evening with Aryanna, Daniel, Devyn, Charity, Dan, and Alice. We hadn't been in the same room for months due to the pandemic. It was wonderful to be together. We prayed God would protect us all from catching or spreading the virus.

Before I went to bed, I texted Eythan and asked him if Jazmin had gone to sleep after supper. He messaged back, "No. She's eaten a lot of food. Talking a bit clearer, but not much conversation. Just one-liners."

Vance and I breathed a sigh of relief.

Emily messaged me. Jazmin was asking for us again. When Emily told her we would be there the next day, Jazmin excitedly said, "Oh, good!"

We went to bed feeling a tiny bit of hope. Maybe the baptismal dream meant God was going to heal Jazmin. With all my heart, I hoped so.

> Do not be far from me,
> for trouble is near and there is no one to help.
>
> *(Psalm 22:11)*

CHAPTER FIFTY-FOUR

Lord,
I Receive This Miracle

Peace I leave with you; my peace I give you.
I do not give to you as the world gives.
Do not let your hearts be troubled and do not be afraid.

(JOHN 14:27)

April 27, 2020

I WOKE AT ONE THIRTY in the morning. and couldn't go back to sleep. So I poured myself an extra-big mugful of coffee, went to my office, and prayed for Jazmin.

Later that morning, I asked Emily how Jazmin was doing.

She texted, "When she woke up this morning, she threw up on an empty stomach."

Jazmin's day wasn't starting out well.

A few hours later, when Vance and I were on our way to Sudbury, Eythan texted me, "Jazmin is up and eating and talking more clearly."

One more day to hold our sweet Jazzy. Thank You, Lord!

We chatted quite a bit on the way to Sudbury. We dreamed of what life would be like if Jazzy got her miracle in the final hours.

Jazmin would write a book.

A movie would be made of her miracle.

She would travel the world sharing her story.

Eythan and Jazmin would have children. I would hold those sweet little redheaded babies.

My heart warmed.

We arrived at two thirty in the afternoon. Jazmin was sitting on the side of her bed. We gave her a hug, then she lay down. We hugged Eythan, and surprisingly, he looked fairly good. We sat around Jazmin's bed, chatting with her as Eythan organized her meds. Jazmin was quite drugged, but we were able to have a conversation with her.

While we chatted, Charity messaged me some photos of Alice. I showed them to Jazmin.

She stared at the pictures for a long time, sadness in her eyes. "Alice looks so old. I'm missing out on so much!"

Jazmin asked to be moved to the rocking chair so she could sit up and eat a popsicle when Vangie came back from the store. Since Eythan was in the bathroom and Sherie and Aaron had gone for a walk, I lifted Jazmin to help her walk to the chair, but I had to hold up her fifty-pound body because she was too weak to stand.

Vangie returned from the grocery store, bringing the treats Jazmin had asked her to pick up. Jazmin chatted with us a bit more as she ate her popsicle.

Vangie desperately wanted her sister to live. She was hoping something good would happen. But we saw her anxiety in the way she moved her restless hands. Death was lingering in their home, and no one knew when it would take our sweet Jazzy.

Eythan fell asleep in the recliner next to Jazmin's chair. No surprise. He probably wasn't sleeping much with Jazmin being so sick.

When Sherie and Aaron returned from their walk, she filled us in on answers to prayer. Jazmin was throwing up less often after switching to the pump and had almost no acid reflux. Knowing she was more comfortable brought us peace.

We asked Jazmin if we could pray for her before we left. When we finished, Jazmin held her palms upward and prayed, "Lord, I receive this healing. Please heal me." Her face looked peaceful. "I feel different," she said as she basked in a moment of glory.

We weren't sure what to think. Maybe the Holy Spirit had come over her and she had felt His presence. Maybe she had a miracle. Only time would tell.

Jazmin laid her head back in the chair and smiled at us.

We said goodbye to her again, wondering if this was our last. I gave Jazzy a hug. "Don't lose hope. The miracle is coming soon." I knew my words were true. She was going to get a physical healing, or she was going to get a spiritual healing in heaven.

Vance hugged Jazmin gently and said goodbye.

I turned to Eythan. "I'm praying for you too."

"Thanks, Mom." He gave me a long hug.

Sherie followed Vance and me outside. Aaron was working on a portable sawmill project. Vance walked over to say goodbye to Aaron.

Sherie wrapped her arms around herself to fight off the cold. "Before you arrived today, Jazmin told us she didn't think she could fight anymore. She said she thinks she is going to go to heaven soon."

"Aw, Sherie, I wouldn't have told her to hold on for her miracle if I knew she felt that way." I wrapped my sweater around me as the chilly air nipped at my skin. If I'd known Jazmin was ready for heaven and wanted to go there, I would have prayed for God to take her home. We had always wanted what Jazmin wanted.

"I'm glad you didn't know, because you encouraged Jazmin to hope for her miracle. She needed that." Sherie looked heavyhearted.

Sherie and I hugged goodbye. Two moms holding on to each other—hoping, wishing, and praying for miracles.

> Sherie and I hugged goodbye. Two moms holding on to each other—hoping, wishing, and praying for miracles.

I waved farewell to Aaron. Then we hopped into our truck and started the journey home.

A few hours later, I messaged Eythan, asking about Jazmin.

He texted, "She sat at the table with everyone tonight and ate supper. She was feeling pretty good. After the meal, the girls hopped into her bed, and they had fun visiting."

Never had I seen friends so devoted as Serena and Emily. They had been a godsend.

As we continued driving home, I wondered if something really happened when we were praying with Jazmin. I hoped so.

We arrived home tired and ready for bed. Devyn told us Kyle had had a good day. We were so thankful he could stay with Kyle so we could do these trips. We'd been bouncing between two cities with kids with needs, but God was carrying us through our weariness.

We rolled into bed, and I prayed for God to heal my daughter. I opened my suitcase, pulled out a pair of pajamas, and mustered as much hope as I could.

The next few days, Jazmin slept about twenty hours a day and woke in between to have a few bites to eat or something to drink. Waking her up was getting harder each day.

Would our Jazzy make it? I placed my trust in God—only He knew the ending to this story.

Dear Lord,

Sustain us when we are weary, sick, or dying. Help us to lean into You when we are at our weakest point. Carry us until we can stand again on earth or in heaven.

Amen.

CHAPTER FIFTY-FIVE

No More Rallies

It has been granted to you on behalf of Christ not only to believe in him, but also to suffer for him.

(PHILIPPIANS 1:29)

April 30, 2020

*T*ODAY WAS THE SIX-YEAR anniversary of Jazmin having a tumor the size of a grapefruit removed.

I sent my regular morning text to Emily and Eythan to see how Jazmin was doing. Emily said she was more coherent than the day before and she'd had a better night.

There'd been a lot of rain the past two days, so we decided to wait until the highway was better to visit Jazmin. I messaged Emily at six o'clock, asking how the rest of Jazmin's day had gone.

She texted, "A good day today! She took a few boluses of morphine, but she's been chatty and coherent. And she's eating dinner with us."

I sent praise and thanks to God!

Vance was in the shower, and Kyle was wandering around with no clothes on, so I took off the long semisheer floral top I wore over my shirt and jeans and gave it to Kyle. He loved wearing other people's clothes. I took a picture of him, being as discreet as possible, and sent it to Jazmin. "Hello from Kyle," I texted.

When Vance came out of the bedroom, he sat in the grandpa chair. I plunked onto the couch beside him. "Jazmin had a good day today. Emily says she's been awake and talkative."

"That's amazing!" Vance shook his head.

I looked at the food on my jeans and tried to pick it off. Taking care of Kyle is messy business. "I hope this isn't a rally. Everyone will be so excited, thinking she's getting a miracle. I can barely handle the up and downs of thinking Jazmin is dying, then a spark of hope that she might live."

Vance looked out our great room window to the forest that was just starting to come back to life after winter. "This waiting has been hard on all of her family and friends. But if Jazmin gets healed, would we actually have the faith to believe it was a miracle?"

I wasn't sure. I felt so frustrated with God. His timing and mine were not meshing well together.

In my mind, Jazmin wasn't supposed to linger so close to death for so long. Eythan looked tired and drawn too. How long can people wait before they see their loved one either die or get a miracle? It seemed like God was making us wait forever.

Jazmin had an incredible evening with the girls and her family. They ate dinner together, and Jazmin talked quite a bit and was actually being funny. They took her out on the back deck, where Emily and Serena posed with her for a picture. Jazmin had on her rust-colored sweater, a little forest-green toque, and a pair of enormous yellow sunglasses—the kind you might see on a clown. The oxygen mask covered her mouth, and she held up two fingers in a peace sign. Jazmin was trying to be the cool girl. Emily and Serena were laughing in the photo. We were happy they had a wonderful evening with Jazzy!

We fell into bed exhausted after a long day with Kyle. The last thing I said before I fell asleep was "God, please heal our Jazzy."

Even though I walk through the darkest valley,

I will fear no evil, for you are with me: your rod

and your staff, they comfort me.

(Psalm 23:4)

CHAPTER FIFTY-SIX

Finally Free

I also believe that God may not give me a miracle but instead call me home to be with him in heaven. If that's God's plan for me, and if that will bring people to accept Jesus as their Savior, then that is what I want.

—JAZMIN HENSON

May 1, 2020

AT ONE FIFTEEN IN the MORNING, my phone buzzed. I grabbed my glasses off my bedside table and looked at the screen.

I'd received a text from Jazmin in response to my photo of Kyle in the floral sheer top. "Looking so handsome! I think I have a pair of black or brown boots pulled out. If I do, bring them, along with a nicer shirt or something. :P And wheelchair, although likeliest is pizza party." She had added two party emojis onto the end of the message.

I wasn't sure what the text was supposed to mean. She was obviously too drugged or weak to gather her thoughts properly. I mulled it over. It sounded like she wanted me to bring some nicer clothes for her and also her wheelchair so she could have a pizza party.

Just hearing from Jazmin in a long message like that gave me hope.

I started the daily live video on my phone at nine o'clock (a little later than the usual six thirty). I talked for thirty minutes.

As I was ending my video, a text popped up on my phone from Eythan. "We can't wake up Jazmin, and her breathing has changed."

I held back tears and said goodbye to my community of women, keeping my face as normal as possible. I ran downstairs and read the message to Vance.

We quickly got our stuff together and headed out the door for Sudbury. Restrictions had eased a bit, and Kyle had his day staff back. Devyn agreed to come stay with him in the evening.

As Vance and I drove, Eythan kept updating us, but nothing was really changing. We prayed. Around one thirty, a peacefulness spread over me like a warm blanket. I knew I didn't need to pray for Jazmin anymore. Something had happened. But I didn't know what that something was.

My phone rang. It was Eythan calling.

"Hi, Eythan." I listened, my heart pounding.

Silence.

Quiet crying.

"She's gone," he managed to whisper.

"I'm so sorry."

"She . . . she . . . just . . . stopped . . . breathing." He could barely get the words out between sobs.

Tears streamed down my face. "We're ten minutes away. We'll be there soon."

Vance and I cried the rest of our drive to the Ayotte house. We had no words.

When we pulled into the long gravel driveway at Sherie and Aaron's house, Eythan opened the front door. As soon as Vance parked the car, I hopped out, crying so hard I could barely walk. I wrapped my son in my arms. His body shook with inconsolable grief. Vance's arms were soon around both of us.

We stood weeping together.

After a few minutes, we went into the house.

I stepped into the living room and saw Jazmin lying in her bed. I slowly sat on the edge of it and held my Jazzy.

Our dear, sweet little girl was lifeless. Her poor body had finally had enough.

I wept and wept as I caressed her hair and kissed her pale, bony cheek.

Peace.

Quiet.

No suffering.

Sleeping soundly in the arms of Jesus.

Vance sat beside me and hugged his little girl. Jazmin had been his third daughter, and he had loved her like our other children.

We found Vangie, Serena, and Emily in the kitchen and hugged them all as we cried.

I went out on the deck and found Sherie, and we wept together—Jazmin's two moms, united by a girl we both loved.

Aaron and Vance spent a lot of time together, talking and crying. A couple of times, Aaron went into the living room and sat with Jazmin and wept. Sherie went in and stared at her in disbelief, wiping tears from her eyes.

A couple of times I heard Sherie say, "It wasn't supposed to happen like this. She was going to get a miracle."

Jazmin had hung on to that miracle for dear life, and so had Sherie.

The funeral home attendants arrived to take Jazmin.

We stood together in the doorway and watched the funeral attendants drive away with Jazmin in the back of the Dodge Caravan. Jazmin's people wept together as she was carried off.

When a loved one's body is taken away, I thought, *they don't take a single possession with them. Only the clothes on their body.*

But Jazmin had left us with many beautiful memories, thoughts, words, encouragement, love, faith, and hope. Treasures that no one could take from us. We would cherish these gifts until we saw her again.

We stood around hugging and crying while Eythan packed his things. He took a little blankie Jazmin had as a baby. She'd slept with it every night. I knew he would cherish that childhood blanket that his wife had loved so much.

I called all our kids and my mom, and Vance called his mom. It was all so overwhelming.

Vance and I were quiet on the drive home. I slept the last hour of the trip. Eythan followed us in his car.

We were exhausted physically and mentally. I had woken almost every night for the past two months, checking my phone to see if I'd received a text from Sherri or from Eythan.

I no longer needed to worry.

Before we went to bed, Vance and I stood in our kitchen with Eythan, weeping and holding one another.

Jazzy had been the love of Eythan's life. His best friend, encourager, and loving wife. Our son would turn twenty-three in five days. And he was a widower.

I went to bed with swirling thoughts and visions of Jazmin in heaven.

God had sent His angels to gather His Jazzy. Our sweet girl was no longer in pain. She had finally received the miracle she'd clung to, and it was way better than she could have ever dreamed.

God had sent His angels to gather His Jazzy. Our sweet girl was no longer in pain. She had finally received the miracle she'd clung to, and it was way better than she could have ever dreamed.

I imagined Jesus holding Jazmin in His arms and saying, "Well done, my good and faithful daughter!" Jazmin would beam as she looked into the face of Jesus, knowing she was finally home and that her Savior had seen how much she'd suffered for His glory.

I could see Jesus gently taking her by the shoulders and turning her around, and Jazmin seeing her grandma Evangeline, her uncle Ben, and her friend Gayle running toward her—the same way Jazmin had run toward us to announce Alice's birth—hopping, skipping, and laughing. They surround her in a group hug, then the four of them walk arm-in-arm into heaven's glorious, beautiful pastures of the wonderful home Jesus had prepared for her.

Lord,

We give You our lives and the life of our loved one who is sick. We offer up our lives as sacrifices to You. Whatever glorifies You most, whether life or death, help us to accept Your will and love You no matter what You choose for us.

Amen.

CHAPTER FIFTY-SEVEN

Tell My Story

Some people wonder how a loving God could allow horrible things to happen. How could God allow me to have cancer and die from it? We are only humans and cannot understand the bigger picture, but what I know is that sometimes God allows bad things to happen because He sees the bigger picture, and it may show something amazing coming from something tragic.

—JAZMIN HENSON

May 2, 2020

OUR CHILDREN ARRIVED AROUND nine thirty the next morning, and we spent the day together. Before breakfast, Vance started to say grace but couldn't get the words out, he was so overwhelmed with grief. Finally he whispered a broken prayer. "God, thank You for my family. . . . Thank You . . . for giving us . . . Jazmin."

We wept as Vance finished his prayer. We passed a box of tissue around and blew our noses and wiped our eyes.

We had a wonderful day remembering Jazmin. In the afternoon, we got out board games and played for a few hours. Jazmin loved games, and we had all loved doing that with her. We honored her by playing her favorite ones.

After the kids left, Vance, Eythan, and I looked through photos of Jazmin. We cried as Eythan told us stories or cute things about her. Then he said something I didn't know. "Jazmin didn't think I should shower or bathe her. She said a husband should never have to do that for his wife."

I'd known Eythan rarely showered her. She always waited for her grandmother or mom to help her. Now I knew why.

Eythan wanted to be needed. But Jazmin didn't want to burden anyone with her care. She had strong ideas of what people should or shouldn't have to do for her.

But all of us wanted to do anything she wanted because we adored her.

Many days, Eythan had been in and out of their room ten times in an hour, getting Jazmin whatever she needed. We never heard him complain about taking care of his dear wife. But we saw the exhaustion, and he often napped on the couch when someone came to take over her care.

"Jazmin said that for my birthday," he started, then wept. Vance and I wrapped our arms around him. Finally he whispered, ". . . that it would be nice if she got a miracle." He continued crying.

I went to bed that night praying that God would heal my son's broken heart and carry him through the hard weeks ahead.

During the week between Jazmin's passing and her funeral, our home was filled with an incredible peace. Our children came over every day and ate supper with us most evenings.

One night I had a dream.

Eythan was holding up his phone and said, "Mom, look at this picture of Jazmin."

I looked at his screen. Jazmin looked beautiful, standing in a field of tall wheat. She was smiling sweetly and had the most precious peace about her. She whispered to me, "Tell my story."

I woke up and instantly knew what the dream meant. Jazmin had willingly suffered for God where her faith and hope had bloomed the most: through her battle with cancer.

Twice that week I wrote posts about Jazmin's faith in God despite her suffering. I wrote of her unwavering faith in God and her desire to embrace His will for her life. Jazmin's faith would spread farther and wider than we could ever imagine.

> For it has been granted to you on behalf of Christ not only
> to believe in him, but also to suffer for him.
>
> ## (Philippians 1:29)

CHAPTER FIFTY-EIGHT

God Has a Purpose

If God wants to use my death for his sake,
I'm happy to die for whatever reason He wants.
If God wants to give me a miracle and use me here on earth
for His sake, then I am happy to wait to go to heaven.

—JAZMIN HENSON

May 7, 2020

HE DAY OF THE funeral, Eythan came out of his room holding a shirt and pants and asked me to iron them. He said Jazmin had bought the clothes for him for Gayle's funeral. Since we were in a pandemic, shopping for clothes was a challenge.

I ironed the clothes, then handed them to him. "You're all 'Jazzed' up now."

He smiled. Jazmin loved fashion and had fun transforming Eythan from a sweatpants kind of guy to a man who looked like he stepped out of *GQ* magazine.

Eythan had been Jazzed in many ways. His wife's gracious and kind acceptance of people's faults and hang-ups had changed him.

Our son had matured a lot since marrying Jazmin. His heart had become more tender and servant-like.

Our family had also been Jazzed. Before Jazmin came into Eythan's life, he had pulled away from us. For a year and a half, we watched him go through a hard time. Jazmin brought him back to us. She loved us and helped Eythan to see the treasure he had in his family, who loved him dearly.

Jazmin cherished the times we all gathered around the kitchen table and ate together. Sometimes we cleared the dishes after and played games, and Jazmin was silly and funny and could easily make us laugh. These were my favorite memories with Jazmin, and I mulled them over often.

We made the trip to Sudbury with Eythan, Dan, and Charity and arrived at the funeral home at noon. We embraced Jazmin's people. Together we walked into a room with a casket and flowers. We all took turns at Jazmin's closed casket, saying our goodbyes.

Sherie and I chatted in the hall before the service. She was still in shock. "It wasn't supposed to happen this way. Jazmin was going to get a miracle."

I told Sherie about my dream of Eythan showing me a picture of Jazmin standing in a field of wheat. "I believe with all my heart that Jazmin's story will bring people to Jesus. Her suffering and love for God will bring in a harvest to His kingdom."

She looked at me with tears in her eyes. Her face showing all the emotions of a broken heart, she said, "Oh, Cindy, I hope so. I have to know that God had a purpose for all the suffering Jazmin went through."

"He does. It just might take a while for us to see the end result."

The funeral was beautiful, with Sherie, Aaron, Vangie, Emily, Serena, Vance, and me sharing our cherished memories and the inspiration we had all been given from Jazmin's faith during her battle with cancer. Our pastor gave a beautiful message and encouraged people to lean into God when they were grieving Jazmin and not to pull away from Him. The service was aired online, where thousands of people witnessed our final farewell to Jazmin.

Eythan brought Jazmin's blankie and asked the funeral home to bury her with it.

I remembered the day I changed her sheets to wash them and found the tattered, well-loved white blankie under her pillow. I smiled and threw it in the wash with her bedding. I tucked it back under her pillow when I made the bed.

When Jazmin realized I had seen it, she sheepishly told me, "I've slept with this since I was little. I take it with me wherever I go."

I told her she didn't need to worry; I thought it was cute that she still had her baby blankie. Her love for meaningful things from her childhood showed me how tenderhearted she was.

Knowing she would be buried with her beloved blankie warmed my mother-heart.

As we drove to the grave site, I saw another funeral going on near Jazmin's. But when we got closer, I realized these were friends and family who would have been at her funeral if there hadn't been a pandemic. People filled the graveyard.

Pastor Wendell shared lovely words of comfort. We each took a rose and placed it on the casket.

Jazmin was buried next to a tree, and a small bird sat in that tree, singing sweetly for us.

I remembered that the day Jazmin passed away, we stepped onto their back deck, and birds in the trees sang loudly over us. I wanted to believe God allowed them to sing in celebration, serenading our sweet Jazzy as she entered heaven.

We went back to Sherie and Aaron's to visit and eat lunch, then said our goodbyes and drove home.

Eythan napped three times some days and slept heavily at night. His digestion had been struggling. Whether it was from stress or an immune system that was down due to lack of rest, we weren't sure.

Since we were still in the midst of the pandemic, he had time off work. Such a blessing. We suggested he sleep as much as he could, to allow his body to heal.

In many ways, the pandemic was a perfect time for Jazmin to pass away. Her parents were off work so she could stay at their camp for a month before she died. Vangie worked from her computer, so she was able to be by Jazmin's side. Serena and Emily took time away from their jobs. Jazmin was surrounded by people she loved for the last two months of her life.

The funeral had been small and intimate, and we were thankful we didn't need to spend a couple of days greeting people and listening to condolences when we really just wanted to be with one another as we mourned. So many blessings we were thankful for.

Jazmin would have been honored and proud that her people had gathered once more and brought one another comfort.

Not one of us would be the same again. Jazzy had changed us all. We were better for having loved her and known her.

Jazmin would have been honored and proud that her people had gathered once more and brought one another comfort.
Not one of us would be the same again. Jazzy had changed us all. We were better for having loved her and known her.

Lord,

When we lose a loved one, pull us close, wrap us tight, and don't let us go. Let us rest our teary cheeks against Your breast and find strength in Your loving arms.

Amen.

CHAPTER FIFTY-NINE

Fan or Follower of Jesus

*What reason could possibly be good enough to allow parents to
watch their children suffer as my parents have, to take a wife
from a devoted husband or a friend away from friends?
I don't know, but I do know that God knows,
and that is good enough for me.*

—JAZMIN HENSON

THE WEEKS AFTER JAZMIN passed away, Eythan went for long walks with his dog, Lacey. Sadness seemed to follow him wherever he went.

Vance and I prayed for him daily. How does a twenty-three-year-old man get through losing a wife he loved so dearly? Only God can carry a heartbroken man in deep grief and help him sort through his mourning.

> Only God can carry a heartbroken man in deep grief and help him sort through his mourning.

We fell into a new rhythm in our home. It was weird to not think of Jazzy needing a place at our table. I couldn't text her anymore or tell her funny things Kyle or Alice had done. We had to adjust to life without her.

Eythan texted Jazmin's parents, letting them know they could come pick up Jazmin's belongings whenever they were ready. Six weeks later, Sherie and Aaron came for a visit. Vance and I were sitting on the front porch when they pulled up with a trailer. My heart squeezed tightly as we hugged. How we loved these two for sharing Jazzy so generously with us.

> "I know our families will be forever friends because of Jazzy. I'm so thankful she brought us all together."

Sherie still carried heavy grief. "I know our families will be forever friends because of Jazzy. I'm so thankful she brought us all together." Tears pooled in her eyes.

"We're thankful too. Jazmin touched our lives in ways we will always be grateful for."

After supper, Sherie and I packed Jazmin's stuff into bags. The room still smelled of her.

"I have dreaded this day. Being in this room is making a lot of my emotions resurface." Sherie had spent a lot of time in that room caring for Jazmin and encouraging her.

"I think it's normal to feel that way." I held a garbage bag while Sherie threw clothes into it.

After we had gathered Jazmin's things, we sat in the living room. Aaron and Sherrie expressed their sadness over losing their daughter and shared stories of her with us.

Aaron extended his arm along the back of the couch and looked out the great room window. "When Jazmin was six, she asked me if God was real. I pointed up and asked her where the sky ended. She thought about it and agreed that there had to be a God since there was no explanation for a sky with no end."

Such deep thoughts for a young girl.

Sherie sat beside Aaron with one leg tucked under the other. "When Jazmin was thirteen, she came back from a week of camp at ABK. She told me about the chapel services, then asked, 'Mom, are you a follower of Jesus or just a fan? Because even the devil admits that God exists. I want to be a follower of Jesus and devote my life to Him.' I thought, *Wow, my daughter is thinking things I haven't thought of.* Jazmin inspired me to really examine my relationship with Jesus. Going to summer camp changed her life, and after that week, her walk with God was genuine."

Sherie and Aaron wondered what God's purpose was in taking Jazmin at such a young age.

Sherie expressed her vulnerability. "After we lost my brother, Ben, to a snow machine accident and my mom to lung cancer, I thought surely God wouldn't take my child. God just had to breathe, and Jazmin could've been healed. We don't know why God took Jazmin, but I have to believe that He has a plan we don't understand."

Eythan sat behind us at the dining room table, eating a snack. "I feel honored to have known Jazmin. Having her in my life for three and a half years was such a blessing."

Jazmin suffered almost every day of those three and half years, and Eythan said she was a blessing—that is true love.

> Jazmin suffered almost every day of those three and half years, and Eythan said she was a blessing—that is true love.

Our family wouldn't want to erase the last three and half years, even though they were some of the hardest years we would ever go through. Jazmin had been a warm breeze across a field of wheat on a lovely summer day. She had brought our family added happiness, joy, hope, laughter, and love.

As we looked through her things, Sherie asked me if there was anything I wanted of Jazmin's. But my heart was full of moments I will cherish forever, and they cannot be eaten by moths or rust or fire—memories so sweet and beautiful, earthly treasures couldn't measure up.

Jazmin's possessions were packed into bags and boxes then loaded in the trailer. The next morning after breakfast, we said goodbye to Sherie and Aaron with tears and hugs and promises to stay in touch with one another.

> Therefore we do not lose heart. Though outwardly we are wasting away, yet inwardly we are being renewed day by day. For our light and momentary troubles are achieving for us an eternal glory that far outweighs them all.
>
> *(2 Corinthians 4:16-17)*

CHAPTER SIXTY

Love in the Chaos

As a Christian, I know that when I die, whether that's soon or when I'm a hundred years old, I am going to be with God for eternity. Some people can't say that because they don't know Jesus.

—JAZMIN HENSON

FTER SHERIE AND AARON left, Vance and I switched rooms with Eythan.

As I sat on our bedroom floor, emptying out Jazmin's portable fridge that had held all her liquids and electrolyte drinks, tears spilled down my cheeks. Memories flooded back of getting her drinks out of the fridge and then standing by her bedside and praying for her.

I missed this sweet girl. Vance and I never thought we could love a young girl as much as we loved our own children, but we did.

Jazmin accepted our crazy household of autism and all the noise and chaos that came with it. Before she got really sick, if Kyle threw something or stole an item, Jazmin jumped off the couch and tried to help us rescue them. If she saw Kyle coming down the stairs, she ran to the fridge and locked it with the bicycle lock through the double door handles. Kyle could empty the whole fridge in seconds. When she agreed to move in with us, she knew how crazy life would be here, and she was okay with that.

Jazmin was really sweet with Kyle, talking to him and showing him she valued him. Every once in a while, when Kyle was in a good mood and she knew he wouldn't bolt or knock her over, Jazmin wrapped her arms around him and gave him a hug.

> In all the chaos and noise of this big house, Jazmin and our family fell deeper in love than we ever thought we could.

Jazmin chose a life in our home—even though it was a bizarre life—because she loved our son. The devotion she had for Eythan was beyond what we ever hoped for when we prayed for Eythan's future wife from the time he was a baby.

In all the chaos and noise of this big house, Jazmin and our family fell deeper in love than we ever thought we could. We also grew to love her family and friends.

People touched our hearts and home in the most glorious ways.

> I found a pair of Jazmin's socks the other day and brought them to my nose. Another day, I opened a dresser drawer and found some of her IV supplies. Another time I saw a photo of the three girls that Serena posted on Instagram. Memories seemed to be everywhere, and I held them close to my heart.

We prayed for her. We ate together and played board games and enjoyed good food, desserts, and way too much Starbucks.

The memories are still vivid to this day, and they flood back when I least expect it. I found a pair of Jazmin's socks the other day and brought them to my nose. Another day, I opened a dresser drawer and found some of her IV supplies. Another time I saw a photo of the three girls that Serena posted on Instagram. Memories seemed to be everywhere, and I held them close to my heart.

Yesterday, I looked at Jazmin's belongings at our front door and thought, *This is what we leave behind . . . meaningless stuff.*

If that is all we leave behind, we've missed out. If we've lived a life that glorifies God, our loved ones' hearts should be full of the beauty of our gifts of encouragement, laughter, hope, faith, and love. Treasures.

What will you leave behind? I hope it's something wonderful!

Yesterday,
I looked at Jazmin's belongings at our front door and thought,
This is what we leave behind . . . meaningless stuff.
If that is all we leave behind, we've missed out. If we've lived a life that glorifies God, our loved ones' hearts should be full of the beauty of our gifts of encouragement, laughter, hope, faith, and love. Treasures.
What will you leave behind?

Let us not become weary in doing good, for at the proper time we will reap a harvest if we do not give up.

(Galatians 6:9)

CHAPTER SIXTY-ONE

Jazmin's Hope-Train

What if my death allows people to see God's light and realize how much they need Him? And through my death, someone comes to know Jesus and therefore finds comfort in the fact that when they die, they can look forward to an eternity in the most perfect place imaginable, in heaven with our Savior, Jesus? That is what brings me comfort and peace and allows me to fully trust God when my sickness deters me from having the earthly life I wish for.

—JAZMIN HENSON

ETWEEN THESE PAGES IS the story of a girl who wanted to leave behind more than just clothes, shoes, makeup, money, or fame. Jazmin wanted to leave a legacy for us. For you. For the world.

Her faith was tested beyond what I hope you will ever have to endure. God didn't cause Jazmin's suffering. But I believe He allowed it so you could see how genuine and unwavering her faith in God was. He knew Jazmin was one of His rare children who could endure tremendous suffering and never give up her faith or hope in Him.

Maybe you're going through a crisis of faith right now. Well, you are holding the story of a girl who lived and died believing God loved her, even though He never gave her a miracle.

Are you willing to become a follower of Jesus and not just a fan? Would you place your life in God's hands? I urge you to say in this very moment, "God, whatever You want for my life, I will accept it. My life is Yours."

Jazmin stepped over the line from *fan* of Jesus Christ to *follower*. She gave Him all she had, and God treasured her offering to Him.

I wish I had been as devoted to God as Jazzy was when I was a young mother with a little boy suffering with autism.

God has different timing for everyone.

He changed my life before Jazmin came into our lives so I could stand strong during the months she was dying. I mourned the most when Jazmin was living. After she passed away, the first week was the hardest. Tears came easily. But I had a peace that surpassed all understanding.

I knew Jazmin was not coming back. But we would see each other again. God allowed me a space and time to mourn while Jazmin was living. Then He told me to clean up, change my clothes, eat, and move on with my beautiful memories of Jazmin and a heart filled with the hope she left me. I was able to be a ray of joy to my family amid their mourning.

I also believe God let me go through the premourning so I could write to you who are grieving over someone who hasn't passed away yet. Let me encourage you to live as though today is your loved one's last day but also live as though he or she has thousands of days left.

When a loved one is dying, we need one foot on each side of the line. Even though God told me to live with hope that Jazmin would get a miracle, He also wanted me to be prepared in case she passed away.

After my journey out of premourning, I chose to lean more toward the miracle side because that helped me to face each day with joy instead of sorrow.

God knew before I was born that I would care for Jazmin one day. I don't believe it was a coincidence that Jazmin married my son and that we took care of her for six months. God knew we would be telling Jazmin's story, and who better to tell you about her faith amid her suffering than one of her people who had been on the front lines with her?

Jazmin had periods of depression and feeling down, but most of that had to do with the drugs she was taking, the tremendous pain she suffered, and the lack of nutrition and sleep. Jazmin never once said she didn't believe in God, and she never gave up her relationship with Him. She had faith that could move mountains. Cancer and drugs dragged her through deep valleys and dark waters. She felt like she was drowning and couldn't breathe. God called His people to pray for Jazmin, and He reached into those dark places and brought Jazmin back up for air.

Jazmin reached a point where she gave her miracle to God. She still kept believing He could heal her, but she decided she wanted to love Him and worship Him even if He said no to her prayers.

After Jazmin died, Eythan looked through the messages and photos on her phone from her last day. I was the last person she texted before she went to sleep for the last time, planning a pizza party with Vance, me, and Eythan. Then she took a selfie. Jazmin took selfies every week. —*In case I get a miracle, I can show people what God did for me.* Both the photo and the text were signs she was still hoping, still believing, God could move mountains, just minutes before she closed her eyes for the last time.

Jazmin went to sleep and woke up in heaven.

Would you like to embrace the hope and faith Jazmin had? Can I invite you to join Jazmin's hope-train? Would you like to step into this beautiful place where Jazmin lingered before she passed away? She suffered tremendously but never gave up hope that God could heal her, right up until she took her last breath.

You may be thinking, *Why would I want to put my hope in God like Jazmin did, when hope got her nothing?* Jazmin caught the butterfly and stepped onto that train one last time, and it took her to heaven. One of our friends said, "I like to believe heaven is like a train station. When Jazmin arrived, God announced to everyone, 'Jazmin Henson is arriving! Come welcome her!'"

I dream of our beautiful Jazzy stepping off that hope-train and Jesus sweeping her into His arms, swinging her round and round until, with her new lungs, she filled every meadow and garden of heaven with the glorious sound of her laughter. Then her grandma Evangeline, her uncle Ben, and her dear friend Gayle all embraced their sweet Jazzy as she walked into a field of people who are in heaven because she showed them that her love for God was unconditional, not dependent on ideal circumstances.

Jazmin didn't love Jesus so she could get a miracle. She loved Jesus because He had loved her, died for her sins, forgave her, and saved her. Many times Jazmin told her friends and family that she hoped her battle with cancer, getting a miracle, or going to heaven would draw people to Christ. "I don't want people to be bitter if I don't get a miracle. I want my death to cause people to lean into Jesus and not to push Him away."

I believe Jazmin wants you to step onto her hope-train. She wants you to live every day believing God can change your life.

I believe Jazmin wants you to step onto her hope-train. She wants you to live every day believing God can change your life.

Hope is a beautiful treasure.

If you don't live with hope, you have no reason to live.

When I met Jazmin, my hope in miracles was a faint beating inside me and needed a massive revival. My pain had caused me to stop believing God could perform miracles. Jazmin lived every day with hope and taught me to do the same, and it was an incredible journey to be on together.

Jazmin wants you to step on her hope-train and ride it the rest of your life, with Jesus as your conductor. Hopefully, one day she will stand in heaven, and Jesus will call out your name and announce you have arrived. After He has embraced you with open arms, Jazmin will meet you at the platform. She will reach her hand out to you and bring you to join the harvest of others who hopped on her hope-train.

Jesus Christ is calling to you from the ashes of Jazmin's life and wants to use her suffering and her story to bring beauty to your life. Today, will you ask Him to forgive your sins and become your Savior? You may be the one person Jazmin dreamed would come to Jesus through her story and her suffering.

I believe Jazmin wants you to step onto her hope-train. She wants you to live every day believing God can change your life.

Jazmin left the beautiful treasure of hope for us so we could live life to its fullest.

All along I have trusted God.
He knows best, and He is the only one
who knows the outcome of all this.
I trust Him with my life, but that is way easier said
than done. It's a constant struggle to decide
to fully put my trust in Him. It's obviously way easier
to have faith when everything in life is going well,
but it is in the bad times when it is so important
to rejoice in the Lord and praise Him
because He is so good,
and He has a plan.

—Jazmin Henson

EPILOGUE

CHARITY, ARYANNA, AND I sat in my office on a gorgeous sunny Friday morning. A couple of years ago, I'd redecorated the room with a soft pink paint and floral wallpaper that reminded me of a bedroom I had slept in as a child at my grandparents' house.

The girls and I had hauled our makeup, curling irons, and beauty products up to my office and sat in front of a couple of mirrors. I looked in my mirror and watched Charity apply Aryanna's makeup.

I smiled. Today was a happy day! Nothing could spoil our joy. We laughed as we listened to love songs and talked about our anticipation of how this special day was going to go.

"Ashley's dress is so pretty. She will look beautiful," Aryanna said as she closed her eyes so Charity could apply bronze eye shadow. We both agreed with her.

"And Meghan is going to make the barn look amazing with her talented decorating." Charity asked Aryanna to open her eyes so she could look at her eyelids.

I applied the waterproof, smudge-proof, cry-proof mascara that the girl at the drugstore said was the best for a crying mom. "Your dad and I have been praying that everything will go perfectly and that the rain will hold off this afternoon while they say their vows."

The girls and I agreed. God was going to rearrange the rain predicted for that afternoon.

We had fun chatting as we finished transforming ourselves into three glowing beauties. We went downstairs to put on the floral dresses we'd bought to wear to the wedding. We passed the great room where the groom and his men were dressed in their gray pants and vests, with white shirts and green bow ties.

"Eythan, that suit looks so good on you!" I admired my handsome son with his fresh haircut and big grin.

Devyn, Dan, Eythan, and a friend of our family named Nathan stood in front of our enormous fireplace. "We'd better head to the farm," Dan said as he grabbed his shoes.

An hour later, Vance and I stood as the bride appeared at the end of the path lined with rows of gold chairs facing the front of the barn at Thomson's Strawberry Farm.

Ashley looked beautiful in her long white dress. She held a bouquet of baby's breath, chamomile, and eucalyptus. Her long dark hair was accented with a white veil hanging to her waist. Her dad, Mike, walked arm in arm down the aisle with her. Ashley smiled the entire way to the front. Eythan stepped forward and shook Mike's hand, then took Ashley's hand in his own.

Pastor Wendell married Eythan and Ashley in a wonderful, God-filled ceremony. Partway through, a monarch butterfly flew over them, then flitted back over them again.

I smiled.

Months before Eythan married Ashley, I started working on the cover of this book and had done a rough draft to show the publisher what I wanted. I had included a monarch butterfly to symbolize Jazmin's faith and hope in God.

Charity and Aryanna saw the butterfly fly over Eythan and Ashley and started to cry.

God had shown all three of us that even though we had been devastated to lose Jazmin, He was honoring her and showing us that she had been the one who blessed Eythan before she passed away with her wishes that he fall in love and marry again. This day, the day Ashley became Eythan's new wife, was blessed by God.

During the reception, various people gave speeches. No one mentioned Jazmin.

Eythan stood to give his speech. He eloquently thanked each member of our family for supporting him and having an influence in his life. Then he surprised everyone by saying he needed to honor Jazmin because she had changed his life and made him into the man he was today. He said it was an honor to have been married to her, even though their marriage had been short, and he was thankful for the role she had played in his life.

Throughout his speech, Ashley stood by Eythan's side, smiling and encouraging him as he cried. This beautiful woman had entered into a relationship with Eythan while he was still mourning Jazmin. Ashley has an abundance of grace most women will never have.

Ashley had a concussion a few weeks before the wedding, and we asked her to stay with us so we could check on her daily and make sure she was okay.

Vance, Ashley, and I had a few hours alone together one day while Eythan was at work. Vance and I told her we wanted her to be herself, that she never had to compete with Jazmin, and that Eythan was deeply in love with her.

We had seen him fall in love with Ashley just as easily as he had with Jazmin. We knew he wasn't going to compare the two women.

He loved them both. But we told her we knew how hard it must be to be the second wife after a man loses a wife he loves.

"Ashley," I said, "if you ever need to talk about the effect Jazmin has on your marriage, you can talk to us. We will understand. We want to support you. And you don't need to pretend it's easy."

We shed a few tears in front of Ashley as we shared memories of Jazmin. She was empathetic and kind. Loving Ashley is easy.

How my son was blessed twice with a loving, kind, and beautiful wife is beyond our comprehension. How we were blessed twice with daughters who are easy to love—God's grace.

My son loves his new wife. Jazmin would be so proud of him for choosing Ashley and proud of herself for praying for his future wife and releasing him before she died so he could love again.

Two weeks after Eythan and Ashley's wedding, I cleaned out his room. He had already taken most of his stuff. But I found a Christmas card on a bedside table, opened it, and found this beautiful handwritten note from Jazmin:

Even though we haven't been together for very long, I wanted this Christmas to be special since I had a feeling it would be the first of many together.

Eythan, you are so wonderful, which I feel like I say often, but I want to share why I think you are so wonderful. So here's a list.

I feel wanted, cherished, and appreciated by you. I admire that you try to be the person who you think you should be. I love that you pray for me. It's so important to me that God is number 1 in your life. And I'm still amazed that you want to be with me even though I'm battling a life-threatening disease. It's also super important to me that you put your faith and trust in

God as I do. And that you trust that God keeps his promises, as I do.

You've seen my super-weird side, but you're a total weirdo too, so it works! I like that we are equally unphotogenic. The fact that you can do a Rubik's Cube in under one minute is pretty hot! I like that you have confidence. And you smell super good all the time. Your eyes are mesmerizing. Not to mention you're a babe. I give you credit for sitting through three of my hockey games, which I know are painful to watch. And rather than insisting you were right when I blatantly announced otherwise, you let me talk myself in a circle to let me come up with my own conclusion . . . which, of course, was that you were right.

When you look at me, even when it's with a ridiculous face, I feel special. I love that not only did you let me shoot you with an Airsoft gun, you also shot me back. And I really appreciate that you don't treat me like I'm fragile (because you know I could take you any day).

It's also amazing that I have the privilege of getting to know you more and more.

I could have put so many more things on this list, but I can't really fit them in this card. I just hope that in like 10 years from now, we can look back on this Christmas and see how different life is. I'm banking on the fact that you will keep me around for a while.

Happy New Year! XOXOXO
Jazmin

Love is blooming.
Life is going on.
We will always have a place in our hearts for Jazmin and never forget how she changed our lives forever.
Love from Jazmin is eternal.
A true treasure.

Jazmin's love and prayers changed Eythan's life. They also led him to fall deeply in love with Ashley. And we did too.

Love is blooming.

Life is going on.

We will always have a place in our hearts for Jazmin and never forget how she changed our lives forever. Love from Jazmin is eternal. A true treasure.

> I have fought the good fight, I have finished the race, I have kept the faith. Now there is in store for me the crown of righteousness, which the Lord, the righteous Judge, will award to me on that day.
>
> *(2 Timothy 4:7-8)*

ORDER INFORMATION

REDEMPTION
PRESS

To order additional copies of this book, please visit
www.redemption-press.com.
Also available at Christian bookstores, Amazon, and Barnes and Noble.

Made in the USA
Monee, IL
22 February 2024

53919380R00204